CH00540952

DOROTHY HEATHCO

biography of a remarkable ...ia teacher

DOROTHY HEATHCOTE'S STORY
biography of a remarkable drama teacher

Gavin Bolton

Trentham Books

Stoke on Trent, UK and Sterling, USA

Trentham Books Limited

Westview House
734 London Road
Oakhill
Stoke on Trent
Staffordshire
England ST4 5NP

22883 Quicksilver Drive
Sterling
VA 20166-2012
USA

First published 2003

British Library Cataloguing-in-Publication Data
A catalogue record for this book is available from the
British Library

1 85856 264 3

Designed and typeset by Trentham Print Design Ltd., Chester and printed in Great Britain by Cromwell Press Ltd., Wiltshire.

Contents

Acknowledgements

I have so many people to thank. Firstly, Dorothy herself, of course, for being willing to share her story and for the patient hours she has spent painting the pictures that have made up her life for me to translate. I feel intense gratitude, too, to all those past students, colleagues, friends and drama teachers round the world who have taken so much trouble to let me have their recollections of Dorothy and her work. Their anecdotes have stimulated, amused, surprised and even shocked me.

Above all I must thank Sandra Hesten whose own studies of Dorothy Heathcote have become an authoritative source for many. She has been my sounding board, reading, correcting and advising on chapter first-drafts and generally keeping me on the rails.

I must also thank Cynthia, my wife, who, yet again, has tolerated fourteen months of my disappearing into my study at what should have been social hours. And thanks, too, to my amenable friends, who were beginning to believe I had only one topic of conversation – Dorothy Heathcote.

Dear Gavin,

You've pulled it off! I laughed till I cried - and sometimes cried till I could laugh again.

When Raymond died and you asked me about a biography, once I got over my surprise that my life would have enough interest in it to invite a reader (I've always thought I just got up every day and got on with it - prascio!) I realised I wasn't really surprised. You in your kindness and wisdom chose your moment well, realising that such a change from a long, happy companionship to an uncertain "singularity" could be a watershed from which one could see behind, and tentatively forward, usefully.

I've enjoyed as usual our encounters and your reassembling this snail's-trail of my (and sometimes our) experiences - especially the laughs. Years ago I wrote of you as an eagle and me a mole. Your talent for seeing the landscape wide and detailed is in no way diminished. You've been miner and archaeologist, finding the deep pattern of theory and locating the tiny jigsaw details I've forgotten to remember. And you've balanced the pros and cons of opinion regarding "D.H. teacher" very usefully for which I'm grateful.

So, as the song says "Thanks for the memories". Now, about that commission model...
...there's this garden in the new N.H.S. Hexham hospital, and I've an idea we could . . . . . .

in gratitude, Dorothy.

Introduction

Today, 25th June, 2001, I have received a letter from Dorothy confirming that she would like me to write a story of her life. We had been together, one day the previous week, in a local church hall where family, friends and past students had assembled to celebrate with Dorothy the life of her husband, Raymond, who had died suddenly a few months earlier. The day had been filled with memories. Over a cream cake, I told her I had been reading some misleading information about her early career in a current journal article. We agreed that there was a danger that this kind of thing was likely to occur more and more. I suddenly said:

> 'Dorothy, is anyone writing your biography?'
> 'Not as far as I know', she said and added 'I wish somebody would...'
> 'I would...'
> 'You're on!'

So, here I am, about to start, with a blank page before me. Even as I write 'blank page', I know it's not true as in a way I have been carrying 'Dorothy's story' around with me for the past forty years. Indeed some people would claim that our stories are intertwined, a perhaps harmless distortion that I for one have done little to discourage. It arose no doubt from our being for so long the only University appointees in the field of drama education, from our operating as colleagues even though we were at different Universities, from our being seen together at conferences and courses all over the world, and latterly, our joint authorship of publications. And to many people we seemed intent on promoting the same praxis, clothing our message in similar language. Only the closest examination of our teaching methodologies and philosophies revealed important differences of which relatively few people have seemed aware.

We met in 1962 at the college flat of a mutual friend, Mary Simpson [née Robson][1], who was in charge of Drama at Neville's Cross Training College, Durham. I had recently been appointed as Drama Organiser to County Durham. Mary had said to me; 'The way you talk about school drama reminds me of Dorothy Shutt ... or Heathcote as she now is ... at Newcastle ... I'll arrange for you to meet her.' And, having met, Dorothy and I organised ourselves to visit a variety of schools, each taking it in turn to teach or watch the other. This began a comfortable relationship that allowed for mutual criticism, although in practice there was more to criticise in my teaching!

We became affectionately known as the 'Laurel and Hardy' of the drama world, the physical parallel not going unnoticed, but in so far as Laurel aspired to emulate Hardy's evident streetwiseness and was the perpetual learner, this underlines the aptness of the description, for my relationship with Dorothy, especially in respect of her consummate skill in planning learning across the curriculum, has been that of master/apprentice. There is no doubt that she is a distinguished educator, master/teacher and artist – a genius, no less, as so many people who have written to me suggest. I hope through this book to tell 'Dorothy's story' in a way that gives us clues to the sources of her artistry and shows how her early inspirations about teaching drama became a life-long mission to educate.

Which brings me to the key question to be asked of any biography – how accurate can it be? The reader may feel trapped into reading Gavin Bolton's version of Dorothy's career and be left wondering what the 'true' version would look like. One way to get round this is for me to interview a whole range of family members, neighbours, students, colleagues, friends and critics and present her life as a kind of balance sheet of perspectives. Another way would be for me to write about 'how I perceive Dorothy Heathcote'. Neither of these approaches, alone, appeals. Both are flawed. Much more interesting to record 'how Dorothy sees herself', balanced by the perceptions of others, including my own. Very occasionally, some contradictions will be detected.

This is the angle I have chosen. Of course, it too could be flawed. Its almost total dependence on honest and accurate recollections leaves plenty of room for self-deception from Dorothy herself and from those who know her. We all carry with us our subtly revised versions of life's stories, some of them conveying more of who we are now rather than who we were then. And the problem is further exacerbated if our stories are retold by someone else. It becomes Gavin's version of Dorothy's version – and he has already boringly declared his admiration of her work! Is this to be an exercise in Dorothy worship to be enjoyed only by fellow disciples, a nostalgic recall of cosy memories? I will try to counter this with critical observations from myself and others.

I am only interested in writing this biography if it creates an opportunity for seeing Heathcote's contribution to education through a different lens, that of her life story. My aim is to tell that story in such a way that new light is thrown on what she and her work stand for. You will find that as much attention has been given to her work as to her personal life. Indeed, for many pages, it has been necessary to hold the flow of the latter in order to summarise significant changes in her educational thinking and her practice. To understand Dorothy, you need to have some grasp of how her work has evolved and, above all, where she stands **now**, what her latest vision of education is today.

So, get a grip, Gavin ... you're an enquirer, not an admirer! But of course a story it remains and, as such, it should also offer the reader some entertainment, for those of you who have met Dorothy know that she surrounded herself with laughter and some of the tales that follow will certainly raise a smile...

Gavin Bolton

Note

1   It is The Mary Simpson Memorial Fund that provides financial help for students and teachers attending the National Association for the Teaching of Drama conferences and courses.

1

Childhood

A protective circle of women

The 1972 BBC documentary *Three Looms Waiting* turned Dorothy Heathcote into a 'star drama teacher' with a public, television face that teachers all over the world could claim to know. But to the people of Steeton, West Yorkshire, the village where she was brought up, she was our Dorothy Shutt, the mill-girl in whose success they could share. One person who asked to see her when she visited her mother soon after the TV showing was Mr. Andrews, the long-retired elementary school headmaster. No longer the formidable figure she remembered, he mused: 'I wonder what you would have done, Dorothy, if you'd passed the scholarship ... you'd have been *trained* as a teacher, wouldn't you ... and you'd have been ruined'.

I interviewed Dorothy for the first time yesterday, July 2001. She was all prepared with the tiny tape-recorder laid out on the dining table – all important events in Dorothy's life seem to occur either in the kitchen or at the dining table. Hundreds of students will have had their tutorials there. We test the recorder for 'sound quality' [my idea], but Dorothy has already done that earlier that morning [she would, wouldn't she!]. Nevertheless she obliges me and I nod approval, at the same time explaining, rather unnecessarily, that we'll start with her earliest memories. 'Well ... when I think back ... it strikes me ... I seemed to spend a lot of time amongst women ... particularly older women.' And so we go on, smiling a lot, me butting in from time to time and occasionally sharing something from my early life ... for two hours ... a rich piece of recording.

And then, today, I go and type out the above paragraph. What I say there is accurate as far as I know, but it captures nothing of the way that information was fed into the tape. Behind my crafted, formal account you cannot see Dorothy smiling nor can you catch the richness of her warm Yorkshire tones, her idiomatic language and dialect. No way would Dorothy phrase it as: 'a star drama teacher' nor indeed 'a mill-girl in whose success they could share'. If you are to understand Dorothy, you must know that that kind of pat phrasing, that mixture of academic and journalistic tone is what she has resisted all her professional life. She has a deep suspicion of so-called scholarly texts that serve merely to promote other scholarly texts and fail to reach the centre of the subject-matter. So as you read on, be aware that there is an underneath to my text ... that I am writing about a person who always stayed centred and eschewed abstract propositions and generalities. As she talks about her life she is seeing images not sentences. But I have to content myself with words...

The headmaster's question about Dorothy's failing, in 1937, to get a scholarship, an examination for 11 year olds which selected a few, probably just one or two from each village school, to 'go on' to the nearest Grammar school, touched on a key circumstance in Dorothy Heathcote's life, for her route to adulthood and her career beyond would have been immeasurably different if she had passed that test. His somewhat startling answer to his own question: 'You'd have been trained as a teacher wouldn't you ... and been ruined' represents more than a cynical remark about his own profession for it goes to the very foundation of Dorothy's professional philosophy as a teacher-trainer, to which this book will necessarily be returning again and again.

> *Even as Dorothy quoted the headmaster I couldn't help but wonder whether her memory has subconsciously transferred the remark to him, for its distrustful view of traditional teacher-training is essentially part of Heathcotian armoury. Checking this account with Dorothy later she confirms that her memory is accurate because she recalls being taken aback by the acuteness of his observation.*

Dorothy's closest childhood friend, Margaret Freeman, however, has come up with an explanation of Dorothy's failure to pass the scholarship that all was not above board – and guilt might account for the headmaster's close interest in Dorothy's career! Margaret has written a charming letter to me about her memories of Dorothy, going back 72 years. While musing on nostalgic reminiscences such as: 'I don't remember Dorothy or I ever falling out ... what I do remember is her kind, gentle manner, her beautiful smile that was framed by that lovely curly hair that I really did envy', she nevertheless includes an 'off the record' paragraph that raises the issue of political corruption or at least of how *suspicion* of such corruption was part of the village culture:

> One other journey we made was to Silsden School one Saturday morning. This was to take our exam for the Grammar School. Prior to the year we took it you had two attempts to pass. If you failed the first test at 11 years old you could take it again at 12. The year it came our turn the rules had changed and each pupil only got one chance to pass the exam. From Steeton

School three students were usually admitted to Grammar School so it was the top three scoring students who went. The year we took it the three who passed were the Headmaster's son (who never scored higher in class than Dorothy or I) his friend whose father owned a mill and the girl from our class whose father managed an exclusive dress store in the next town and who eventually married the headmaster's son.

But significant as failing the scholarship became at the time, corrupt or not, for Dorothy it was a matter of sheer relief. How would mother have paid for the uniform? Clothes weren't something you bought but her mother, clever as she was with a needle, making Dorothy's clothes usually from the outgrown garments of other family members, could not have made a school uniform. A way would have been found, of course. The women in the family would have pulled together. And here we have a long list, for those early years until she was 11 were spent in Granny's house shared with Aunties Ellen, Lucy [with whom Dorothy shared a bed] and Edith. Grandad, a warp dresser, whose warps as the foundation for men's suiting were often on show at trade exhibitions and whose craftsmanship at the loom Dorothy was later to emulate, was out at work all day. Her own mother, Amy Shutt, widowed before Dorothy was born, was away in service earning ten shillings for a full week of housekeeping for a local farm where she baked, churned butter, and carried all the water from a pump.

On Saturdays she and Dorothy would go to the cinema – 'going to the pictures', as it was called – or the shops in Keighley. If it rained, they would stay at Granny's and sew dolls' clothes for Dorothy and her many friends, a motherly routine Dorothy was to adopt years later for her own daughter and her friends. On one occasion there must have been enough money to take them on the bus all the way to Harrogate, twenty miles away, their eyes sucking in the hillside views and Dorothy wonderingly commenting 'and there are still seven miles to go!' Her mother knew Harrogate very well because one of her employers, a farmer's wife, did her shopping there and travelled in a Ford car with an outside bucket seat in which Amy Shutt sat. Dorothy and her mother did manage a holiday occasionally – in Morecambe where Auntie May and Uncle Harold lived, but each morning of their stay Amy Shutt made beds in local boarding houses for a few hours – to pay for the holiday and contribute to Auntie May's food bill.

Granny and Grandad lived at 35 Whitley Head. It was always referred to as Granny's house, for she was the centre of that household of women. It was a rented, stone-built terrace house with scullery, living room, two bedrooms, an attic, a cellar for storing food and coal and an outside closet. A central feature of the house was the big black iron range, a magnificent oven to one side of the fire and at the other side a set pot for hot water. Blackleading the stove and white-stoning the front and back steps were routinely marks of pride in one's house. Dorothy still does her front door step today, when she has time. In winter it was at first lit by oil lamps and later, gas, followed by electricity just before the war, and heated with a coal fire, their only means of cooking. It was also their only means of heating water for their nightly 'wash-downs' – Dorothy still recalls having her neck scrubbed – and their weekly baths, Dorothy in a round tin bath in the kitchen and the rest of the family in the 'long bath' in front of the fire in the front room. Thursday night was the women's bath night, taken in turn in privacy, while the men, Grandad and uncles were discreetly out of the house. The used water was emptied onto the plants in the garden. This was a weekly ritual, with its unspoken code of modest behaviour. Dorothy did not have a bathroom until she moved to Newcastle at the age of 24.

They were poor but Dorothy was barely aware of it, perhaps vaguely conscious of the headmaster's son being at 't'better end'. The local Cooperative Society – Granny was among the first people to shop there – was an important factor in finances all over northern households. You saved your 'divi' [dividend] to buy shoes and other clothing and then collected it on 'divi' day. In Steeton the Coop delivered coal up the hill to Whitley Head where the family lived – the colder the weather the better the 'divi'!

They were part of a tight community – her friend Margaret labels it bluntly as a 'class conscious society – where people knew their place within an almost feudal pattern of landed gentry.' There was the chapel-going headmaster, the vicar and, above all, the mill-owning benefactor, Sam Clough – also 'chapel' – whose family had virtually built the centre of Steeton. 'Clough mill', as it was always known even with a new owner, and John Dixon's bobbin mill together provided the major source of work in the village and Dorothy's family, like many others, were dependent on those mills for their livelihood. Indeed, weaving was 'in the blood', as Dorothy's great grandfather had actually been a 'home weaver', working in his own cottage. Dorothy's mother, also an experienced weaver, knew that she could rely on Sam Clough to provide her with work.

> *It's here I wish I could translate Dorothy's dialect onto paper. The phrase a would-be employee would put to Sam Clough was: 'hev-ye-onny looms?' and the reply seems to have been something like: 'Aye, tha can start reitchin in'! Got it? [No, I haven't either! Likewise it took me a few moments to take in what Granny meant when she would instruct Dorothy 'Whisht!' It turned out to mean: 'Sit there, don't move and keep yourself to yourself'].*

The reason Amy Shutt, Dorothy's mother, had temporarily turned to employment other than the mill was that she was blinded in her right eye with a hay seed when she had been helping her husband's family with harvesting. Soon after her husband's early demise in 1920 she and a friend built – actually designed and got friends and relatives to build – a fish and chip shop outside the entrance to the bobbin mill. The two young widows sought advice of Harry Ramsden, the famous Yorkshire fish trader, at that time still running his first fish and chip shop in Guisely, who generously delivered fish daily from Hull to Amy Shutt without charge. This project lasted only about a year. It unfortunately coincided with a bad potato harvest and they realised too that handling the cold, wet fish and lifting weights was affecting their health – so she had been obliged to give up the business and go 'into service'. Not until 1936, when Dorothy was 10, did her mother risk returning to the mill.

From a toddler, Dorothy attended Anglican church for two services on Sundays, singing in the choir and giving many concert performances at St. Stephens and the Methodist and Baptist chapels and other places in and around Steeton. 'There was always something going on', including visits from well-known soloists such as Kathleen Ferrier who lived a few miles away, near Blackburn. Auntie Ellen would point to the two trees outside the church door, a yew and a holly. 'Ten men,' she would say, indicating the yew, 'had taken their bows to Crecy from that tree' and nodding in the direction of a holly, 'You'll always be safe' assures Auntie Ellen 'if there's a holly outside the church' And this feeling of history and protection was enhanced by the closeness of the community. As Dorothy says, 'You knew everybody ... you spoke to everybody ... and if you did anything wrong ... they knew who you were – that was a mark of Steeton.'

And yet there were important times of freedom, for Dorothy and her many village girl friends were allowed to play out in the streets or countryside, or in the attic if it was raining. They made the environment their own, making dens, building dams, and some – not Dorothy – climbing trees. Dorothy says: 'Whitley Head was full of children. We never stopped playing ... and inventing things ... mostly with girls.' One unusual environment for climbing, hiding and disappearing into was the massive site of John Dixon's timber yard which housed hardwood, teak and mahogany from all over the world, huge trees in towering stacks awaiting the hand-saw and then the slow seasoning, so that some were never moved during the whole of Dorothy's childhood.

Some events, and Dorothy feels that her childhood seemed to be full of *events*, were only too real. She remembers a particularly scary one when Granny yelled after her and her neighbours' children one day as they were all setting off for school: 'Rishworth's horses are out!' Their narrow, sloping street was to be invaded by black and white iron-clad shire horses madly, wildly escaping from the farm right at the top of the hill. They were just setting off for school but no child on the road would be safe from the advancing pack. 'Walk on t'wall!', cries her grandmother. They scrambled on top, heard the thundering hoofs and Dorothy still remembers this charge of phantoms, like, as she sees them now, the Horsemen of the Apocalypse.

Another, rather different but no less dramatic tale is to do with toilets. The linked outside closets, as they were called, in the backyard of each house in the terrace were a feat of engineering and plumbing. The flushing system operated from each kitchen sink, feeding into the shared drain-pipe that ran well below the toilet seats. When there was sufficient water collected, the 'tippler tippled' and flushed away the waste. One day two of Dorothy's uncles, Harry and Alfred, motor-bike enthusiasts like many young men of the time, were carrying out a cleaning and oiling job on their machine – just outside the open toilet door. Harry must have accidentally poured a drop of petrol down the toilet – nobody knows quite how this could have come about – and Alfred, a smoker, cast his cigarette end down the same toilet. The explosion that followed caused the two men to gasp but that was nothing compared with the scream from the young lass two doors down who was blown off her toilet seat! That young lady was Irene Teale whom Uncle Harry was courting, or rather, whom Uncle Harry *was* courting! Whenever Dorothy now visits Aunt Edith, at 96, the one remaining relative of that generation, the old lady reminds her of this story: 'Were you there, Dorothy, when Irene Teale was blown off the toilet?'

If the hub of Dorothy's childhood offered security and protection and plenty of events to gossip about, its edges were tinged with the extraordinary, a rim of strange goings on that you did not talk about but could enjoy half-knowing about, like ...

'the witch' next door ...

the man's house across the way you must never, never enter 'even if he offers you sweets'...

the gold sovereigns and half sovereigns Dorothy found in the sheepskins and which she put in her apron pocket thinking they were only buttons...

as Annie Emmet's brother Jim lay dead...

that's Ann Emmet, suffering, according to Granny, from being 'crossed i' love'...

Ann, who always bought half a loaf of bread from the store with the agreement that she could go back for the other half two days later...

And so on...

Such domestic mysteries could only be matched by mysteries of the mystic kind. There was Auntie May in Morecambe who had second sight, who got messages during the war from the recently dead to pass on to others ... Dorothy as a child would hear of this comfort to the bereaved, but not until adulthood did she have direct experience of Auntie May's gift. When Dorothy's mother died suddenly in 1972, Auntie May already knew it had happened and when it had happened even before Dorothy phoned her, the first to phone her, with the sad news. And Auntie May went on to say in her business like, matter-of-fact way: 'I have a message ... You're to go on your journey ... Take the box – meaning 'take along the appropriate legal documents to register the death' ... and go on your journey ... She's with her mother ... the funeral will be on Thursday...'

Dorothy got a word in, about to explain they couldn't know which day...: 'But I've not yet registered...'

'... it'll be on *Thursday* ... I'll be over.'

Dorothy was about to visit the States to give a key-note address at a conference, and thus with her mother's blessing she flew to Albany, New York State, four days after the *Thursday* funeral.

And there was the ghost story. In late adolescence Dorothy would sometimes return, fairly late at night, to the 16th century mill shed, the upper floor of which had been turned into a cosy home, rented to them by Charlie Fletcher who took over an old mill in Silsden. 'You'd come round the corner ... up the steps that were so worn ... you couldn't say you *saw* it ... you *sensed* a shadow ... the feeling would be of a very large bulky male ... would move aside with a kind of courtesy ... no threat.' This happened fairly regularly as she arrived home in the dark but once inside she would immediately forget about it. She never mentioned it to any one, not even her mother. And yet a few years later, she was returning home from her University work in Newcastle and as she opened the door she overheard her mother chatting to a visitor, telling him about 'the ghost at the door'. It dawned on Dorothy that her mother had long been aware of the same gentle haunting and she then recalled how her mother was always reluctant to have that door shut – 'in case he wants to come in', her mother now felt free to explain. And some years after that a young relative casually came out with the news that 'they've pulled down the haunted house' – it had obviously been a piece of local legend of which Dorothy and her mother had at first been unaware.

There was another unusual feature characterising Dorothy's childhood, just the opposite of mysterious but rich in crisis, at least through the eyes of a young child. Her Granny, Sarah Ann, was always fetched. [What was that again,

Dorothy? Fetched? Yes, Fetched, sent for.] She was the Whitley Head woman other women of the village would send for if there were a minor tragedy, an accident or sudden illness or even death. Granny would keep a basket of clean linen, probably old, washed sheets, and always a large apron and soap ready to hand. Alone at times with Granny, Dorothy would have to go with her – not to be left with the coal fire burning – whenever Sarah Anne was 'fetched'. 'Whisht!' was the instruction and Dorothy, all eyes and ears, sat on a buffet as if she wasn't there. And Dorothy was good at not being there and not asking questions. So she probably saw and heard more than she understood.

Even within the house the adult circle of Granny and the Aunts, forever reporting to each other the latest goings on and weighing up the credibility of each new story, gave the young girl privileged status beyond her years. And when Granny and her friend Mrs. Mawson went on one of their regular summer afternoon walks with Dorothy up to 'the waste piece' – Heather moor – they would speak of: 't'yellow dog's out.' Dorothy could see it in every detail, not its yellowness, but its slavering, loping figure, bringing its forewarning of death. She glimpsed the very edge of her protected world and never said a word.

It was some years later that Dorothy read an account of the yellow dog, which the author, Halliwell Sutcliffe, described as a legendary creature of the dales, an omen of foreboding. Its image was to stay with Dorothy into adulthood, changing its colour to black but still a slavering, loping phantom dog figure, lurching at one's shoulder, not wanting to be seen, ready to jump if you give it a chance. It became linked in her mind with loss of confidence and self-esteem, especially relating to how one felt about oneself as a teacher. Losing your nerve because you've let the class get the better of you or coming up against a colleague's criticism, someone with a different agenda from your own. Dorothy would say to her students who were suffering self-doubt; 'It's the black dog – knock it off.'

But there was one mystery in Dorothy's life her family circle never talked about in front of her. Never good at Maths, she nevertheless worked out that the man who had died several years before her birth could not possibly have been her father! She cannot recall at exactly what age she did this sussing out, perhaps 7 or 8. At some point she questioned her mother about this and had to be satisfied with the assurance that 'her real father was a gentleman' – and he was never discussed again.

Grandad, the mildest of men, who 'wouldn't hurt anyone', seemed to Dorothy as a young child to be on the edge of the goings on at 35 Whitley Head. He worked long hours and rarely drew attention to himself when he was at home – except, that is, when he came home drunk on a Friday or Saturday evening. Not loudly, aggressively drunk, you understand, but 'overly happy' – and never sure where he had thrown his hat on his journey home from the Goatshead Inn. He had three 'billy-cocks', as the brushed felt hats were called. It was the 'middle billy-cock' he would lose, the others being the one he wore for work and the 'best' for funerals. Grandma would say: 'Which way did thee come 'ome?' And then, next morning, on the way to church, Aunt Ellen and Dorothy would retrace that route until they found it, usually discarded by the wayside, but once in the middle of the tarn!

Learning to read and to imagine

When Uncle Alfred was too ill to work – he later died of a brain tumour – Dorothy, as a pre-school child sat by him while he read the local *Titbits*, a favourite family paper of the time. As he finished with each page he would drop it in her lap – and that's how she learned to read. The material may not always have been suitable. She can still recall the silence, followed by 'I'll tell you about it later' from her Granny, when she asked at a time when the living room happened to be full of male and female members of the family: 'What's a sanitary towel?'

Not only did she learn to read very young, she could read as she walked. And when she did go to school she would sometimes be reading as she walked there and back if there was no-one else around to walk with. From a very young age she won prizes at Sunday-school and her Auntie Ellen had some books kept in a hatbox, one being *Pilgrim's Progress*, she recalls. She liked all the subjects in her Elementary school or 'big' school as it was known locally, especially English, History and Geography, but an unexpected opportunity for self-education occurred. It was Sam Clough's daughter who invited Dorothy to borrow books from her private library, kept in the billiard room of Steeton Hall, a soundly built Victorian mansion amidst wooded grounds and stables. A vast collection of set volumes of classic texts presented themselves. She even read books on horse riding, a keen interest of Miss Clough. An arrangement was made whereby she could, through the maid, borrow a book long before school started in a morning – by now she was living in Market Street with her mother who had to leave her with a neighbour to go to work. She would take the book to school to read until school started, read in the breaks, read in the lunch hour and evening, read as she walked home – and return it, finished, next morning.

Schooling after 'failing' the 11+, was a comfortable routine for Dorothy who found learning very easy. She enjoyed the requirement of 'getting and re-membering facts'. Not having a Grammar School education deprived her, how-ever, of the chance to learn foreign languages. The pronunciation and spelling of continental words remain a mystery to her to this day. Two teachers she still remembers well. One she liked to be with was Miss Bray, who, Dorothy noted, always brought her embroidery to school with her. [This will have stirred the memory of those of us who know Dorothy well – I can recall that she was inclined also to bring her embroidery or knitting to social events such as house parties. And she achieved notoriety 45 years later when she gave an interview for a television programme called 'Heroes' and embroidered throughout.]

Not long before leaving school Dorothy became attached to a friendly teacher, who had been evacuated with her class to Steeton School and was very popular, always surrounded by a group of girls, but she was taken seriously ill with TB. Dorothy would cycle the fifteen miles to the Grassington Open Air hospital to visit her, impressed with her courage in facing the long confinement in hospital.

Dorothy Clough was more to Dorothy than a source of books. She was also the District Commissioner for the Girl Guides, an organisation Dorothy stayed with for eight years until she was 19. Weekly meetings were held in commissioner Clough's stable block. A great deal of badge work was done, Dorothy finishing up with a sleeveful! During the Mill holidays they went camping, learning all the outdoor 'correct' ways to survive – tents, fires, cooking and camp songs – and enjoying all the rituals of grace before meals and prayers.

Two strands brought a balance to Dorothy's childhood, her imagination that took her away and her sense of responsibility that kept her here. From the age of 6 she divided her energies equally between these worlds, enjoying both and appreciating the distinction between them. Sewing and baking are – as they are still – regular occupations. She had a sure hand and eye, so that when they all joined in making tab rugs, great family talking time, she was the one who cut out the pieces of material from old clothes, each piece the same size. Sometimes the sewing was related to special events such as Harvest Sunday, the Gala Queen or the Rose Queen. These domestic activities represented more than a way of doing something useful; they fulfilled her perpetual need to be busily engaged. Even when she was reading, it had to be seen to others and to herself as *busy* reading.

She was always aware that she mustn't add to her mother's worries and make unnecessary demands on her. Thus she mustn't let on that she was upset when her mother left on Saturday night to be back to work for another week, so she used her 'busy-ness' as a way of disguising her feelings. As her mother came to say good-bye, Dorothy would turn to some task, like 'needing to play with Granny's gas pennies' – as though she were preoccupied. She was intensely conscious that there was no spare money and recalls gazing at her shoes in church, praying that her feet wouldn't grow any more, because although her mother could extend stockings, shoes remained obstinately the same size. What a relief to be able to start work at 14, so that she could give her mother the £1 a week wage from the mill. And yet, it must be reiterated, they never *felt* poor, but rather, as Dorothy puts it 'rich enough for it all to go round.'

There emerged another side to her sense of responsibility. She was drawn to a girl the same age as herself, a girl who in those days would have been thought of as 'backward' or 'slow learning'. Characteristically, Dorothy befriended Gladys Lund not in any patronising way. She simply took to her, while recognising that she was 'different' and needed help. This ability to see directly to someone's essential humanness without judgement was to become a mark of Dorothy as a teacher. When, as so often happened, she met classes that she had never met before, they appeared to sense straightaway that she was seeing them as people worth getting to know. They may have been carrying other teachers' labels of 'nuisances' or 'a difficult class' or 'you'll not get anything out of them' or 'retarded' or 'emotionally disturbed', but they saw her reading beyond any label – and a trust began. She herself, without necessarily articulating it in these terms, understood that all teachers needed this basic human gift.

The imaginative aspect of childhood took Dorothy in many different directions. She played on her own a great deal, becoming 'someone else' as she tried on her aunties' hats. On one occasion she cut her hair to suit the hat. Even playing with the cat, 'I was kind of performing ... me and the cat ... and somebody out there.' Dorothy describes such playing as 'self-conscious playing fully aware and in control'. *Who* she chose to be was influenced by the latest cinema show, although she was Robin Hood for something like three months – wearing her green waterproof cape. She was more likely to experience some *loss* of control, however, from her intense reading of stories, equally intense today. She recalls allowing herself to be frightened on one occasion by a story from *Pilgrim's Progress* told by the vicar at one of her confirmation classes. Walking home, she was sure Appollyan was lying in wait for her as he did for Christian and Pilgrim, and that night in bed the candle suddenly went out and she screamed, arousing her mother. Only her aunt who owned the copy of *Pilgrim's Progress* understood what Dorothy meant when Dorothy had whimpered 'Appollyan' as an explanation of her terror.

This particular memory of terror has stayed with Dorothy throughout her life, causing her, for instance, to temper stories she reads to her own daughter. It has noticeably affected her work with very young children, especially when monsters of some kind cropped up in their drama. She would insist that the class created its own monster, planning it, designing it, technically devising it ... anything to make sure it was *theirs* and that they knew what they were making – with a 'cool it' or 'opt out' exit clearly visible!

Her early stage appearances were cool pieces of entertainment. She had great confidence that she could pull it off. She knew how to make an audience laugh, how to grip their imaginations, as she did more informally with her cousins when she entertained them with made-up stories. Her first experience of being in a play was at the age of 5 in the infant school and she continued right through each year until she left at 14. There were many church concerts at which she would recite longish ballads such as *Sir Patrick Spens*. As she approached teens she started to play adult roles. Again there was a 'self-consciousness' about her performance, using the term in its best sense of searching for the most economical way of creating an effect. She recalls playing Sir Peter Teazle when she was 14 and trying hard to 'think male behaviour', while recognising the need for style and timing.

Even as a seven-year old she became more and more absorbed by how something was achieved. She gazed with her Grandfather at the two lithographs hanging in the living room, of Gladstone and Disraeli and other Members of Parliament being received by Queen Victoria, her attention drawn to how the artist illuminated the queen and shaded down the other figures. That the angle of light brings a particular meaning to a picture could be said to be one of Dorothy's earliest realisations about art. From a very early age she grasped that artists do more than paint an image of a landscape or portrait – they purposely direct the onlooker's eye. There were other pictures and items of interest in Grandad's possession – two china dogs, green paperweights, Staffordshire figures – suggesting, perhaps that he had once been more affluent. Auntie Ellen's story is that he actually owned a row of forty terraced houses, which somehow he 'lost' or sold foolishly!

I can recall that when I first met Dorothy she would occasionally read rapidly through whodunits or James Bond novels, but always start at the end. Her explanation was that if you knew how it ended then you could settle to watch the mechanisms by which that ending evolved. This way of perusing a novel is not merely to satisfy some intellectual pursuit. It is self protective. Dorothy reads with such intensity that she can become overwrought with emotions of grief or despair or fear, unless she shields herself in advance by knowing the ending. As she later put it to me: 'I must know the worst first so I can survive it.' And, presumably keep Appollyan from her dreams.

She has never been able to cope with watching television drama or a video film. This is not a matter of taste but of terror. It is a fear of drowning in what is happening. The only way she can watch is if the context allows her to think technically, so that when she watched a video of *Citizen Kane* with her son-in-law, Kevin, she could comfortably adopt the role of educator, pointing out to him, for instance, how the use of camera angles represented an advancement in film-making. This 'seeing it at one remove' allowed her to feel safe.

That same need, although not as raw as the domestic confrontation of a TV screen, is also part of her theatre-going. Thus when Dorothy went to the theatre, as she did in her teens each Saturday to Keighley Playhouse, she enjoyed the relationships between the characters and how they formed the events of the plot. She was fascinated by how the same actors adapted themselves week after week to different roles. She does not mean greying the hair and stooping, but how they found other people in themselves. Her concentration was also on how the theatrical effects were achieved.

Perhaps the greatest influence on Dorothy from the arts was the richness of words and other means of communicating, such as sound and colour and movement. The richness and subtleties and shades of difference made up a rainbow of meanings in a word/colour/sound/movement spectrum. Choice of word and choice of colour became compelling crafts. Her awareness of the need to discriminate came to Dorothy as a young child when her grandfather, the expert warp dresser, would sometimes bring home tangled silk threads used in weaving the expensive Bradford suiting. It was catching sight of the subtle herb and aniline dyes amidst the snarled-up greys, blues, greens and reds that she learnt from her grandad to identify peacock blue, ruby red, rose and lime. She found that colours inspired distinctive words and words were like distinctive colours. So the infant Dorothy played in her mind with these distinctions. Similarly, when she went to church as a young child, she was fascinated by the coloured stamps given for attending Sunday School, the colours representing the church year's calendar. As she explains in an interview with Sandra Hesten:

> So at Lenten times they were purple ones and at Easter they were very deep purple, and at Christmas they were red and white. And this symbolism had great effect on me. I remember loving these stamps, looking at those pictures, looking deeply into those pictures. I suppose to me they were illuminated manuscripts, although I had not heard of that kind of thing then.

There was another kind of imaginative world that Dorothy was nurtured on. She was ever conscious of the history that surrounded her. Steeton was in the Domesday Book in the parish of Kildwick, the mother church known as the Long Kirk of Craven. The monks of Bolton Abbey, three miles away, were a thriving community dating from Saxon times to the suppression of the monasteries. 'Our history at school was 'real' – we lived among Bolton Abbey stories, the legends of the strid (Wordsworth's White Doe of Rhylstone), Robert the Bruce's raids on the Abbey, failing to find the treasure which was really hidden in Thorpe, a 'lost' village'. Ritual walks in Easter bonnets were organised to Bolton Abbey, from St. Stephens to the Abbey Church. At weekends the Abbey grounds and river, with its famous stepping stones used by the monks, were visited by the local people. 'If ever I had a day off from the mill I rode my bike there and wandered around the ruins and graveyard stones.' One is reminded of the number of times that monks crop up in Heathcote's classrooms.

The more secular, feudal past was represented by the Elizabethan manor, Steeton Hall, dating back to the Domesday book, 'a manor gifted by William to Sir Thomas Stiveton'. The gentry still occupied it in Dorothy's day. She recalls that Sir Alex Keighley provided the prizes for the school Prize Day, and arrived on a sleigh and dressed as Father Christmas to give presents at the end of the autumn term. On special days, such as crowning of the May Queen, he would open his grounds to the public. Old Alex, as he was called although not really old at all, was in fact a famous photographer. Curiously, there was a second Steeton Hall, a Victorian mansion amidst wooded grounds and stables and adjacent to the first Hall, where the Cloughs lived.

Her concerns

What deeply troubled Dorothy throughout her childhood was her size. She saw herself as too tall, too broad, too heavy, too fat, so that she always looked older than she was. She felt ashamed when her mother was challenged on the bus about wanting half fare. Only when she was acting could she be any size she wanted to be. 'I'm going to be a film star', Dorothy announces to her first year elementary school classmate. I ask her whether she was ever teased about her size by other children. 'Nobody ever laughed at me – of course I was top of the class', she replied. And yet, according to her friend, Margaret Freeman, they were known as 'the two fatties' and 'were the brunt of many nasty hurtful comments'. Margaret goes on to say 'I think that is why we retreated into a make-believe world'. Dorothy was to be conscious of her size for the rest of her life, often meeting people of whom she would say: 'that's how I would like to look'.

Fear of swimming was another of her worries but that was something she could avoid having to deal with. But her terror of birds has stayed with her all her life. One of the most panicky moments of her teaching career was when a child brought a wounded pigeon into the classroom. I recall once, when we were engaged in an animated conversation as we crossed Trafalgar Square, wondering why we appeared to be zigzagging across the pavements. Whereas her fear of birds is something she never got over, she overcame her anxiety about swimming, helped by a student and life-long friend, Joan Hilsden, and was motivated to learn because she did not want her baby daughter to have the same fear. And then she taught me to swim!

One might have expected that not knowing who her real father was might have caused some misery to Dorothy as a child. But this was not so. One reads of so many instances where children seek their 'real' parents into their adulthood, feeling a sense of incompletion or, worse, deprivation until they know the 'truth'. Only the mildest curiosity arises for Dorothy when, *very* occasionally she has vaguely wondered, when reading about some man in a novel, 'whether her father was like him'. Dorothy's childhood was secure and complete. She was at the centre of a circle of love and support in which the figure of a 'real father' barely featured. Her mother's and aunts' version of the story will now never be told.

There was an aspect of her relationship with her mother that became more special to Dorothy as she grew old enough to appreciate its significance. At her birth the doctor who had delivered her, childless himself, had offered to adopt her. Thus Amy Shutt had been given a choice of immense consequence to herself, her baby and to the doctor. Her decision lived with her for the rest of her life, an expression of commitment and love that few are asked to make. Always to know that it could have been otherwise surely gives an awareness to a mother/daughter relationship that is profound. That the headmaster understood that if Dorothy had passed the scholarship her life would have taken a totally different route pales in significance compared with the 'what if' that Dorothy's mother lived with – the effect of adoption by the young doctor and his wife and how that would have been. To live with such a memory is almost beyond imagining.

Dorothy's early life was circled by love; no middle-class doctor could have given her more. But this was not an indulgent, spoiling upbringing. It was a tiny community in which the rules were made clear and were not to be broken. Dorothy, even today, is more comfortable going along with whatever appear to be the rules, especially the rules of officialdom. And yet the unshifting presence of those 'adult' rules appeared to allow Dorothy as a child to be free of them, or rather, to be free within them. She has always had the courage, as she puts it, 'to be *me*'. She tells Sandra Hesten in an interview: 'I think I knew from an early age that I was somehow remarkable; I don't think I have ever wanted to just fit in with everybody.' The story of her childhood has been one of growing independence of mind and her career, as we shall see, has broken all the rules.

Astonishingly, Dorothy has now discovered who her father was. Having read a draft of this chapter which includes the comment: 'her mother's and aunt's version will never be told', it occurred to her that that need not be the case for Auntie Edith is still alive. Thus Dorothy stirred herself to write to her cousin, Auntie Edith's daughter, to see if she could find an opportune moment to ask her mother about it. And so, in the middle of one of their usual mother/daughter arguments, this time with the rather querulous old lady refusing to agree to have her bed taken downstairs, Cousin Ann asks: 'Can you remember Dorothy's father?' 'Oh yes...' came the immediate response 'it were ... and he lived in ... and he had a fish shop ... we knew he was chatting our Amy up' – and the arguing about not having the bed downstairs resumed.

Thus in the week of her 75th birthday, August 2001, Dorothy has learnt the name of her father ... and the story is completed. A few weeks later, her Aunt Edith died, and it only took a few weeks for Dorothy, 'fittingly', she believes, to forget completely what name she had been told.

2

Three Looms Waiting

At t'Mill – for the rest of her working life

'Weaving was a prideful job – it really was you know'. Towards the end of July,1940, a month before her fourteenth birthday, Dorothy left school and went into the mill the next day. These two events, leaving school at that age and entering employment in Sam Clough's mill, were as routine as night following day for the pupils of Steeton, all except the odd one, including the headmaster's son, who'd gone off to Grammar School. The possibility of a career was not part of anyone's thoughts, least of all Dorothy's. In any case there was now a war on and there was a shortage of weavers, as most of the men were called up. Dorothy's mother was working in the mill at this time, in spite of her 'blind eye', although a year or two later 'bad legs' obliged her to give it up.

Rationing, the blackout, the absence of sons and fathers, the occasional rumble of tanks passing through the village at night, and regular news of bombing in Leeds and Bradford provided the war-time background to Dorothy's five years [1940-45] in the mill. Hours were long, 6.30 a.m. until 5.30 p.m. with two half hour breaks and, when the firm was obliged to switch from suiting to parachutes, the employees worked a 48 hour week, including Saturdays. Early each morning, mostly in the dark, Dorothy would join hundreds of other girls and women walking to the mill, an old stone building with huge chimneys, covering a massive acreage. A hundred looms would be silently waiting in the cavernous, white-washed section where Dorothy worked. The engine man would start the master belt, the smaller ones would follow and then, once all the belts were moving, the tremendous din began, as each weaver turned on her loom. The looms crashed into action for the rest of the day, the noise deafening to any visitor but, curiously, not heard by the weavers themselves. The floor bearing the looms was stone, the looms close together. 'You got used to rushing between them to avoid catching the shuttle and tearing your black apron'. Each weaver, usually wearing clogs for comfort, stood on a small platform of wood in front of each loom, carrying on conversations with the fellow workers at looms on every side in a general atmosphere of friendly industry, pitching their voices with careful articulation over the noise.

After a year of being a 'reacher in', handing threads one at a time from the big warp suspended above for the 'warp dresser' to thread them through the healds, she was given her first loom. Dorothy was lucky to have Emily, an expert weaver to train her on the loom. Or perhaps it wasn't luck – as granddaughter to Irving Sugden they may have expected Dorothy to inherit his skill. Moving to Fletcher's Mill in Silsden, she was transferred from dobbies to jacquards, a more complex process that allowed for the weaving of flowers and abstract designs and she was given the usual three looms to watch. By now she and her mother were living in the 'haunted' house – right against the mill chimney.

Knowing that Dorothy was to become a famous drama teacher, it is perhaps difficult for us to understand the contentment she found in the work. It demanded both high concentration and skill. She drew considerable satisfaction from her ability to control hand and eye, always aiming at perfection, for mistakes were costly in time and money – and there was a war on. She belonged to the mill and did not set her sights beyond it, until she met up with Mollie Sugden...

Dorothy, the adolescent entertainer

Mollie Sugden – now known as a successful TV actress and comedienne in the UK – was a young elocution teacher living in Keighley. Dorothy kept a shilling and her bus fare back from the £1 a week wages she handed over to her mother and started having lessons. (The £1 rapidly rose to £5 a week – 'good money' because of the war.) Fortunately Miss Sugden's teaching veered towards helping her students with interpretation of texts rather than elocution in the narrow sense of artificially correct speech. 'Mollie must have recognised I was good at things ... giving me quite complex things to do.' Dorothy would stick sonnets or longer poems on her loom and learn them off as she worked. When Mollie Sugden left the area three years later Dorothy had further lessons in Skipton from a man who stimulated her interest in the literary side of texts such as Shakespeare's sonnets. Soon after starting work, Dorothy was invited to join a little amateur concert party, just four of them, for which she performed many of the recitations she did with Mollie Sugden. She gradually extended her repertoire by performing speeches from plays. With a good ear and a contralto voice, she was part of the quartet that sang such stirring pieces as *Oh Peaceful England*. Her knowledge of songs from musicals was rapidly extended and her social life broadened somewhat as the quartet would be invited to supper after the performance. She enjoyed the experience of a different kind of adult company who engaged in friendly chat about music and musical theatre. They presented their show in different parts of the region at the week-ends, mostly in church halls, for the village churches were the centres for village culture and entertainment. Thus Dorothy found herself visiting places in the Yorkshire Dales she had never seen before.

Soon after starting work she joined the Bingley players, which at times demanded five nights a week and occasional Sunday afternoon rehearsals. Of this period Dorothy says 'At this time I knew I really could act'. And for Dorothy, this was a matter of self-consciously selecting pitch and gesture etc. in carefully gauged control of her acting behaviour. For the first time since fantasising as a child about becoming a film-star, she began to see the possibility of a career beyond the mill, or at least alongside the mill, as an elocution teacher and amateur actor.

So there was no sudden break for Dorothy in seeing herself as a performer. Throughout her childhood and now during her teens she developed her ability to captivate an audience – lucky are the people who have the chance of being entertained by Dorothy today when she revels in the telling of some personal anecdote. One of the things her past students remember about her courses is how much they laughed.

The Audition

The elocution lessons, the concert party and her weekly Saturday afternoon visits to Keighley Repertory and rehearsals with the Bingley Players appeared to fulfil her thespian interests in her spare time, but such theatrical fare suddenly seemed inadequate when, one day early in 1945, Dorothy read in the local press, the *Yorkshire Post*, an advertisement for the opening of a new Theatre School which was to train both actors and teachers. The Principal was to be Esmé Church, a well-known director and actress in her late forties whose work was influenced by Michel St. Denis.[1]

Dorothy's immediate reaction was: 'I'd like to go there!' Of course she couldn't go, as she was the sole bread-winner, her mother having had to give up work because of her bad legs but she was keen to go to the audition to see if she had any talent. Her mother insisted on attending with her and sat at the back of the Bradford auditorium behind the audition panel, which included Esmé Church, J.B. Priestley[2] and Rudolf Laban. Dorothy, realistically avoiding heroines, presented Volumnia and Queen Margaret for her audition pieces. Immediately after the audition Esmé Church offered Dorothy a place. Dorothy apologetically stammered:

> 'I can't come to Theatre School. I haven't any money for the fees ... but I wondered if I have talent.'

'You certainly have talent.'

At this point her mother's voice could be heard from the back, announcing that she had some savings. Esmé Church made it clear that the decision was theirs and that Dorothy was to let her know if she wanted the offered place. Returning home on the bus, she knew now, more than ever, that she wanted it!

Dorothy makes no mention in her interview with me of not having any 'proper' qualifications for a further education course, having left a non-selective school at 14 with no examination successes behind her. Was this lack of paper evidence of her ability raised as an issue at her audition? One would have expected that a minimum qualification at that time was five subjects at School Certificate level or at least some sort of grammar school background. Was this waived because it was to be a theatre vocational course? Emergency teacher training courses that started about the same time as Bradford Civic Theatre School opened required at least School Certificate. Perhaps it was assumed that those who passed the teaching course would go on to teach classes of adult amateurs, as indeed Dorothy was to do.

Dorothy was later to appreciate that she was incredibly lucky to get a University post, but it had not dawned on her that her lack of grammar school education was perhaps something the Bradford Civic Theatre School management were obliged to overlook, especially when she went on to the teacher course. It is likely that the students' qualifications were as varied as their ages, for whereas one or two were as young as 16 or 17 there were a number of mature men and women just demobbed from war service.

The headlines in the *Yorkshire Post* next morning – Esmé Church was not going to let a good student slip out of her fingers so easily – read as follows:

WEAVER GETS CHANCE
OF STAGE CAREER

Fellow mill-workers showed the newspaper to the boss, Charlie Fletcher, who sent for Dorothy:

'Is this thee?' [pointing to the newspaper heading]

'If it says what I did in Bradford yesterday...'

'Hast tha onny brass?'

'Well, no ... I can't go ... my mother's only a bit of money ... In any case she's not very well.'

'Could she take the looms?'

'Well, she doesn't weave jacquards ... she only does dobbies.'

'There's a couple of dobbies ... she can have dobbies ... and I'll pay thi fees. How long will it be?'

[Apologetically] 'Two³ years'

'Well, that's all right ... and there'll be three looms waiting for thee, when tha's finished.'

The offer of 'three looms waiting' was not heard by Dorothy as a piece of wry cynicism from a man who was 'chapel' and did not really approve of theatre. She and her mother just assumed that once this chance to train properly was over, she would indeed be continuing with her 'real' job. Her mother thought it necessary to warn her: 'When tha comes back ... I doubt there'll get *three* ready for thee ... newly set up'. No doubt Dorothy acknowledged the wisdom of this, banishing as best she could a tiny, niggling fantasy that she could become a 'proper' stage actress.

With one more week to work, Dorothy's attention was drawn to an unusual weaving phenomenon occurring in front of her. It appeared that by Friday all three warps were going to be finished, all three at the same time. It had never been known for three warps to empty at once. And on the Friday, the very day she was due to leave, when normally someone else would have to take over the completion of a piece of work, 'the three warps ran out ... and the three beams became completely empty ... it had never been known to happen before.' And to Dorothy this had to be 'a sign!'

Theatre School

Theatre School began – and a new kind of life. In an interview with Sandra Hesten, Dorothy talks of her mixture of feelings about this 'new life':

> My memories of theatre school are that it was a very dangerous and very worrying time. Remember, I had left a mill which seemed secure. I was worried conscience-wise because I had put my mother in a position where she had to be the only bread earner again. It seemed to cost an awful lot, and of course it went against that puritanical strand in me, that is, you must *work* for what you want. Somehow, being at theatre school seemed so much like play...

Thus guilt turned her training into what she describes as 'a despairing struggle to be sure it was worth leaving the mill'.

Dorothy made herself two dresses out of black-out material, Bolton sheeting sold off cheaply by the church as the war ended. She decorated them with braid. They were to last her until after theatre school, although one of the staff, Barbara Crabtree, who looked after speech training, occasionally gave her a dress. Esmé Church provided her with a new dress when she wanted Dorothy to do some amateur evening class teaching for her. The Shutts missed Dorothy's mill earnings while she was at Bradford, but frugality, care over not wasting money or resources were part of their nature, so they always 'managed'. This abhorrence of waste has stayed with Dorothy all her life and has, indeed crept into her professional work, whether it is a matter of economy in the use of materials and time or 'parsimony', Dorothy's term for a high degree of selectivity, in her artistry.

The quality of the course was guaranteed by the people who staffed it. They were an enthusiastic, enterprising collection of theatre practitioners, loyal to Esmé Church and excited by this new project in the North of England, the first of its kind. Church had worked with Michel St. Denis in setting up the Bristol Old Vic, which she used as a model for her new school. Such was her connection with the leading professional world that she was able to invite Sir Lewis Casson, Dame Edith Evans, Marie Ney and Michel St. Denis as visiting speakers. It differed from established theatre schools in opting to give emphasis to children's theatre, touring large-scale public productions for children's audiences, along with classical productions of *The Rivals, Androcles and the Lion* and *Julius Caesar*. Rudolf Laban, Geraldine Stephenson and Lisa Ullman gave the course its philosophy, basing their training of actors upon Rudolf Laban's approach to characterisation. His way of perceiving people was not in terms of their temperament or psychological history but in terms of efforts and levels as expressive movers. Dorothy learnt to appreciate this way of seeing others and when later she was to work with amateur groups on stage she used Laban's principles as a basis both for characterisation and fluency of movement on stage.[4]

The course was entirely practical with no theoretical element of any kind. It included regular children's theatre performances that were sometimes toured. On one occasion they presented *The Tinder Box* at Toynbee Hall, in front of the Lord Mayor of London, Sir Bracewell Smith, to whom they were introduced. He was a distant relative of Dorothy's, Granny's nephew. They didn't know each other and had never had anything to do with each other, but she knew of him. His history had been a kind of mythical family tale. Like the rest of his family, he worked in a Yorkshire mill, but he somehow became the owner of the one he worked in. An enterprising man, he borrowed a million pounds from the bank in the late 1940s and, with his eye on London, he recognised that now that the tourist industry was restarting following the war, there was nowhere for wealthy Americans to stay. So he took up residence in London, built the Park Lane Hotel, following that success with the Mayfair. His reputation led him to be appointed as official caterer to the House of Commons. A knighthood followed and he became London's Lord Mayor, paying an official visit to Toynbee Hall as part of his duties in 1947. Dorothy could have said to him on that occasion, 'I am your second cousin, Dorothy', but she didn't. She could have said: 'One branch of your family has no money', but she wouldn't! He died, a public benefactor, in the early 1950s, leaving his money to many causes, including leaving a mansion in perpetuity to the citizens of Keighley. It is a flourishing museum today. Sir Bracewell's portrait – with 'granny's face' – hangs in Cliff Castle, near Keighley.

Towards the end of the second year when Dorothy thought her course of training in acting was near completion, a conversation in the Principal's study about Dorothy's unmistakeable preference for stage work went as follows:

'My dear', says Esmé Church 'you're very talented – quite fearfully so at times [almost an accusation!] ... However, you are not the right size for your age, for the roles you can play ... I think we have to face it...'

'I know that' interrupts Dorothy.

'One day you will be, but in the meantime ... teaching... [in presenting this dialogue to me Dorothy is now caught up in giving a fair impersonation of Miss Church, adopting a rich, somewhat nasal tone – I wonder if she used to take off her principal in this way to entertain fellow students? No, she wouldn't have dared!]

'No thank you.'

'My dear, I'm making a serious suggestion.'

'I don't want to teach – I'll go back to the mill.'

'My dear ... I'm going out of the room ... and when I come back ... you'll be going to teach.' And she left the room, locking the door on Dorothy, returning shortly afterwards.

'Let me tell you what you'll be doing if you teach...'

Esmé Church proceeded to plant in Dorothy's mind an image of future drama work in schools, calling it 'The Drama of the Mind'. Instead of schools preparing the occasional play for performing to parents and friends on open day etc, pupils would get together to make up their own plays about things that mattered.

Thus, in 1947, Dorothy is presented with the image of curriculum drama that she was later to develop into a distinct methodology.[5] One man who shared this vision was A.L Stone, recently appointed Physical Education Organiser for the West Riding. Esmé invited him to advise the students on classroom teaching. She no doubt realised he came to Yorkshire with a national reputation as a leader in progressive education.[6]

The third year teacher-training, however, was a huge disappointment to Dorothy – she describes it as 'ridiculous', no more than a group of theatre professionals attempting to share with students their vague notion of what schools were like. She seemed to learn very little from it but in her free time she seized the opportunity to watch Esmé Church direct plays, plays that she couldn't take part in because she'd opted for teaching, a profound training of a different kind. It is curious that Dorothy quotes A.L. Stone as an example of the inadequacy of the advice given about teaching. He suggested to Dorothy: 'All you have to do is to get good lessons ready and teach them over and over again.' Some students, dreading school practice, might have felt relieved by such pragmatism, but not Dorothy Shutt, a mature young woman of 21, who, without realising it, was already formulating in her mind a kind of classroom practice that challenged all previous conceptions of how drama should be taught.[7]

The third year at Bradford Civic Theatre School, now with its name changed to Northern Theatre School, required Dorothy to take the external examination of the Royal Academy of Music, London, L.R.A.M., in order to attain its Licentiate. Dorothy regarded this qualification as 'ridiculous', but now sees that having such a qualification at the end of the three years gave both the course and 'teacher' students some clout. Although this was the first examination she had taken since the 11+, she felt little apprehension. Indeed she actually enjoyed it, including the theoretical paper, for it covered matters such as verse form, for which she had been ably helped by Mollie Sugden in Keighley years earlier and Barbara Crabtree[8] at the Theatre School.[9]

A kind of school practice took place each Friday afternoon in a secondary school[10], over two terms. On her first visit the Headmaster, who had obviously forgotten that she was coming, spotted the usual knot of boys sent out for bad behaviour dotted round the hall at various classroom doors, called them over and announced that 'This is Miss Shutt – she's going to do Drama with you.' And Dorothy did what she was to do for the rest of her career. 'Out of the blue' she found the unexpected question that startled, intrigued and straightway overrode the fact that they weren't a 'proper' class, reaching well beyond their immediate mid-Yorkshire background yet appearing to trust that they would be just the ones who would know all about it: 'If you were Captain of a ship...' she began 'what would you look for in the men who were going to sail it?'

And that is how Dorothy's teaching started: pupils selected at random, a make-shift arrangement. And somehow this was to set a pattern. Throughout her career she was to find herself in circumstances sometimes quite bizarre, that most teachers would be appalled by. To understand Heathcote as a teacher you have to see this capacity to rise above normal teaching expectations. But it is not so much a conscious effort by her to counter adverse conditions, as a failure to recognise them as adverse, so that in any teaching circumstances she finds herself in, its *opportunities* present themselves to her and what others might see as shortcomings she can, apparently naïvely, blissfully ignore.

What did she do next? Every teacher reading this book will know that however apt your first question, you have to know how to proceed from there! I pressed Dorothy on this and her answer took me by surprise. She explained that with this, her first class, her hunch that 'controlled conflict' was needed led her to draw on her Theatre School instruction in fencing with foils. A 'fight choreography' followed.

> *This strikes me as an insufficient answer, not really telling us very much. Could it be a fanciful memory of over fifty years ago? Or is this Dorothy's way of sharing with us the central image, that is, the need to defend, using a fencing foil as a symbol, around which she set the action for the class? It is possible that it is but the symbol she remembers and none of the details. So I pressed her further...*

It turns out that she brought in the two foils and masks for the *second* lesson, with much the same group. She had followed up her initial question in the first lesson by asking them what kind of ship they wanted their Captain to run. Choosing 'a ship of olden times' brought piracy to the fore. Her next step is to ask each young man, lined up facing the same way as though they have turned up to join the Pirate crew: 'What would *you* be prepared to do to defend us?' But the question was not a 'teacher' question: intuitive theatre skill and potential teacher skill combined to create a moment of abstract theatre. She stood *behind* the line of boys and delivered the question with a force (those who know Dorothy can imagine the dramatic change of voice from that of the nice Miss Shutt!) suggesting the power of this Captain. And each boy answered 'to the air', self-conscious without feeling stared at by either the teacher or the other lads, and without having to adjust to the sight of this young woman looking far from captainish. And Dorothy found herself doing what she was to do effectively for the rest of her professional life: using a gentler, encouraging voice, always impressed by what she had just heard, she would make a brief response after each reply that sought to tilt all thoughts towards the *implications* of their answers. Each boy understood that he had said something important, something that had implications for a future. The *mode* of the interaction was dramatic, the educational intention affirming and philosophical.

This is not to suggest that Dorothy finished her final year feeling confident that she knew how to teach in schools. That she did things that 'worked' in her school practice lessons did not mean that she knew what she was doing. She was an artist following her instinct and she discovered she enjoyed it. Nevertheless, what with the, in her eyes, spurious Speech and Drama qualification and the unsatisfactory, unsupervised school practice arrangement, she no doubt felt that the final part of the three years was something of an anti-climax. Nevertheless she acquired the School's Honours Diploma at Bradford Civic Playhouse Theatre School, duly signed by its two Presidents, J.B. Priestley and Tyrone Guthrie.

Dorothy Shutt, teacher of adult classes and private teacher of elocution

Dorothy could indeed approach with confidence the kind of work she was to take up after finishing at Theatre School. Her training in theatre had been solid and creative. She knew what she was good at: acting, directing, speaking verse, interpreting scripts and making costumes and props. This was to be her element from which she was to build a new identity, a new sense of who she was. Early in her Theatre School training, she had given private lessons at home, charging two shillings and sixpence for an hour to friends and others who wanted help, for example, with public speaking. Two evenings a week during the third year she ran a Theatre School evening class for Esmé, an indication of the kind of respect the Principal of the School had for her protégé. Her classes were adults who were involved in local amateur dramatic societies, church or school groups. She loved this work and extended it to other amateur groups in the Yorkshire Dales. And by now she was acting and producing regularly with the Bingley, Bradford and Ilkley amateur societies.[11] The adult education work gained her a teacher qualification issued by the County Council of the West Riding of Yorkshire. Its curious title reads as follows: Certificate of Definite Recognition as Teacher in Technical and Evening Institutes. It is dated 1st August, 1949.

Living at home with her mother in the upstairs apartment of the haunted house, Dorothy was still in touch with the family circle but they had long since ceased to be her only models. In fact one thread of her maturing towards womanhood was the companionship and mentoring she enjoyed with a series of individuals, all women, who had no connection with each other.

Living in the apartment below was Annie, who allowed Dorothy, when she was at Theatre School and afterwards, to use her sewing machine. Annie was a none too popular mill worker living alone who treated Dorothy as an adult in her talk, sharing without boundaries her wisdom about men and family responsibilities and life in general whilst Dorothy sewed. No-one had talked to Dorothy like that before. She listened ... and pondered.

During the second year of the theatre course, Barbara Crabtree had introduced Dorothy to Margaret Robinson, who was beginning her career as a puppeteer and professional artist, and who later offered Dorothy the chance to work alongside her. Margaret made exquisitely designed marionettes but although extremely artistic, she was less confident over the dramatic skill needed to operate a show with a good story-line. In fact Dorothy's relationship with Margaret started with her as teacher, trying to improve her speech for the puppetry work. She writes:

> Anxious to improve my dramatic skills, I requested lessons at the Bradford Civic Theatre School. In my best coat [30 shillings – made by my mother] I was interviewed by Barbara Crabtree who said she had someone good lined up. It would cost ten shillings *to begin with.* To Dorothy she said: You'll be all right there, dear' – meaning money. She had been taken in by the professional-looking coat, trimmed with a fresh button-hole from the garden – when you're on the breadline you've got to look opulent. Dorothy knew this and was not taken in. 'Is ten shillings all right?' she asked and never put it up.

This was a time when Dorothy was still happily doing the theatre course, so Margaret knew how devastated Dorothy became at Esmé's refusal to let her be an actress. It was partly as a way of cheering her up that Margaret suggested they combine on a puppetry project. They devised a programme of entertainment together to be taken round locally. Dorothy and Margaret shared the 'voices', deliberately swapping types – Dorothy, by now morbidly conscious of her size letting her down, playing skinny little boys and the thin ugly sister while Margaret played the heavies. Margaret writes: 'I have never had such a sense of collaboration in performance as when Dorothy and I teamed up.'

When Margaret was invited to take a puppet play to Germany, Dorothy wrote a version of *The Reluctant Dragon* as typifying British humour. As Margaret puts it: 'The Germans were a little puzzled by the irreverence – their fighting saints are all heroic!' They presented it in a youth camp near Stuttgart and it was a great success. While they were there they were invited to visit Margaret and Lola Eytel, daughters of Baron Eytel who had served as ambassador to various countries, but had lost status when Hitler came to power. Lola had been a theatre designer and wood carver and had helped carve the many 'women in grief' masks for Rudolf Laban's new ballet *Motherhood and War*. This work influenced Hitler to banish Laban for introducing 'impure' techniques into the Berlin Classical Ballet. Dorothy was befriended by these sisters and began on subsequent visits to hear of the atrocities of the war through German eyes for the first time.

They were very musical and cultured women. Margaret Eytel had worked for the American embassy in Stuttgart before the war and Lola had worked in the stables looking after Goering's horses. They played in the Stuttgart State Orchestra and had helped many Jewish friends gain the affidavits required to leave for the USA. Margaret frequently had to visit Himmler's office for his signature and hid the Jewish ones among the authentic documents. During the war they had both been allocated to work in POW camps with English prisoners, an opportunity for them to smuggle out letters in their closed umbrellas.

Both spoke many languages, having lived in many embassies. Lola was interested in English poetry and asked Dorothy at various times to record on Lola's small reel to reel tape recorder a range of English poetry, including long ballads. During one of these visits, Lola gave her the last remaining 'women in grief' masks that Laban had given to Lola as he departed Germany for good in the year of the 1936 Berlin Olympics. Dorothy still has that mask today.

Margaret Robinson writes:

> That visit to Germany was important to both of us. We had both been at the receiving end of snobbery. Six years older, I was beginning to shed the chip on my shoulder, but Dorothy seemed still to be ill at ease with those who considered themselves our betters, particularly the 'jumped up', the *nouveau riche.*

When, at around that time, Dorothy was greeted at a bus stop by a smiling lady who introduced herself as Marion Lawrence, she had no idea that they were to become so close that Dorothy would eventually regard Marion as her 'other mother'. Marion helped to run a thriving amateur company in Chapeltown, near Leeds. One of Dorothy's new sources of income after Theatre School was giving some theatre training to members of the company for two sessions on Saturday evening and early Sunday afternoon. Dorothy recalls being met off the Chapeltown bus for her first visit by this charming, urbane, easy-going lady who explained that Dorothy would stay at her house over each Saturday night. And that was where the company would return for refreshments after each Saturday session. They were happy, friendly and quite talented and for the first time Dorothy found herself in a social gathering in which talking about theatre was the norm. Dorothy explains to Sandra Hesten in an interview:

> There were teachers and lawyers, professional people, joined in this camaraderie of the theatre ... There was an ease and sense of tolerance with each other ... she [Marion Lawrence] was open and free and had no secrets ... I felt so astonished to be trusted ... these people were surrounded by their comfortable objects ... while to me at home they were our very precious relics ... I think the people that I value have been those who just accept me as I am and have not criticised me nor have they judged others around me.

But it was Marion herself who offered friendship to Dorothy in spite of what Dorothy recognised as a middle-class world far beyond her experience. As she says, 'My mother would have been a cleaner in her house'. And yet she was taken in to join Marion's family, including husband and surgeon daughter Rosemary, as if she were part of it. And so for the first time Dorothy became a regular overnight visitor in a household where money and middle-class comfort were taken for granted, where books, business, education and political issues were the general currency of family chat. The friendship was to last for many years, Marion and Rosemary often visiting Newcastle after Mr. Lawrence died. It was here too that Dorothy was introduced to an Aga – a domestic feature that has been central to her home life.

A pivotal connection for Dorothy, the one most affecting her choice of career, was Sheila Sanderson, a member of Dorothy's adult class. Dorothy admired Sheila's input to the work of the class but sensed an underlying grief even though Sheila smiled a lot and sometimes engaged in comedy scenes. After several weeks Dorothy felt comfortable enough with Sheila to say to her: 'There always seem to be tears in your acting'. Taken aback by this perceptiveness, Sheila asked Dorothy if they could walk to the bus-stop together after the session. She later explained to Dorothy that she was indeed grieving – for a husband who with no warning had suddenly left her and her two daughters. This sharing of a confidence began a friendship lasting until Sheila's death in 1999.

Sheila Sanderson was Head of English in a Secondary Modern girls' school and was keen to promote the school Drama productions. She herself had an English Literature background and had joined Dorothy's evening class in order to get ideas for play production and poetry work She started to seek Dorothy's advice, inviting her to school to help with rehearsals and so enliven the chorus of *Trojan Women* and advise on costumes, lighting and props. Thus for the first time Dorothy found herself in a school because her skill and experience were needed. This was not a Friday afternoon session in a school doing her a favour with a trumped up class. This was her first taste of being received and respected by a school as an expert. She took this new role in her stride.

Sheila was the first person to give Dorothy some insight into the working of a school, the first person with whom she could discuss education. Whatever her dreams of a future career at this time, she could not have anticipated, however, that Sheila would one day thrust a *Times Educational Supplement*, which she'd never heard of, in front of her and point to Durham University Institute of Education's advertisement for a Staff Tutor with qualifications in Speech and Drama.

Sheila Sanderson is the last in a long line of women who had a powerful influence on Dorothy's life. The first chapter described the family circle of Mother, Granny and the Aunties. And then came her first mentor, Dorothy Clough, whose personal library opened up a wonderland of reading; Mollie Sugden followed, offering insight into interpreting scripts and poetry; then Esmé Church with a Theatre School almost on Dorothy's doorstep. And others became part of this new circle of women: Annie, who lived under their flat by the mill chimney; Margaret Robinson the puppeteer; the aristocratic German sisters; Marion Lawrence, her 'second mother' and now Sheila Sanderson, the teacher. But we shall see in the next chapter that it was a man, Professor Brian Stanley, who brought about the most dramatic change in her life. I was tempted to say 'who gave her a new identity', but this is not true for Dorothy Shutt of Yorkshire in important ways remained the same whatever she was required to do and whoever she appeared to be in the eyes of other people.

Notes

1   It has puzzled me how it came about that a London based actress and director determined to set up a theatre school in the North. I am grateful to Libby Mitchell [née Dewhurst], a fellow student of Dorothy's for researching the background for me. Apparently The Old Vic, where Esmé worked as head of the School of Acting under the Principalship of Lilian Baylis, was moved up to Burnley during the war. Libby explains: 'During this time she must have become enthused by the idea of bringing theatre to the provinces and became involved with the West Riding Arts Movement, led by the West Riding Drama Adviser, Gerald Tyler.' She was appointed as paid director to the Bradford Civic Playhouse, a prestigious amateur theatre and she found enough supporters for the idea that the 'Civic', as it was referred to, should also become a centre for actor training. All students were to sign on as members of the Playhouse. There was however considerable resistance to the idea and Libby recalls that in the first year they were instructed to attend the Playhouse's AGM to sway the voting in favour of retaining the Theatre School. However, the Director of Education for Bradford, Thomas Boyce, a keen supporter of Esmé, was President of Bradford Civic Playhouse at that time and swung the meeting in favour of a deal between the two functions. Money for the Theatre School may always have been difficult, but it is thought that such people as Edith Evans and Lewis Casson, friends of Esmé, contributed. Esmé died in May, 1972. E. Martin Browne, contributing to her obituary in *The Times*, described her as 'one of the most gifted teachers in the theatre, and this small professional school, run on a miniscule budget, but with a first class staff ... produced a number of theatre men and women now established in various fields.'

2   J.B. Priestley was there as chairman of Bradford Civic Theatre – later to become The Priestley Centre.

3   The teacher course would be an extra year, but Dorothy at this point had no intention of being a teacher.

4   In 1945 neither Dorothy Heathcote nor Rudolf Laban, who had been forced out of Germany by the Nazis, could possibly have foreseen that each of them, passionate about *theatre*, was to become famous enough to have books written about them as *educationists*. This was but Laban's ninth year in England. Whereas he, [according to Peter Slade] was eventually to regret his association with education, Heathcote's self perception has never wavered from that of educator – not since she was bullied by Esmé Church into staying on for the teaching year.

Laban travelled to Bradford from his home in Manchester where he had lived since 1942 when he had collaborated with a Manchester industrialist, F.C. Lawrence, on the 'Laban/Lawrence Test for Selection and Placing' operatives with the most appropriate machine, based on their natural movement. It was not lost on Dorothy that his scheme for observation of people's natural expressive behaviour went beyond theatre and dance, She was later, for instance, to use it when she worked with Audi/Volkswagen managers in the 1980s.

5   The first journal in the UK to link drama to education had been out for twelve months, Esmé Church being one of the leading innovators in children's theatre whose name was associated with it. It was given the title Theatre in Education, a quarterly publication described on its front cover as devoted to 'Drama in University, College, School or Youth Group'. Esmé was also on the first ever Drama in Education Advisory Committee, although she admitted privately to a fellow committee member, Peter Slade, that she wished she wasn't as 'I know nothing about education'.

6   To contemporaries in education Stone was perceived as sensitive and creative, a pioneer in the arts. Indeed he had recently moved to his position as PE Organiser for the West Riding on the strength of his experience in teaching movement and drama as part of physical education. Trained as a teacher of physical education, he had become a headmaster of a Birmingham Primary school, where his experimental work in these arts drew the attention of Her Majesty's Inspectors. They invited him to write up his experiences there in the form of an HMSO document. He called it 'A Story of a School'. It came out a year after this meeting with Dorothy. He claimed to have discovered, during his time as head teacher, that giving classes of young children regular experience in moving to music and creating stories through group mime built in his pupils a 'readiness' for more academic learning.

7   For an ex PE teacher, repeating a programme of exercises was customary, so there would be nothing odd to Stone to see this as a way of giving a student security for a first school practice.

8   It was Barbara Crabtree, a staff lecturer and a director of the Theatre School, who wrote a strongly supportive reference for Dorothy when she applied for the post with Durham University. Esmé Church, however, wrote an astonishingly bland testimonial:

Dear Sir,

Dorothy Shutt was a student of this School for three years and obtained our Honours Diploma.

She was a very good teacher indeed and I hope your committee will consider her application sympathetically.

Kind regards,
Yours truly

9   That Dorothy was required to take such an examination, almost entirely based on solo performances of pieces in front of an examiner, is an indication of the value placed on training in Elocution, or Speech and Drama, as it later became, during this period. There were two other institutions, Guildhall College of Music and Drama and Trinity College, offering similar paper recognition. Indeed they were at that time the *only* available means for a teacher of speech or drama to be seen to be qualified as a specialist in the subject. It did not however automatically gain a recognised Ministry teacher qualification

10   Again, it seems strange that a course that appeared to be preparing students to lead adult amateur drama classes should use a local school for 'school practice'.

11   This was a period when amateur dramatics was thriving. In 1949 The Carnegie Trust appointed a full-time Drama Adviser, Leo Baker, to organise courses in Amateur Drama and to supervise the setting up of an Examination Board. The West Riding of Yorkshire, led by its renowned Director of Education, Alec Clegg, later knighted, was among the first authorities to take advantage of the local authority scheme for the arts. It is possible that the courses Dorothy led in the Yorkshire Dales were among the first to be set up by courtesy of Carnegie's money.

3

Dorothy Shutt, Staff Tutor at the University of Durham

I've dragged Dorothy from the garden for today's interview. She is trying, with some frustration, to meet the high standard she and Raymond set together.

Ignorance is bliss?

Thus on Shakespeare's birthday 1951, at the age of 24, Dorothy turned up at the University of Durham for an interview in Newcastle. She had scrabbled around for three references and Sheila Sanderson had organised ten photocopies of each. They were posted off to Durham on the final day for applications.[1]

From the first year of the Institute Brian Stanley, the youngest Institute Director in the country, had included on his staff a speech specialist, Susan Pearson. When she left to return to children's theatre work, the vacancy was temporarily filled by Margaret Fraser Stevewright, then there was a year's gap during which Professor Stanley had tried but failed to fill the post. Determined, he re-advertised, and the story goes that having gone through 300 applications he looked at Dorothy's and said 'I want this mill girl'.

His vision for the Durham Institute was somewhat unorthodox. He was far from a typical director, giving himself a small room in the building, keeping his door always wide open, and demonstrating considerable faith in his staff whom he encouraged to pursue their own ways of doing things. At the same time his open door allowed him to feel part of what was going on, to tune in to the work and the attitudes of all who were around. He always showed great respect for his staff, while maintaining that he himself had been a rather ineffectual teacher. And he insisted that they should have the title 'staff tutor' rather than the conventional 'lecturer', for many of their students were older and far more experienced in school work than they were. Indeed in the early days most of them were primary school headteachers. The purpose was to promote classroom practice, not lecture. Thus the relationship between Institute staff and their students was without precedent in a University. But even against this unconventional backdrop, Dorothy Shutt's appointment must have seemed risky, if not bizarre. She had no formal education, no national teacher qualification and virtually no experience of teaching children and yet her job would be to improve the practice of experienced teachers. Professor Stanley broke all the rules of this traditional university. He was a remarkable man and appointed a remarkable young woman.

Fortunately for Dorothy, she found the other six staff very friendly. Mabel Wilson, a very fine teacher of music, stands out as a person of singular ability. Mary Atkinson, the Froebel expert, had written to Dorothy immediately after her interview to say that the head of 'an innovative nursery school' in the east end of Newcastle, Alice Hand, would be pleased to have Dorothy as a lodger. It turned out that Alice was also wardrobe mistress at Newcastle's prestigious People's Theatre. This connection between her landlady and the local amateur theatre at once gave Dorothy a social and artistic niche from which she could satisfy her personal love of acting and directing. The lodgings were to be temporary until she could find a house for her and her mother.

Dorothy discovered that the staff spent a great deal of time in local primary schools, always those where the headteacher or members of staff were attending the Institute's evening courses. Their visits were seen as giving the staff encouragement in trying out new ideas discussed in the evenings. Dorothy was only too happy to follow this enlightened procedure. She didn't know of any other procedure and thought that all in-service training was like this.

Such a close liaison between Institute and schools created a curiously ambiguous relationship with the officers of the local education authorities. It is no wonder that, for example, Silas Harvey, highly respected and well-established Drama Organiser for Northumberland, treated Dorothy with polite suspicion, for it could be said that his function in schools was being usurped. How different the situation was by 1973 when Roger Hancock, a talented teacher from the London Borough of Redbridge, was appointed as Drama Adviser to Newcastle L.E.A. He knew of Dorothy's reputation when he took the job and spent many years supporting her work in Newcastle schools.

Dorothy took the chance to go further than her colleagues by asking actively to teach the classes of her students. It made sense to everyone that new approaches discussed in class should be tried out in schools by Dorothy herself, but such a reversal of normal roles was unheard of. One knew of someone like Peter Slade or Brian Way asking to be given a class to demonstrate with, but for someone from a university to step into a classroom and actually teach children was wildly unorthodox.[2] Dorothy was so ignorant of what went on in universities that she did not realise that she was asking anything unusual. To her, it was the obvious way to find out about helping teachers. Her apparent disingenuousness became a strength. It saw her through the frigid arrogance of academia, where the un-written rule was always to appear to be well informed. She learnt to silence university professors, directors of education, senior inspectors and other dis-tinguished members of the intellectual hierarchy with 'Well, of course, I don't know...' They either disbelieved her or paused to wonder whether she possessed some alternative 'knowing', a different wave-length, that they had better wait to learn about. Either way, they didn't know how to deal with her.

To the headteachers attending the Institute of Durham's two year part-time course, however, Dorothy's 'I don't know how to teach young children ... I would be happy to try out some of my ideas in your school if you like...?' struck the right note. This was no upstart telling them what to do. This was a young woman who sought their cooperation and relied on their experience, and yet conveyed an astonishing self-assurance, directness, humour and commitment. The com-bination of her genuine appeal to *their* expertise combined with that warm, confident smile was disarming.

Stories were her safety net when she started teaching young children. It gives a ground base for the drama and makes sense to the teachers watching – always teachers watching, for the rest of her life. That other teachers were always present when she taught gave a public setting to Heathcote's teaching that must at times have affected her and those she taught. Likewise, that she was always a guest in the school almost guaranteed a ready-made status for her work. She never faced the tasks of taking the register or checking on absentees, writing reports, meeting with parents or dealing with severe behaviour problems. Rarely was she cramped by the time-table – no half-hour lessons for Miss Shutt. Head-teachers were often generous with the time they allocated her, laying the normal time-table on one side. But then in the 1950s, when 'creativity in the arts' was in the air, such flexibility was expected of a headteacher. One of her past students writes, however: 'Her main weakness was the fact that she had never taught in a school ... she was always the honoured visiting teacher and time and facilities were put at her disposal in an unrealistic way.' That she was mostly a stranger to the pupils must also have coloured her initial approach to them. Together, these circumstances add up to an unusual, some would say artificial, setting for her teaching. I have often heard despairing observers comment, 'It's all right for *her*.'

A few glimpses of Miss Shutt in the classroom

The most traditional drama activities of the time – and the North East of England was not exactly known for innovative practice – would have required the drama teacher to cast the story, to bring out the selected children to the front by the teacher's high desk, and invite them to enact the set script or, more daringly, make it up as they went along. One can imagine the surprise of the teachers when desks were pushed back to make a bigger space for them all to sit on the floor *with* Miss Shutt, who doesn't say 'Would *you* like to act the story', but '*We* can try this story'. When the action starts it involves all of them, Miss Shutt included, getting up and doing something. This immediately shatters a precious axiom of the most progressive drama: that whereas it was in order for teachers to join in with their classes in the actions of, say, singing games, when it came to drama, the teacher properly remained outside the action. How otherwise could it be the children's own creativity?

Dorothy did not know about the favoured idea of the time that children doing drama should start as individuals and express themselves in their own separate spaces, initially without contact with each other. For her, classroom drama required a *collective* starting point in which *we* have a job to do: we are not acting a story; we are creating a context parallel to it. And she does not necessarily tell them the story, for, as she was later to perceive, the story format is a 'telling' mode that works against dramatic form. If the story situation – note, the story situation, not the story sequence – were, say, *Beauty and the Beast*, then they might all be the Beast's slaves who have to keep the pathways clear of weeds, leaves and broken branches. Dorothy would with her own actions provide a model of what to do, a level of belief with which to do it. They were to pick it up from her, not be shown by her or told by her.

There was another basic feature of her approach that she was barely aware was innovatory. In the 1950s and 1960s much drama teaching across the Western world took the form of dramatic exercises, in which the activities, often seen as 'fun' activities, retained qualities of practising something or preparing for something or trying something out. For Dorothy such incidental qualities did not and could not belong to drama, for drama by definition operated in **now** time. The Beast's slaves are clearing the pathways now, actually getting it done, with all the implied consequences of failing to get it done. B.J. Wagner says that the first time she found herself in one of Dorothy's workshops she had to learn 'to shun the self-indulgence of even thinking that it is a mere exercise, and to live this new moment to its fullest'.

As the area of responsibility for the Durham Institute was spread towards Middlesborough, Darlington and Cumberland, each week Dorothy would find herself in Carlisle, Silloth, Millom and Cockermouth, staying overnight in order to fit in as many schools as possible. She recalls an occasion when two teachers on the course begged her to teach in their school and, to ensure that no member of staff should miss seeing her teach, they gave her all 175 primary school children to work with. Undeterred but feeling somewhat exploited, she introduced the idea that they should all be circus workers having to prepare the circus for coming out of its winter quarters to start on the first journey of the new season – all the wagons had to be got ready, cages checked, water buckets filled, animals groomed. And Miss Shutt would start, convincingly worried that they'd got so much to do and not much time to do it if they were to move off that day. 'Anybody need another bucket? ... there's a pile of them still in the shed here...' and so on. The children gradually pick up the idea, see where Miss Shutt is filling her bucket, and queue to fill theirs or get brushes from 'the shed' to clean out a cage. Thus a sense of pre-departure and urgency is established and shed, tap and cage gradually build a locality. Together they enter fictional time and space.

One can see how this unorthodox approach appealed to primary school teachers such as her own adult students. But one can also understand that it was anathema to drama specialists, both the traditionalists who saw her work as rejecting real theatre and the progressives who thought she broke all the new rules on which Child Drama was founded. What hardly anyone realised was that it was Heathcote's visceral understanding of theatre that underpinned the way she intuitively set about structuring a drama lesson, for here were the very elements in which she had been trained, the creation of tension, the selective use of space and sound, motivation, 'now time' and so on.

I believe she did not make this sufficiently clear even to herself and certainly many of us who came to work closely with her failed to grasp the theatrical basis for her work. The result was that it came to be seen by the outside world as a peculiar version of Child Drama or as therapy or as only a way of teaching other subjects and certainly nothing to do with theatre. It was not seen for what it was, a new genre of theatre that could be harnessed for many purposes. If the word theatre had been retained in descriptions of her methodology, then the condemnatory dismissal of Heathcote's work by Peter Abbs in 1991 as 'devoid of art, devoid of the practices of theatre' might never have occurred.

It has not been easy to tease out a true picture of Dorothy's early teaching in the 1950s. There is something about the above example, relating to the Circus, that sounds too pat, too accomplished and educationally focused. The accounts emerge as an experience recalled with the language of hindsight, as though she knew exactly what she was doing. This is clearly going to be a trap for a biographer. Each report of a teaching episode will tend to rely on smooth narrative. The reader should perhaps be warned that a drama session that on these pages turns into a good story was not neces- sarily a good lesson! I asked Dorothy to give me another example which I hope takes us nearer to the kind of experiment she engaged in.

She recalls telling the story of Cinderella with a class of infants and then setting up parallel actions with all of them. By inviting comments she would find out what the story meant to them and, responding to what she hears, set up a dramatic context related to the aspect of the theme that appeared to have caught their interest. On one occasion Dorothy recalls that it was Cinderella's drudgery that caught their attention so Dorothy finds herself saying something like: 'Have you heard? ... they're needing more cleaners at the castle? ... what shall we tell them we're good at? ... [she listens carefully for she will be repeating their ideas to an imaginary steward] ... shall I go and tell the castle steward we'd like to work for the king? ... [she does so] ... he says we can start!' And the cleaning starts enthusiastically enough, perhaps with the children all helping to roll a carpet, Dorothy using her voice, words and gestures to establish a sense of place – 'We'll have to be careful when we move these statues ... clean these paintings ... carry this heavy china' ... And then the cleaning goes on ... and on ... Dorothy starts to get restless and tired and wanting a break ... and they realise no-one is going to let them go ... they are not employees, they are slaves! And 'nobody will let us off duty ... and we've got children coming home from school ... and we can't go home to them ... because *he* keeps us here.'

This setting became typical of Heathcote's approach in the 1950s and 1960s – there's a bigun who's giving a hard time to us littl'uns. Thus in Dorothy's version the children experience a long session of fretting and fuming, with Dorothy subtly stirring them into taking some kind of action. She had already warned their teacher that she wanted them in this lesson to understand the meaning of implication, so that she knew that whatever ideas they might put forward, she would not challenge them but, rather, would wonder about the outcome: 'That sounds like a good idea ... but d'you think ... he might ... what might happen ... d'you suppose there might be implications ... would he ... might he ...? Their suggestion of 'telling someone that we want to leave', through looking at these things called implications, became 'asking someone if they could leave'. Then Dorothy, as their spokesperson, returned with the news that the King says, 'You go home when I say' – thus inviting them to bounce back from a temporary set- back. And they did ... they held a meeting, instructing their fellow slave, Mrs. Heathcote, to be firmer.

Thus started a generation of drama classes 'having meetings' as part of or even as their entire drama. Neither the freely expressive mode of Peter Slade's Child Drama approach nor the exercise structure of Brian Way's Personal Development allowed for such a framework. Having meetings, however, became a false trail for those who wanted to take on the Heathcote approach. Drama classes throughout the country too often began with 'What would you like to make a play about?' followed by a rush into holding a meeting. A device used sparingly by Heathcote became the principal method for many of her followers.

A further misreading of Dorothy's teaching would spring from this Cinderella type episode. I used the phrase above 'subtly stirring them into some kind of action'. This ploy made sense to drama teachers since it obviously moved the drama forward, but sometimes they failed to realise that for Dorothy this ploy is moving the *learning* forward. She knows that her stirring creates opportunities for the children to learn to reflect on potential solutions. Those of us who were trained in keeping the drama going at all costs, could only see the dramatic priority. In her Cinderella, the pupils experienced triumph in the end – and they understood implications. Proof of this was demonstrated in their meeting when Dorothy yet again started to voice some doubt and a boy said: 'If this is another implication coming up, I don't want to be bothered!'

In those early days Dorothy would plan to round up the experience with a sense of success. As she grew more experienced, any class, even infants, had to earn that success by working towards a solution. It could not, must not, be a gift. It is possible that the idea of going into a second role is something that Dorothy still had to develop. In some circumstances she might have said: 'Shall I be the King's Steward for a while so that you can talk to him?'. In this particular lesson, however, she probably said something like: 'Shall I go to the Steward's office and say what we think?' – and move away from the corner of the hall where they were working, while, perhaps, narrating: 'So she went to the Steward and came back with the news that ... '. She might not yet have been aware that there was a choice of strategies.

Using a story base for drama work was a secure way for Dorothy to try out what teaching was really like. As she gained confidence, however, she would ask her teachers what they were teaching in other parts of the curriculum, so that the drama work might fit in with those broader objectives. Thus tying the drama to a particular story seemed not always to be appropriate. At some point she discovered that asking the class at the beginning of the session 'what they would like to make a play about', an approach that mistakenly became identified as authentic Heathcote methodology, would give the class a strong vested interest while providing a context which she could subtly manoeuvre into having some bearing on the curriculum.

It is at this point in our interview that I ask about failures.

'Did you have any failures in those early days? Did you fall flat on your face like the rest of us do sometimes?

No.

No?

No.

To ask Dorothy about failures seems to be asking the wrong question. I prod her into telling me of some past teaching that she made a mess of or at least was inadequate. I used phrases such as 'Did you ever make mistakes?'; 'Were there times when you made wrong judgements?' Her answers came swiftly: 'I'm sure there were ... ', but as she pondered it became quite clear that she had no ready recollection of any such thing. And then came 'There was a time ... ' I prick up my ears and pick up my pen and she proceeds to tell me ...

There was an occasion when she began teaching teachers. One woman attending her evening class took out her knitting when the practical work started, explaining: 'I don't come on courses to join in'. This threw Miss Shutt, who responded with: 'If you don't join in you won't be able to understand the experience – I think you'd better not stay.' Dorothy, known now for her seemingly unbounded tolerance – and her knitting – still feels the shame of this today. But it indicates some of the uncertainty she felt at that time about what the rules in her adult classes should be. The teacher concerned withdrew from the course. Dorothy was very upset but Professor Stanley remained unperturbed.

'But Dorothy, did you ever make any misjudgements in your teaching?' I ask, focusing firmly. 'I'm sure there would be ... ' she again replies.

She recalls the regrettable mishandling in the middle of a drama lesson of a somewhat bumptious infant whose teacher had described as 'an awkward one'. He was one of these children all teachers recognise, an independent thinker who can manage to throw everybody else. Echoing the comments of the child's class teacher, Dorothy found herself challenging him with: 'You always have to be different don't you!' and shuddering at her mistake even as she heard herself say the words. 'I was wrong,' she now admits – and also regrets that it happens to be caught on video.

I have noted some of the ways in which Heathcote remained apart from common classroom practice: that she was a visitor, overriding normal timetables, not knowing the children etc. The anecdote about mishandling the cocky infant reveals a more fundamental aspect surrounding her visits to schools: in the eyes of the pupils she always appeared to stand outside the school's unwritten behavioural code. She and they knew that everyone was starting with a clean slate; neither she nor the boys and girls she taught brought past punitive luggage with them into the classroom. She did not appear merely to reflect the 'real' teacher's authority or to speak for the school, which is how most other adult visitors to the school were heard. That she stood apart in the eyes of her pupils freed them to be who they wanted to be, at least for the length of her visit.

Neither of these examples of professional mistakes supplied by Dorothy is directly linked with the work itself. It has taken me some time to accept that she is not avoiding the issue. To ask about failures in setting up the drama is to ask the wrong question – from her perspective. One might wonder how anyone can say, as Dorothy confessed after further pressing from me: 'I don't admit to failures'. It is one thing to be self-assured but her stance surely amounts to arrogance or blindness. It is neither of these. It is partly, in my view, the self-perception of a performer. A professional singer, for example, is unlikely to talk in terms of failure. He or she might feel dissatisfied with a performance, not getting it quite right or lacking magic or even hitting a wrong note, but even this self-criticism would tacitly assume that there was still something there that was worth listening to. I believe Dorothy has always relied on there having been something worth thinking about and learning from, so failure just can't be the right word.

She also has enormous resources for recovery. She works slowly enough to recognise a wrong note coming up and gives herself time to improvise round that bit of the tune so that that particular note does not have to be struck. To anyone casually observing, it seems that it was always intended that way, so smoothly is the re-scoring handled. Just as the singer uses her knowledge of the art to make such an adjustment skilfully, Dorothy uses her knowledge of dramatic fiction and smartly introduces a new dramatic pathway to her class when she recognises that the one she had set up was flawed. She never suggests to them that they are not doing something right and that they should try it again – that is a teacher/pupil thing to do. Her method will operate from within the fiction, perhaps 'discovering some new priority that *must* be dealt with' or using the surprise of her unexpected arrival in a new role. As part of the fiction, the class abandon their attempt to struggle with a poor structure and, with energies refocused, pursue the new goal.

Dorothy has the power to mesmerise a class with her eyes, her stance and above all her voice. For instance, she can retrieve a difficult situation by narrating a different aspect of the event while they in role are having a temporary rest from their tasks, or simply by notching up the intensity and therefore the impact of her role or introducing a new role. Her stage training means that she has many voices to draw on and if a class have become restless, bored, obstreperous or over excited, she selects the pitch and tone that will temporarily spellbind. Temporarily, for enchantment with her performance is not what she is after – but it comes in useful at times! It is mandatory for her that *they* should win through, though not without labour and struggle. People have told me, however, of times when her teacher-in-role was what one observer described as over the top, leaving the class bewildered.

To see Dorothy's lack of admission of failure entirely as analogous to performer, although useful, is incomplete. There is something about the way she conceives of the teaching/learning process that rejects failure as an option. For to her a session of drama is a journey of enquiry. And right or wrong, success or failure is irrelevant. If her class have totally different expectations of drama, then it will take time for them to see it in these terms. And what if the adult observers have different expectations of drama? Dorothy can see the accusation of FAILED written in their eyes and how can she even begin to persuade them that she is on a different plane altogether, when she can see they are angry, disappointed and protective of her class?

David Griffiths, Drama Organiser for County Durham and later Inspector for South Tyneside, recalls a number of occasions when observers – or, perhaps audience is the better word, for Dorothy used to find herself faced with halls full of teachers for a one-off demonstration lesson – were somewhat mystified by her patience. He writes:

> Another unusual factor was her slow build-up of belief in the chosen theme. She would wait patiently until all the children were on board. I remember one lesson where she waited for more than twenty minutes for the children to make what appeared to be a minor decision. The teachers became restless as nothing appeared to be happening. She later explained that she was empowering the children to take responsibility for their actions, and that this technique would bear fruit in future lessons. She was very single minded when teaching, and carried out her plan without deviation, and seemed indifferent to the audience.

> I did question the value of these sessions as a means of modelling strategies for inexperienced teachers, as they were so idiosyncratic and demanded such a high level of skill and flair. They were invaluable, however, in demonstrating the value of drama in education and I saw my role as con-

structing a series of steps, starting from where the teachers were confident, to follow on from Dorothy's example of what was possible at the highest level.

The ploy of persuading an audience that nothing happening in a lesson was nevertheless laying foundations for future work sounds rather like an excuse or wishful thinking, but I think it has to be accepted that this kind of work can be slow in fermenting, too slow for one-off audiences who want just a quick drink. Nevertheless, Dorothy was not entirely without guile, as Griffiths explains:

> Finally I can recall a lesson which didn't work at all, a rare event. I felt for her and wondered how she would cope with the discussion. I need not have worried. She convinced every one that the lesson had been successful and everyone went home happy!

Less happy were observers in a Yorkshire School many years later. Derek Stevens, who acknowledges that his life was changed when he took Dorothy's Advanced Diploma course in 1968, and who stayed in touch with her for the rest of his career, recalls a less than satisfactory experience when Dorothy visited his school. He writes:

> Her experience and that of her students working in the school was not always the happiest or most fruitful. I recall a series of three afternoons with a class and observers when nothing was forged. It was the first time I had witnessed an occasion when nothing from her could break down the negativism and recalcitrance of the group. It was profoundly shocking but salutary for me. Like most people who had done the course I had gone through the sequence of moving from initial delight, awe and admiration of what she does through dismay at ever being able to be like that to realization that one had to find one's own way. She has never wanted others to be imitative Dorothy Heathcotes, but commends everyone to struggle on one's own road. This I was endeavouring to do, but it was a relief to observe her struggling still, because it was clear one would have to accept this kind of struggle would be lifelong and never laurel-resting.

A disfigured hand

Dorothy was in the passenger seat of a colleague's car travelling to the University Senior Common Room for lunch. A second colleague was on the back seat. Part way there, they stopped to have a word with someone, the colleague in the back seat leaving the car and, when he climbed in again, he courteously shut Dorothy's door but accidentally trapped her little finger in the hinge – her little *gloved* finger. The sliced off section accommodatingly stayed in position, held by the glove and, it was discovered, a slither of skin. They just happened to have parked right outside the Royal Victoria Infirmary. And what's more, just opposite its Hand Clinic – a constant flow of injured miners came here in the 1950s.

Thus within minutes after the accident Dorothy finds herself anaesthetized while a doctor puts the finger back on. But it did not take and ten days later they were talking about a false finger. She attends the appropriate clinic, somewhat embarrassed, feeling out of place sitting in the waiting room full of men needing new arms and legs, men who look suspiciously at her evident full-length limbs! In her turn she went in to the little man who, demonstrably expert, measured with diligence and enthusiasm the missing digit for a replacement. Five weeks it would take before a fitting – apparently the fitter brought his limbs in a suitcase on the train once a week. Patience rewarded, the moment came for the trying on of life-like fingers. Alas, it had been made for the wrong hand!

The only solution seemed to be that she could make do – after all it was National Health. The surgeon was intrigued to know whether it would survive wear and tear. So Dorothy persevered with a strange attachment, a false finger, which had to have its garish colours toned down each day with make-up, until one day when she was teaching a class at Aycliffe Approved School – as the institution for young offenders was then known – she had a youth in her class with a glass eye. Over a number of weeks she had got to know him quite well so that on one occasion, when he kept taking out and putting back the new eye he had been given that day, she felt able to remark: 'Do you mind not doing that? I find it disconcerting.' His reply was: 'I'll stop if you'll stop taking your finger on and off; it makes me sick' Dorothy had developed a habit of playing with her unfeeling finger end without realising it. From that day she did without it, throwing it away only when, years later, her daughter Marianne was frightened by the sight of it in a drawer.

But that's not quite the end of the story, for I can recall watching a number of drama sessions that have begun with Dorothy inviting the class to say what they notice about her physical appearance and if they failed to notice or preferred not to mention the absence of a finger, she would point it out. Part of Dorothy's teaching is always to train her classes to look for *implications*. This is her automatic way of connecting seeing and thinking. Everything we observe has a potential for meaning. A foreshortened finger – what is the story there? And that kind of question will be posed again and again about whatever is created during the subsequent drama experience There is another side to it too. It is to do with deliberately making herself vulnerable, as if in drawing attention to her injury she is giving a little of herself, perhaps again providing a model should they ever need to draw on it. It sets the tone for later discussing 'how we are getting on'.

Acting and directing – and riding

Much of Dorothy's leisure time was related to theatre. She joined the prestigious People's Theatre for which she both acted and directed. She recalls one occasion when she was so heavily disguised as the whore in *Pericles* that her mother thought she'd lied about claiming to be in it! And there was a Newcastle-based University Theatre Group, mainly English lecturers whose love of textual work led to some tedious productions of obscure classics. She took part in these and felt sorry for the audience who politely supported what was really 'dreary, boring stuff'. Equally supportive and equally polite was Vice-Chancellor Bosanquet who gave the official thanks at the end of a performance.

One year she was invited to direct a play of her own choice for them. She knew she needed to choose a text that would lend itself to a vibrant production while being undemanding on these 'literary' players for, as she explains, 'they couldn't act.' She chose John Masefield's *The Witch*, a play that began and ended with a witch hunt and had a large-scale banquet in the middle act. Screaming characters made their speedy entrance through the auditorium, so that, from the start, the audience were assaulted with hysteria. But the banquet, by dramatic contrast, opened as a Rembrandt painting, a still picture, out of which, one by one, the characters began to move in stylised, slow motion ... the audience holding their breath in the quietness and stillness. And then the third act raged its way to the final curtain.

But at the actual performance, Dorothy did not see that final curtain. Nor did she see the middle act. She left after the first act, sick with anger. By tradition, the University productions had always been preceded by the singing of *God Save the Queen*. Dorothy, however, foresaw an unbearable incongruity between the formalised, respectful rising from their seats of an audience whose attention moments later was to be caught up in mediaeval anarchy. So she put it to her cast that for once perhaps a note of respect for the monarchy could be included in the programme instead of singing the anthem. It did not occur to her that they would be less sensitive to the inappropriateness of the ritual. Indeed she intended her suggestion to be heard as an unchallengeable request.

And the evening started with *God Save the Queen*. She had been ignored and they had not even told her. She was furious. So angry that she felt sick. And left. Her mother, at home in the flat, looked at the clock and asked, 'Is it over?' to which her daughter replied by way of explanation: 'They played *God Save the Queen!*'

However, the next day, Dorothy heard that Vice Chancellor Bosanquet had made his usual speech, but confessed that whereas in previous years he had been somewhat unengaged by the productions, this time, *this* time, it had been real theatre. And he was kind enough to phone Dorothy later that day and thank her.

Life was not all drama, however, for 7 a.m. Mondays to Fridays, whatever the weather, would find her, dressed in proper gear, riding on the Town Moor. A colleague from the English Department of the University had suggested Dorothy would make a good horsewoman and had persuaded her to join a stable run by an Irishman named Danny. In fact she wasn't all that good on horseback, as confirmed daily by the expression on Danny's face and she wonders whether it is worth including in this book, but then she adds: 'Unless you give it as an example of my risk-taking!' But I think I can guarantee that an image of Dorothy cantering astride a large mare, disturbing the tramps sleeping rough, trying not to get rubbed off by a tree branch, desperately checking an old race-horse from galloping when it found itself on the race-track that used to go round the Town Moor, is a picture that most of us did not have among our memories of Dorothy!

'I reckon I'd quite like to marry you'

In 1954 Dorothy met her husband to be, Raymond Heathcote, pronounced *Heth*cote, as she was to insist for the rest of her life. Dorothy had made friends with Flora, a head of History at Washington Grammar School, who was desperate for a drama course so attended the only one offered in the area, the Froebel course at the Durham Institute. Dorothy would occasionally visit her school and work with Flora on history texts using drama. As the school was short-staffed, Flora pleaded with Dorothy to accompany her on a school trip to the Farne Islands, a bird sanctuary off the Northumberland coastline, even though Dorothy had a phobia about birds. Dorothy agreed on the understanding that she herself would not have to go on the islands.

In the car going up – the schoolchildren were going by bus – was a stranger who had also been persuaded to make up the number of adults needed. He was Raymond Heathcote, an engineer who worked for the firm of Reyrolles, which built power stations all over the world. Some years earlier he had met Flora's son on a train and when they realised Raymond had spent the entire war in India where Flora and her husband had once lived, the son said 'You must meet my parents', and a friendship had started. Dorothy recalls that when they stopped on the journey for a break, she and Raymond talked about war, Raymond impressing on her that the atrocities of modern warfare paled against past slaughter. There was something about the vivid images he drew that caught her attention.

Dorothy was encouraged to visit the first island, where eider ducks 'just sit', but when she chose to stay on the boat whilst the rest visited others, Raymond was worried and reluctant to leave her. Persuaded that she was okay reading her book, he went off with the group to take some remarkable close-ups of nesting birds, with a camera that was to last him his life-time. Returning to Flora's house, Raymond offered to take Dorothy home in Sarah, his 1931 Lanchester. When they reached Dorothy's flat, Raymond said in the voice of someone making a cautious, albeit risky, enquiry: 'I reckon I'd quite like to marry you'.

Dorothy's reaction was to tell him that she was illegitimate. 'I would not be marrying your mother,' he said. And so began a period of low-key courtship during which they didn't see much of each other and arrangements to meet were mostly unplanned – Raymond would just 'turn up', for example, to meet her from the People's Theatre after a show. Being Dorothy she did not try to demand anything more than that casual arrangement, although she was taken to meet his parents. After a year, they became officially engaged, Raymond proposing to her when they were passengers on the Ratty Steam Train, shunting its way through the Lake District, as steam trains were one of his hobbies. Dorothy was then somewhat formally introduced to the rest of his family, an impressive line-up of doctor uncles and their wives, who gave Dorothy a warm welcome. Raymond's pedigree has been traced back to the 14th century, and includes people of some distinction, including a 17th century farmer described as 'the richest commoner in England'. It was intriguing how many 'Dorothys' past Heathcotes had married.

Dorothy was fond of dancing and had had a couple of male companions but she did not see the ballroom partnerships as serious. Oddly, the first thing she thought of when someone did propose to her was her illegitimacy. Perhaps she had always wondered whether this would disqualify her for marriage. I also wonder whether, having been told by Esmé Church that she was the wrong size for the professional stage, she feared that she would also be the wrong size for marriage.

Once engaged, they started house-hunting, knowing they wanted a house big enough to accommodate Raymond's parents, 'with separate kitchens', his mother wisely insisted. And so, in October 1956, after their marriage at St. Paul's Church, Newcastle, they moved south of the River Tyne to Highburn House, built in Gateshead in 1830, to be their home together for forty-five years and a second home for many of the students from other parts of the British Isles and abroad who desperately wanted to study with Dorothy Heathcote.

You will appreciate that for Dorothy this last few weeks, answering my questions about how she first met Raymond and their marriage together, has not been without its pain.

Notes

1   Soon after the war (1948) all UK Universities were invited to establish Institutes of Education in order to promote in-service training for experienced teachers. Money was to be made available for practising teachers to take a year's sabbatical on full pay in order to follow an Advanced Diploma course or, and this was where most Universities (including Durham) started, local teachers could attend evening courses spread over a longer period. Such institutes were to be run as separate departments from those existing departments of education offering one year teacher-training for graduates [PGCE – Post Graduate Certificate of Education]. They were additionally to co-ordinate the work of any two year teacher-training colleges in the locality. They were to have their own staff and could, if they wished, give the new Institute a specialist bias. Professor Brian Stanley was alone in choosing to give the Durham Institute an arts education bias.

The University of Durham, one of England's traditional universities, established in 1832, spread itself across two cities, Durham and Newcastle. For the first time Universities were given the chance to be linked with the education of younger children and Brian Stanley's first appointments reflected contemporary approval of Froebel training. His first appointment, Mary Atkinson, set a tone of innovation in the field of primary education. Others who followed brought their art specialisms, including art and music ... and drama. He chose staff for their talent rather than their conventional academic qualifications. After they had been employed for a few years the staff, including Dorothy, were 'given' higher degrees, so that the entry for the Institute in the annual University Calendar matched that of other University departments in academic standing.

The job description that Dorothy sent for specified that 'Staff tutors are required to pay visits of consultation to their students in their own schools.'

2   I have a personal interest here, for when in the early 1960s I became a Drama Adviser and then moved to Durham University, having Peter Slade, Brian Way and now Dorothy Heathcote as my models, I too just assumed that teaching other people's classes was the expected and obvious thing to do. Only later, when I visited other teacher-training institutions did I realise that tutors were expected only to advise. I was lucky in the people I happened to meet.

4

Staff Tutor, University of Newcastle-upon-Tyne

Derek Stevens, a student who took both an early diploma course and Dorothy's final part-time M.Ed course, travelling some 140 miles round trip twice a week to attend lectures, writes:

> I did not immediately understand or even appreciate her statement to me that all she had in her life were her family and her work. At that moment to someone coming from a vigorous social and cultural life in cosmopolitan Bristol that stand seemed very bleak, but, of course, it took me some time to learn and appreciate how rich and enriching her work and family life both were: how horizons could always be shifted; how she seemed and still seems to be able to move anywhere [geographically and spiritually] and anywhen; to absorb through her permeable spiritual and intellectual skin and to give back at least as much as she takes; how work and family life feed each other and set standards for each other in a continuous symbiosis.

At home in Highburn House

Sharing their home with Raymond's parents worked out very well. Dorothy particularly enjoyed having a 'father' around and for Raymond it was quite a novelty living under the same roof as his own parents, as public school, serving in India for the full extent of the war and university had kept him away from home. Sadly, his mother's health was poor, as she suffered from Parkinson's disease. For a number of years she needed caring for. This proved no problem, however, as Mary, who looked after their house from the beginning of their marriage, kept an eye on Raymond's mother when Dorothy and Raymond were both out at work, and Dorothy gave her much love and attention when she was at home.

When Dorothy sees that someone, friend or family, is genuinely in need of help, she becomes passionately committed to caring, with a command of detailed routine and meticulous support that has to be perfect. She consciously dedicates herself, like a nun taking vows or a knight swearing allegiance. It is as if she sees looking after someone as a way of saying thank-you for the life she has been given.

It became a disappointment to Dorothy and Raymond that they had to resign themselves to being childless. They occasionally discussed adoption, but Raymond was unenthusiastic about the idea, never feeling sure that he would 'make a good father' and Dorothy herself was not sure that that was the route to take. Getting medical help did not enter their heads in those days. I remember going to a London theatre with Dorothy in the early 1960s to see *Who's Afraid of Virginia Wolf* and her telling me afterwards how painful she found this reminder of being childless.

One worrying incident occurred while Raymond's parents were living with them. A stranger – they were to learn later that she was a care assistant in an old people's home – inveigled herself into their house while Raymond and Dorothy were at work. His father fell for her tale that she had lost her handbag in a shop in Newcastle, with all her money. Sympathising to the extent of giving her £50, Raymond's father had invited the woman in and then driven her home, not noticing that she still had her house-key conveniently in her pocket. It is likely that he had it in mind that the money was a loan, offered out of old world courtesy of 'not to leave a lady without means'. Indeed, he was always checking on Dorothy in this respect, as he had noted that she tended not to carry much money around with her.

The intruder became a regular visitor until Mary turned up one day to find her in a bedroom. She reported this to Raymond and the matter was brought to the notice of the police, especially as Raymond's mother's engagement ring was missing. His father, who had previously been scrupulously wary of strangers' tricks, confessed that he had been duped by this woman, even arranging that when Dorothy next went abroad, she would come and stay and look after him and his wife.

The woman turned up when a policeman was visiting the house. She was taken home and a policewoman found, bizarrely, two large silver medals won by Raymond's dad's egg-laying hens in her shoe cupboard. She had not realised, because she had not lifted the 3' diameter silver medals out of their tight velvet cases, that Dad's name was on the obverse side, the hen's breed name being on the upper side. Raymond was very angry about his father's failure to live up to his own past standards of common sense and quietly warned him that if ever he should do anything like that again, he and mother would be put permanently into a nursing home. Some time after the court case, items of jewelry were found hidden in odd places – the engagement ring, for instance, turned up in the turn-ups of a pair of dad's trousers – as though the woman expected to pick up carefully planted items later.

Both Dorothy and Raymond found building a home together a joy. They furnished it gradually, as they found they could afford carefully selected items, mostly antique. They both had an eye for quality and craftsmanship, but Raymond's engineering background took account of quality of function. He used to say, even of ordinary plastic items, 'Is it fit for purpose?' They took pleasure in visits to the flea market on a Saturday morning to pick up unexpected oddments. One of the games they played in their early days together was gazing into antique shop windows and choosing what they would to buy if they had enough money. Often their choices coincided. They tended to like the same kind of painting or drawing and would enjoy 'reading' a picture together. Bidding at auction salerooms became a shared venture. Together they created a home of distinctive furniture and pictures, partly through their astute bidding and partly through inheritance. But they did not think in terms of the unaccustomed affluence, for they saw beautiful possessions not as capital but as artefacts for which they were privileged custodians.

Margaret Robinson, Dorothy's friend from the puppetry years, remembers that when she first visited them in Highburn House soon after their marriage, 'Dorothy consulted Raymond about even the most trivial matters: a placid man, he would have let her take control, but she had the wisdom to avoid the trap – was it wisdom? Low cunning? Manipulation? Does it matter? It made for harmony.'

Raymond was keen on playing bridge, but he gave it up, for although Dorothy tried to learn, she found competitive games meaningless and pointless. Nevertheless she persevered, inviting friends, including the Boltons, in for a game, but as looking after Raymond's mother became more demanding, such socialising became rarer, soon petering out altogether. Raymond seemed not to mind, however, contenting himself with a lunch-hour game when he worked at Reyrolles and, after that, studying the games in the *Financial Times*. Dorothy confesses to still feeling some residual guilt about it.

In the early days of their marriage Dorothy and Raymond led an active cultural life, attending the theatre a great deal in Newcastle and Sunderland. They were also members of Tyneside Film Club and visited art exhibitions at the Laing, Shipley and University Art galleries and any public University lectures. Raymond, as an alumni of Faraday House, always had tickets to their prestigious lectures, given at but six venues in the UK, one of them the Newcastle City Hall.

These were unique 'state of the art' engineering lectures, superbly presented, visually and technically. These were memorable occasions for both of them and he obtained tickets for their house-guests too. They also attended many concerts. Raymond particularly loved music, his mother having been a fine singer and pianist, a long-standing member of the Halle Choir in Manchester under Thomas Beecham.

> Going through Raymond's vast collection of memorabilia recently, Dorothy
> has come across all his mother's Halle programmes since she was 16. She
> has passed them on to the first full-time student to stay in their home during
> her year's study with Dorothy, Margery Peel, who is a member of the Halle
> now. These last few months Dorothy has spent much time going through
> Raymond's things, carefully selecting to whom they should be passed on.

Growing fruit and vegetables in their garden as well as shrubs and flowers became a passion they shared. More than that, it was a responsibility, an act of husbandry bearing a moral impulse. The garden was to become a feature of their lives, a place of productive toil. Marianne, their daughter, recalls answering the telephone to a colleague of Dorothy who, when hearing that 'her mother was in the garden', commented 'Oh I wish I had time to sit in the garden!' The caller obviously did not know Dorothy – the idea of asking her just to sit in a garden would be like asking Gandhi to give up politics.

One aspect of cultivation did not interest them: the product of the vineyard. Rarely in their married life did a bottle of wine appear on their dining room table. Dorothy never drank anything alcoholic. Raymond would occasionally offer guests a sherry, but only on some celebratory occasion that prodded him into remembering that there was wine in the cellar. And it was good wine, for visitors from all over the world would bring Dorothy vintage wine from their region to show their gratitude to her, which was duly accepted by Dorothy with becoming courtesy. Down it would go into the cellar, carefully laid on its side ... and be forgotten. But when John Carroll was successful in achieving his doctorate with Dorothy as his supervisor, the time seemed ripe for opening a bottle. John had to find a way of breaking the news to Raymond that it had been kept too long and turned to vinegar. After that, John conducted a survey for Raymond, sorting out what was worth keeping and what was likely to have gone off.

Raymond's great passion was cars. He belonged to the Lanchester/Daimler Owners' Club and 'Old Sarah' was a Lancaster 10 saloon of 1931. He looked after his cars himself, as he was the only engineer he could really trust. Raymond was intolerant of sloppy work of any kind. In this respect they were alike. Both demanded the best possible work from themselves and from others. The manifestations of this exactitude were markedly different, however. Raymond could work in an untidy mess; Dorothy had to have everything laid out in order. Raymond was slow and ponderous. He never said anything he had not first weighed up in his mind; Dorothy was quick-thinking and discovered what she meant from the words tumbling out of her mouth. Raymond did not like to be rushed.

Slow and ponderous might well describe how people saw Raymond, but not in a real emergency. And how swift he could be. Dorothy tells me: 'He once saved me from a dreadful burning when we were working in the garage, with the old iron stove lit in winter. I put an oily rag on it and it flared and burnt my arm. Raymond was actually under the car at the time and he was up, out, and threw me literally onto a rug and rolled it round me. Otherwise ... well, it doesn't bear thinking about.'

My wife Cynthia recalls another example of Raymond's speed of reaction, when a careless oncoming driver would have caused a nasty accident had it not been for Raymond's skill in promptly reversing out of danger, almost before his passengers could take in what was happening. He used regularly to keep in trim for road skids by practising at the Police Skid Pan. This paid off when he was driving back from their holiday in North Wales, and hit a great oil spill. He kept the car upright by driving into the skid, just as he had practised.

Both found the large dining-table, suitably covered with protective layers, to be the best working surface in the house. Raymond didn't often bring car parts into the dining room, but he did manage to fill the table with papers, such as journals and the *Financial Times* or files from work and Dorothy recalls serving meals round two headlamps for a year! She learned always to leave him a little note saying things like 'This space will be needed on Thursday'. Dorothy is addicted to notes, most of them reminders to herself. She orders her life and, by recording, mostly in a line of tiny slips of paper on one of the kitchen surfaces, what needs to be done in the next 24 hours or at some points during the coming week, she guards against the fear she has of forgetting something. On the surface, this looks like ultra-efficiency, but she explains that she has this built-in paranoia that somehow next day's work has to be achieved today! Neither was she very good at throwing things away, which harked back to her upbringing. For Raymond it was an inbuilt archival sense, although it took Dorothy about eight years to appreciate that what looked like clutter was Raymond's method of filing. They both accumulated and eventually accepted and respected each other's accumulations.

Their way of dealing with petty authority differed enormously. Whereas Dorothy would make tentative, unassertive responses if someone was trying to throw their official weight about, Raymond would see red and determine to reduce the 'little boss' to size. When a long line of passengers were not allowed to embark on an empty train in front of them but were kept waiting under the dripping roof of Newcastle station, Raymond stepped forward after a while, quietly opened a carriage door, got in and sat down. Another time, when he witnessed a bus driver nearly knock down two elderly ladies crossing the road, he got out of his car, stopped the bus, removed the bus keys and sent for the police. Present at these and other incidents, Dorothy grows smaller as Raymond, unmistakably angry but very controlled, grows bigger. Any workman doing shoddy work had better watch out! And in the Raymond book of rules, there is no point in paying a bill until the last day and every point in checking what the Income Tax officials charge you.

Dorothy was extremely well organised at both work and home. Home seemed to centre round the kitchen and at the heart of that kitchen was the Aga. This should be written **AGA** or even bigger, if the name of the cooker is to look anything like its standing in that household, for, as she explains, 'it dries clothes, cooks perfectly, warms hands and backs and self cleans!' Saving enough money to buy such a treasure carried its own story. Impressed by the Aga in Marion Lawrence's kitchen, Dorothy vowed that should she ever have her own home, this piece would take centre stage. As soon as she got a full time job in Newcastle, she saved £100, the price of an Aga when she first discovered them. But when she and Raymond set up house, instead of that money going on an Aga, it had to go towards buying her mother a cottage in Yorkshire. 'I've taken your Aga money', wailed her mother. They found the £250 now needed for the cooker and it was duly installed. It stands proudly, still functioning perfectly, some 45 years later.

Since Raymond's death Dorothy is being persuaded by her daughter to move nearer to Nottingham where Marianne lives. Each time she steps into a possible property her first thought is 'Can I get an Aga into here?'

While he worked at Reyrolles, their holidays together were limited to Raymond's two weeks' annual leave. They often went to Europe, visiting countries that were opening up to tourists for the first time since the war. Food was often limited and sometimes of doubtful source but opportunities for exploring of historical and cultural Europe were plentiful. Raymond had an astonishing flair for nosing out what was available and for gathering background information about historical sites. Dorothy recalls how he searched and found a gravestone of a Roman soldier's wife in Czechoslovakia. He knew that at Hadrian's Wall, separating England from Scotland, there was a plaque made by a soldier to the memory of this wife. Sometimes they would take an officially arranged tourist trip to some site of interest and Dorothy learnt to expect that at some point Raymond would desert her, going off on his own investigation, leaving her with the tourist group. 'He has always come back ... ' she found herself explaining to an anxious coach driver.

Combining the responsibilities of professional career and married life required careful time-tabling. She would plan and as far as possible prepare a whole term's meals – stuck in the second-hand, commercial size deep-freeze and neatly labelled. She hates regular 'house-wifely' shopping apart from winter vegetables, but warehouse shopping became routine. Buying toilet rolls, shaving soaps, toothpaste, flour, sugar and all the staple foods – and Raymond's clothing – for the year meant that she could then dismiss these domestic necessities from her mind and also feel some satisfaction at saving money, But the drive to save time did not stretch to an electric washer. The sink in the kitchen, deep enough for sheets, was all a good housewife required. Not until 1999 did Raymond announce, prompted by Marianne, that 'We need a washer'. As her professional work became more demanding, Dorothy regularly started her day at 4.a.m., for she was determined that evening meal time should be family time, with no concession to the stack of teaching responsibilities awaiting her attention.

Dorothy who?

The chance for Institutes of Education to attract people from further afield arrived with the Ministry of Education's ambitious promotion of Advanced Diplomas, encouraging the introduction of specialist courses with Ministry approval over one academic year, for which experienced teachers could be seconded on full salary. The notion that drama could be given such status came to Professor Stanley by accident. The story goes that the University of Durham wrote to a Mr. Slade of Birmingham inviting him to be an examiner in Agricultural Engineering. But the letter was addressed to the wrong Slade and Professor Stanley duly received a letter from the Drama Organiser for Birmingham, Peter Slade, explaining that there had been a mistake but might he respectfully suggest that the new Advanced Diplomas he'd heard about offered an opportunity for Drama to be given its proper attention. And if only Durham would consider it he, Peter Slade, the leading authority on Child Drama in the UK, would be prepared to give such a project his personal backing and, if appropriate, some practical support.

This was all Professor Stanley needed to launch a unique course, the pattern for which was not followed anywhere else in the country[1]. Dorothy was at first reluctant to run such a demanding course. It was one thing to relate to and gradually build up a bond with local primary school headteachers attending evening classes; it was quite another to provide a full year's course for people who were giving up their jobs for a year to take up residence in the North-East of England, uprooting themselves, leaving their families and increasing their expenses. They would have quite different expectations of what a course should look like. It made sense to Dorothy that it should be a two-year course, one year full-time, followed by a year's part-time during which the students were visited in their schools in various parts of the country by Dorothy, who would advise them for the required dissertation.

Again it was the Froebel policy of giving direct support to experienced teachers that led to the two-year rather than the more usual one-year structure. It also required Dorothy to travel the country to visit applicants to see and understand teaching circumstances. And, as Dorothy says, 'they could see whether I appealed to them'. One of the problems for the University was finding accommodation for a full-time drama course. Nothing like it had been required before; the idea of a large empty space made no sense to University professors. They had to scout round for a place to hire, and found one in a local teacher training institution.

Early in 1962, before the full-time diploma course was fully worked out, Dorothy travelled to Birmingham to meet Peter Slade. I travelled with her. We were invited to attend one of his famous free movement sessions with adults in the hall at the Rea Street Drama Centre. A stirring record was put on the gramophone, and people whirled round the room, sometimes picking up a chair for a dance partner. Dancing with a chair was seen as a test of grace and strength. 'Are you going to join in?' invites Peter. I am shaping my mouth to say, 'Sure!' when a voice from Dorothy, squashed next to me on a wooden chair, says firmly: 'I don't think so'. And my 'ssshure', becomes 'ssshall we just watch?' Sylvia Demmery, Peter Slade's blonde nubile slender 'princess', pirouetting in front of us in her close-fitting black leotard, seemed particularly drawn to our vicinity, twirling on the spot as others sailed round the room. The expression on her face was rapturous. I sensed Dorothy pressing backwards in her chair. Luckily we were against a wall or she'd have toppled over. I daren't look at the expression on her face! When it was all over and we were invited to Sylvia's for drinks, I insisted on taking her a box of chocolates. 'Whatever you think's best, Gavin – I'll go halves', agreed Dorothy in an effort of cooperation. 'And to make matters worse,' Dorothy tells my wife the next day when we got home, 'the chocolates were called *Contrast!*'

Brian Stanley himself visited Slade in order to discuss the final structure of the course which, it was agreed, included a six week visit to Birmingham by the Newcastle students so that they could, as Peter Slade put it, 'study Child Drama'.

Soon after this, Ray Verrier, an experienced teacher of English and History in a Bristol school who was later to become a colleague and co-author with John Fines, was looking for a course. While attending Peter Slade's Summer School in Child Drama, he asked Peter if there was a longer course in school drama available for which a teacher might get a sabbatical. Ray writes that Peter's response was:

> I have a little lady who runs a year's drama course in Newcastle. At the end of the year her students are sent to me for polishing up. That course would be very suitable for you.

Ray continues:

> A year later I attended an interview at Newcastle University. Remembering Peter's 'little lady', I greeted Winifred Fawcus (who was interviewing with Dorothy) as Mrs. Heathcote, only to learn that Dorothy was not exactly a little lady in any respect.

As a university course it did not come under the direct jurisdiction of the Ministry of Education, but it was of interest to the Inspectorate, especially those responsible for the Arts, that such an innovatory course was being set up in the north and by a virtually unknown woman called Mrs. Heathcote, with a Yorkshire accent. Apparently she had been there some thirteen years. And it was reported that she joined in with the children's own drama – very dangerous. They were no doubt relieved that Peter Slade had somehow become involved in the course and they gave him their informal support.

Slade was not deceived into thinking that he and Dorothy shared a philosophy of drama education. He has written to me as follows:

> I gradually became aware of some differences between us over attitude, approach and theory in our work with and for children, but I cannot remember this ever interfering with our personal relationship. On one visit to Birmingham she suddenly said: 'I must be honest, Peter, you were not the inspiration for my work.' I replied: 'I know' – and I resolved to get used to North Country honesty!

Although it was generally welcomed that Drama in the classroom had become a subject for study at Newcastle and Durham Universities, there was some suspicion among a few LEA Drama Advisers that these seemingly prestigious appointments might rival the established leadership. Even Brian Way felt some loss of stature. Dorothy's and my students would sometimes collaborate in a trip to work with Brian in London. I recall being taken aback when we had just arrived at his centre with our group to join a larger audience assembled for his talk and he began: 'I see we have the intellectuals from the North here now,' a barb that was as unexpected as it was misplaced. But it gave me a glimpse of how we were perceived.

One of Her Majesty's Inspectors who respected Mrs. Heathcote's work from the start, without claiming to understand it, was John Allen, who became Senior HMI responsible for Drama. A leading Canadian educationist, Helen Dunlop writes:

> I first met Dorothy in June of 1967 ... I was doing research on Drama in Education ... and turned for advice to John Allen ... I had met him the previous year in Canada when he came out to adjudicate a drama festival and he proved most gracious and helpful. He sent me all over the country visiting various programs and one of my last stops was Newcastle. I now suspect that he arranged this deliberately, keeping the best until the last, so to speak.
>
> Nothing I had seen before prepared me for Dorothy. Her dynamism and complete involvement as well as her philosophy about improvisation captured my imagination. As I subsequently reported to John Allen, here was the very essence of drama in education as an aid to learning.

Helen Dunlop was among a growing number of visitors from abroad whose attention was directed towards a certain drama tutor at Newcastle University. They had no vested interest in supporting her or giving credence to her work. They were often extremely experienced educators themselves. One would expect that some might disapprove, but on the contrary, many responded much as Helen Dunlop did. Some did not appear to see beyond Mrs. Heathcote as a charismatic teacher whereas others could perceive the unique educational potential of her approach.

Her methodology is given a label – Drama as 'a Man in a Mess'

Past students who have written to me about their visits to Birmingham express their disappointment. They describe the experience variously as 'frustrating', 'a waste of time' or 'disappointing'. Peter Slade was a genuine pioneer and had a great deal to offer teachers, but the two philosophies were incompatible. And when Dorothy's teachers were struggling to come to terms with the demands of the Heathcote methodology was the wrong time to become deeply engaged with a totally different approach.

The contrast for the students between the Sladian and Heathcotean classroom practices must have been disconcerting. Although the language that these two pioneers used occasionally overlapped in relation to child-centredness, the importance of child play and the avoidance of stage acting, Peter Slade's overall style of narrating an action sequence for the children to follow as individuals in their own space in the service of self-expression, appeared painfully at odds with Dorothy's teacher-in-role manipulation of the whole group in the service of her conception of drama as 'a man in a mess', a definition of drama she adopted from Kenneth Tynan.

Dorothy believed in the value for her students of seeing other people's work, although I think this did not extend to herself. Indeed she appeared to keep herself distinctly 'uninfluenced' by others' approaches. She used what others did merely as an indicator of where she herself stood. David Griffiths concludes: 'Had Dorothy undergone the traditional course of teacher training, she may never have achieved such success. She came to the classroom with an open mind, and was able to chart her own course, unencumbered by established theories.'

This biography does not give detailed examples of Dorothy's teaching. You will find vivid accounts of it in B.J. Wagner's book[2]. But I do try to capture the essence of her teaching through selected examples in an attempt to give the reader an image of what she did and how her work appeared to others at different times in her career. A Man in a Mess fairly conveys the way in which others, and she herself for a few years, perceived her approach. I believe that most teachers studying her work at that time came away with the understanding that a teacher's aim was to take the students into some experience that amounts to a state of desperation.

Cecily O'Neill summarises a lesson she observed that typifies the approach.

> The most 'dramatic' experience I saw her operate was in London. The kids wanted to be 'bad kids' locked up in a borstal. She became the Warden, and ran a very tense session, where she just called out their numbers, instead of names. Every so often she would stop and check with the kids that they were happy for her to be so severe. Of course they egged her on to greater severity! I was excited by the dramatic tension and simplicity of the session, as well as Dorothy's going in and out of role, each time deepening the experience for the kids.

This description of the lesson and Cecily's response to it epitomises teachers', including my own, assumptions about the Heathcote methodology. If asked to say how her work differed from Peter Slade's, we were likely to answer in terms of exciting tension, powerfully effective teacher role-play, and instant reflection brought about by constant interruption of the dramatic flow. And such impressions of her approach continued, so that for the rest of her professional career, Dorothy suffered from a misalignment between her current thinking and that of the people who remained stolidly attached to her man in a mess dramatic structure after she had discarded it.

A teacher's course must be based in the classroom

Dorothy may have claimed that she was still learning what a full-time drama course should be like but she was adamant that the course was about what takes place in the classroom. And not just 'what do you do in the classroom?' but 'who are you when you enter a classroom?' and 'what and whom do you see?' Each year's full-time students found that the course was firmly based in the bank of schools in the North-East, where Dorothy's reputation was already well established. She was popular among local teachers who eagerly offered their classes for her to teach so she could demonstrate to her new students what drama teaching was about. The experienced teachers on a year's secondment from their education authority could not know much about Heathcotian drama teaching unless they happened to live in the area. One candidate even thought he would be learning how to do stage falls! Dorothy had not written anything and nothing had been written about her. Teachers wanting secondment discovered that the only full-time drama course on offer was at Newcastle, run by a 'Dorothy who? ... ' As students from abroad trickled in, some came with almost mythic images. One from the Caribbean had heard that Mrs. Heathcote was so large that she couldn't walk and was carried everywhere in a litter, rather like the Queen of Tonga!

Not surprisingly, many of these experienced teachers suffered an undermining of confidence in their own abilities. For many, Dorothy's approach was so incompatible with the drama skills they had acquired over many years of teaching that their confidence ebbed and, because their grasp of the new methodology was partial, they initially appeared to be less able as teachers. Their uncertainty went beyond matters of drama. As Sandra Hesten puts it: 'The teacher on Heathcote's course often felt disorientated in that his/her accepted views and values on teaching and on life had been shaken.' Sandra calls it 'the fog-weed' factor', where a student might face continual crisis and intellectual fog.

Dorothy was well aware of the problems facing her students and mindful of the danger of merely supplying easy answers, leaving the learners with a mistaken impression that they understood the methodology. Teachers on her short courses who picked up the surface features of her methods faced disastrous consequences when they failed to grasp the underlying philosophical and artistic values. Her full-time students, however, were never allowed to delude themselves into thinking that the skin of the apple represented the core. Dorothy tried to set up experiences that led them to examine their own values, their credo as teachers and their own humanity. She worked to help them recognise the limits of their perception and to extend their skills in reading, reading for form, for interior meaning, and for how an artist has achieved his purpose in poetry, in film, in a script, in a play performance. She would say, 'Go to the theatre and do not allow yourselves to be enchanted'; 'Look at the three minute opening of this film and know what the camera is doing'; 'Read this first paragraph and pick up the pointers the novelist has laid there'. This is not to suggest that she would claim to know what the content of the course should be. Such a 'perception' task is but one example of Dorothy's life-long search to discover: 'how does one help people to learn?', a search she continues still.

She did not believe in mollycoddling her students. One of them writes: 'Dorothy seemed to expect all of us to be like her in her Spartan, stalwart, physical strength ... totally impervious to weather, cold or heat, hunger, bodily functions, and needs of rest, breaks, or weaknesses like that'. Another ex-student puts this down to Dorothy's theatre training which made no allowance for human weaknesses. Tiredness was no excuse for anything. I can recall one occasion when attending her class – she invited me to drop in whenever I was free – when I had twisted my knee the day before. Sitting watching what she was doing, I volunteered to be used by her as a demonstration of something or other. I hobbled with my stick into the position she wanted me to take up. She talked us through a lengthy exposition of a point she wanted to make, leaving me standing there straining to keep upright without putting further pressure on the damaged leg. Eventually she released me. Her students commiserated afterwards, saying they could see the strain in my face. So I wondered afterwards: 'If others could see the agony I was going through, why couldn't Dorothy, especially with her reputed skill in observation of people? Or was there a vindictive streak in her?' The answer is that she was working and presumed that minor inconveniences and discomforts should and could be overlooked.

During the first week of the full-time courses she would invite the students to take the group through a way of teaching drama they would have used back in their own schools. She did this not because she wanted to expose a weakness but to show how to look for the values implicit in someone else's approach. She wanted them to see differently – just as she wanted them to look at children differently. Teachers brought up to expect judgements to be along the lines of success or failure found themselves looking anxiously to Dorothy after their lesson demonstration for her approval or disapproval. Just as she never looked at her own teaching in those terms, she always saw possibilities in their work.

At first, she would undertake various teaching projects in schools with her students watching the lesson at a respectful distance from the edge of the hall or classroom. She soon discovered that having their eyes riveted on her prevented their reading what she was seeing in the children's behaviour. They did not really see the class. To overcome this, she started to devise school projects that drew her students into the drama, using neutral roles such as 'press' or 'witnesses' or even 'silent statues', to be referred to but without power to initiate. This close proximity to individual pupils obliged them to adapt to the children's behaviour while taking their cue from Dorothy. This was the beginning of seeing themselves through the behaviour of another, which eventually led Dorothy to the idea, discussed in Chapter 6, of having her students work in one to one relationships with handicapped children, as they were called in the UK in the 1960s and 1970s.

Taking part in role, Dorothy discovered, was a rich learning experience for her students in other respects too. They could share the pre-planning; they could be made responsible for providing or making their own distinguishing properties – usually a token hat, jacket, helmet, cuff, badge, armband or weapon. To select the material, the right colour and make the right cut became an important exercise in authenticity and economy. And, also, an exercise in asking oneself 'what will the infant, the adolescent, the city/rural child, the engineering apprentice, the battered wife, the trainee nurse, the A stream pupil, the educationally disenchanted see in the choice of glove, knife, quill pen, or silk drape?' Thus having the students carefully prepare their supportive roles in class teaching led by Dorothy became an integral part of all her major courses. I recall the words of someone watching Dorothy teach for the first time and seeing her students participate: 'Can't she do it herself?'

Other features of Dorothy's first full-time courses

One feature of Dorothy's courses that did not always appeal to her students was the work she did on Laban 'efforts'. Her intention had been to use Laban's system for creating characters as an aid for the students who would go back in their schools and a means of helping their pupils to act in school productions. A few of her students laugh when they look back at these sessions, which seem to have mystified them. Some in the first two or three courses were unhappy about the time she spent on improvisation. In answer to the question in the questionnaire I sent out to many past students: 'Were there uncomfortable moments?', Robert Hornby, despite his fulsome praise and admiration for her, wrote:

> Working with a disparate group of fellow students on seemingly interminable improvisations instigated by DH invariably involving disasters and/ or journeys.

He goes on:

> In those rambling improvisations ... a few of us students would involve DH in them to relieve the tedium (or perhaps just in desperation). As far as I

remember, she would always adopt the role of someone very old, very fat, very slow-moving for whatever reason, hard of hearing or gormless. This, we believed, was a crafty ploy to give herself plenty of time to think and/or make it more challenging for us ... Serve us right for dragging her into the impro!

It is interesting that Dorothy does not remember doing this kind of improvisation but I know she did, because I recall taking part in some of them. Derek Stevens, who attended a year or two after Robert Hornby, found his first experience of such improvisation painful but timely. He writes:

> In the market situation that Dorothy and Eve Carr set up, my hesitant approach, as it was the first time I was not teacher in charge of class, swiftly led to my being treated in role as the market inspector. Before I knew it, one of the class charged D.H. in role as a stall-holder of malpractice, and I was having to confront her with the charge. To my absolute terror D.H. pulled herself to her full height, froze me with a baleful glare and thundered, 'Are you accusing me of cheating, young man?' I flinched, felt I had disintegrated, had no way out of the awful desolation I was in. Well, somehow I must have emerged – and with a tougher skin, I suppose, and some kind of awareness that there would be many more occasions like this when I would need to undertake a proper stocktaking of myself as a teacher and as a person. Because, of course, by stopping the action in order to resume one's breath and to enter a space of discussion and reflection, she never lets the group forget the 'virtuality' of the event.

In fact Dorothy soon dispensed with such improvisational exercises as having little to do with her philosophy. She had been conforming to the fashion of the time, which was to treat improvisation as a proper activity, associated with the work of Stanislavski in the theatre and Slade in the classroom. It is probable that her students would expect such a course component in any progressive course. In 1967 she herself wrote an article on improvisation, but the word gradually disappeared from her drama vocabulary. Although most of her drama was indeed improvised, more and more this became a means to an end rather than improvisation as a genre.

Reading the draft of the above paragraph, Dorothy is sure she did not ever think of improvisation in the fashionable way of the time, but my perception is that improvisation, being the very oxygen of 1960s' drama courses, was breathed in by Dorothy, as it was by the rest of us. I shall never forget running a week-end course for a group of teachers in the South-West, who were aggrieved that once I had started them off on an improvisation, I dared to interrupt. They complained that I was 'ruining their natural creativity'.

Dorothy was moving rapidly away from improvisation for its own sake. Most of us who were privileged to lead groups in improvisational methods up and down the country and abroad would see week-end or summer courses as a useful opportunity to set up a dramatic experience, often over several sessions, for the teachers themselves to enjoy, based on their choice of theme, their input and their means of bringing matters to some kind of satisfying resolution. This was followed by reflection on what issues had been opened up and only then would discussion follow on how the strategies we had used in our own creation might be applied to various kinds of classrooms and age groups. Thus, it was argued, the experience provided a model of what might be achieved for children. The feel-good factor was also a key indication that the course had been successful.

I anticipate that Dorothy will wince as she reads a draft of this. The approach I have described would be anathema to her – feeling good has nothing to do with learning to teach, I can hear her say. Experiencing is but indulging, she would add. After the first few years of including such improvising in her course, she dropped it. If she ever set up a group experience with her students, you can be sure it would be interrupted every 15 seconds by Dorothy wanting them to notice something.

There was another activity she avoided. Perhaps the one activity that grew most rapidly in popularity during the 1960s and after was 'games', a genre in which one of Dorothy's students, Donna Brandes, was a creative expert. These were invariably introduced as pre-drama warm-ups, although one year when I was examining Drama students on their final school practice, every drama lesson I saw consisted entirely of games – and the staff on the examining board raised their eyebrows when I complained that I had not seen any drama! Dorothy remained totally untouched by this fashion. Carole Tarlington, a dynamic Australian teacher and entrepreneur in Canadian Youth Theatre, involved in writing a text for publication, sought Dorothy's support for the concept of using games. The opportunity to ask Dorothy for ideas came while attending a course in Victoria, BC in which Mrs Heathcote found space for ten-minute one-to-one tutorials with each teacher on the course. Carole writes:

> Never one to waste time, she sat, of course, deeply involved in her embroidery while I burbled on trying to get her to bless this approach we had taken. After all, if the guru said it was a good approach then we must be right. 'You see Dorothy,' I explained with some enthusiasm, 'We just feel that the teachers need these little drama games and exercises. Don't you?' There was a pause as she inserted her needle and tied off the stitch, and then she said 'I don't know any little drama games and exercises, Carole.' I left the room and collapsed in hysterics. What was I thinking?

From the first of the full-time courses Dorothy included work on scripts with the aim of helping students probe more deeply the interior interaction between the characters and inculcating the feel of an actor's line as responsive to what another character has said or done. Of the students who have answered my questionnaire only one refers to this particular work, recalling some frustration at Dorothy's 'constantly interrupting and talking at you too much'.

One inevitable feature of her full-time courses was that a group of students from all over the world who didn't know each other did not necessarily get on together. A number of past students write of 'a clash of personalities' that held the work back. Donna Brandes, blaming the men on her course for 'loving heady arguments', tells the following anecdote:

> One week, Dorothy went away for a few days, leaving us to complete the plans for a Shakespearean presentation [Hamlet] we were doing for GCSE students at Hexham Grammar School. While we were planning, we got hung up on whether to wear full Elizabethan costume or go for a more trendy set of black turtlenecks and jeans. Three days later Dorothy found us firmly entrenched in two camps ... I have never seen her so furious. She gave us a tirade about the wasted time, and about how we were acting like small children, and since we couldn't decide she would decide for us!

> She paced the floor, not wanting to come down on either side and give one bunch the satisfaction of winning. We sat in disgruntled and fearful silence, waiting for the verdict. Finally she slammed to a stop, and shouted 'SLEEVES!!!' ... 'What???' 'SLEEVES!'

> And so it was, we wore the black turtlenecks and jeans ... we all wore fantastic colourful Elizabethan sleeves, joined front and back with broad bands of colour. It worked. A prime example of DH's resourcefulness and determination – and of her sense of artistic 'rightness'.

Several students have indicated that it was sometime *after* the full-time course, in the protective context of their own employment, that they found they truly integrated Dorothy's practice with their own. For some it was a kind of 'eureka' experience as Kathleen Berry vividly relates:

> Even twenty years later, there are many moments in my teaching drama, literacy, and other areas that Dorothy's articulations echo throughout my consciousness and sometimes change or enlighten my actions.

> One particular moment I remember was during a drama episode I was doing with a group of Grade 6s on the topic of coalmining in Lethbridge, Alberta. I was walking the students through the river (the school hallway becoming

the river that Lethbridge miners always had to penetrate to get to the coal), feeling that the experience of the original miners was being sensationalized and trivialised by the students-in-role. Suddenly, Dorothy's voice echoed through my body even to the point I felt I was Dorothy. In a split second, I stopped, turned with my 'Dorothy stance' and resolutely declaimed: 'There are people depending on us for black stones to heat their homes and cook their food – responsibility given only to we miners'.

I thought at first this was a bit corny but immediately the tenor of the drama and the posturing of the students changed – we had moved to a deeper level. I laughed at myself as in that moment several of Dorothy's tutoring sessions took shape in my work. I heard her tutoring session on archaic language and questioning and keeping in role when disciplining and keeping the action going, and the role of 'teacher-in-role' all fall into place at that moment. No methodology or prescriptive lesson planning could have prepared me for that moment and that decision – it was the accumulation of Dorothy's tutoring sessions that bounced into that moment to create a true dramatic action.

Reading Kathy Berry's account, I think there are many past students who will recognise what she is talking about, who know what it is like for all Heathcote's teaching suddenly to bounce into the dramatic moment. Claire Armstrong Mills, Head of Drama at Kings Norton High School in Birmingham, writes of a similar moment of excitement :

I think my happiest moment was when I first used teacher-in-role and realised the work had entered another dimension – the sensation of energy and engagement for the pupils was quite scary.

For nearly all her students, the full-time course was the greatest professional experience of their lives. Perhaps the most difficult aspect for them was how they too could attain Dorothy's level of artistry. How can they learn, they asked themselves, to think like her, to stay centred with an image or theme, so that their work too stays 'true'? How can they acquire that speed of seeing a range of possibilities and selecting the precise one that will be right for this class at this time? Dorothy would occasionally give them practice exercises in making connections, testing how many directions their minds would take them in. For some students their only hope was that close proximity to Dorothy the artiste would be sufficiently sustained for osmosis.

An invitation from the British Council

Suddenly Dorothy's career became international, not in drama but in education. In 1964 she received an invitation from the British Council to look at the education of girls in Sarawak. She went down to London for a briefing only to discover that they had switched the country to India – for four weeks and two more in Aden – because they had mistakenly lined up a male educationist for India, forgetting that purdah would forbid him entry into girls' schools. At the briefing a pre-war colonialist type gave her pre-war advice on how she should conduct herself and what she should wear, including a pith helmet – as if she were about to join a tiger shoot in the days of the Raj.

It was a happy coincidence that Raymond knew India, having spent the whole of the war there as an airman. At the end of the war he was officially recorded as having 'gone missing', but he and an army friend had made an expedition into the foothills of the Himalayas in Kashmir, equipped with camera and two horses. He had had no leave for years and after landing himself for three months in an army hospital, he eventually discharged himself and took some of his well-deserved leave. Asked how he had fared without money, he explained, 'As long as you had your air-force or army cap, people fed you willingly.'

Thus Dorothy went home from the London briefing to a husband who was ready with practical advice and a great deal of enthusiasm for the enterprise. The following January and February, armed with Raymond's camera she travelled long distances in India, mostly by train, visiting mainly private girls' schools. When she asked to visit schools in the poorer districts she was met with reluctance as they really wanted her to confine her visits to schools teaching English. The state schools were huge and open for 24 hours, the pupils arriving in shifts – slaves had the night shift. She was always well attended by a chauffeur, a long-serving driver for the British Council, who waited patiently outside in the car however long her visit took.

When she returned home she assiduously prepared a two hundred page report covering her six weeks' observation. The British Council seemed taken aback by such conscientiousness, as though completion of the project was a matter of filing rather than studying. For Dorothy and Raymond this was the first of many lengthy separations that marked their married life, and as for her full-time students, they were relieved to be back in Newcastle with Dorothy after a long six weeks in Birmingham.

Open house at Highburn House

When Dorothy was pre-visiting the teachers for her first Advanced Diploma (1964-5) she came across Margery Peel, a teacher who did not qualify for full salary while she attended the course because she did not work in a local authority school. Dorothy's immediate response when she heard this was 'Well, you could live at our house, if you don't mind living in. I'm just an ordinary cook.' And she was to say this to subsequent applicants, housing them mostly free of charge, except for the few who insisted on contributing toward the cost of food. Raymond was equally accommodating, finding them interesting guests and happy to put himself out at week-ends, occasionally arranging their visits to historical sites in the North-East.

By the summer term of the first diploma course, the Heathcote household was affected by the rapid deterioration of Raymond's mother from Parkinson's disease. Dorothy was extremely fond of her and Raymond's father. Marianne Heathcote, whom his father always called 'Marie', died in early August, 1965.

One day, some weeks later, Raymond was away and Dorothy, bending over the car to wash it, suddenly felt a twinge ... and knew that she was pregnant. She knew this for certain, just as she was convinced that it was 'a life given back to them' in return for 'a life taken away'. In May a baby girl was born and they called her Marianne. Dorothy's sure touch with planning ensured that the teachers on Dorothy's second full-time course conveniently spent their weeks with Peter Slade in Birmingham during the month of May.

Notes

1   By the time the first Advanced Diploma Course in Drama in Education started in 1964, Durham University had split into Durham and Newcastle, so that it was to Newcastle University that the first group of five full-time drama students travelled. The separation had occurred in 1962, so that Durham now found itself without an Institute. I was appointed to Durham University's newly set up Institute of Education in 1963. No other universities took up the idea, so the North-East became seen as a focus for educational drama.

2   Wagner, B.J. *Dorothy Heathcote: Drama as a Learning Medium* Portland, Maine, Calendar Island Publishers 1999 [first published 1976]

5

Working mother and media star

Dorothy's first experience before the cameras

There was a curious overlap in the timing of her baby daughter's entry into the world and Dorothy's first appearance before professional cameras. Dorothy emerged from hospital soon to enter a classroom all set up for filming. It was June, 1966.

Several months earlier I had received a visit from Joe Reid, BBC's Education Officer for the South West who, along with Ron Smedley, made school programmes for the BBC and was currently looking for quality school drama work. Joe had explained to me that he was conducting a film series related to the use of improvisation in schools, and, although he had worked with some people who were highly recommended as drama teachers, he had found the quality of the work disappointing. He had been building his hopes on this Mrs. Heathcote of Newcastle, but now he had heard that she was expecting a baby in May, just the time allocated to his filming schedule! When he began to sound me out about my taking Dorothy's place, I said: 'Hang on, don't give up so quickly on Dorothy Heathcote – you obviously don't know her! And if you have no luck there, the man to contact is Tom Stabler, a recent student of Dorothy's whose approach reflects hers.'

Ron Smedley phoned Dorothy from London the day before she went into hospital, to ask if she would be willing to view the film he had prepared, based on what he had seen so far in other parts of the country. He would like her opinion. An hour later he was flying up to meet Dorothy in the tiny, darkened film theatre of Newcastle University's Medical School, a venue with which Dorothy was to become very familiar. And he listened to her comments in the dark. About John Hodgson, Head of Drama at Bretton Hall her remarks were not complimentary – 'he was a person thinking clever; his questions were those of an English teacher using a novel; his technique was a sort of watered down producer who loves his play; and, of course, he's afraid of the class'.

Ron asked if she could suggest where he might see some better work, and when once more he heard Tom Stabler's name – alongside Dorothy's suggestion of Sister Bridget and Maurice Gilmore, two more of her students – he opted for a visit to Hartlepool. Ron had written to me as follows about their disappointment so far:

> He [Joe Reid] and I set out to be thrilled. To say the least we weren't. Now, let me emphasise that this was 35 years ago, much of the work was new and experimental and we may have been unlucky ... but nonetheless! The work we were recommended to see seemed shapeless, boring and sometimes un-intentionally funny. No one seemed to be going anywhere. The Emperor was naked!

Thus Ron, somewhat dispiritedly, found himself visiting this former student who had taken the Newcastle Primary Diploma course, not Dorothy's drama course, although Dorothy was currently working with him in his Hartlepool primary school. Ron goes on:

> I still remember exactly what happened. I sat down with a notebook and a pencil in the awful, gloomy hall and waited to make notes – notes like 'Another wasted journey'; 'There really is no series here.' My notebook was full of them. Tom informed me that he had previously told the class a Bible story, they had talked about the story and they were going to show me the play they had developed out of their discussion.
>
> I made no notes.
>
> These little scruffy, pale, deprived children ('You almost expected them to have no boots', said Dorothy later) in one of the poorest parts of a poor town began to act out, at some length, a real play, a real and complicated argu-ment, in what was obviously their own words, while Tom said nothing. His work, for the time being, was done.
>
> I don't think in forty years of programme making, mostly with and for young people, I've ever had an experience like it. Tom, learning from Dorothy, believed that children were surrounded with language that they were never called upon to use. By telling a strong tale, telling it well and dis-cussing its meanings and its implications with the class, he gave the children the chance to use this locked up language.
>
> If this had been a Hollywood film there would be a close-up of a moist-eyed producer writing in his note-book 'There is a series, after all'. Well I didn't write it but I felt it.

He returned to film Tom's work but had some misgivings about Dorothy's offer to go before the cameras herself. After all, she was a lecturer, not a teacher, and had just had a baby! It was only when pressed by Sister Bridget, a worldly-wise nun and ex-student of Dorothy's who instructed him to film Dorothy, that he 'did as he was told'. Sister Bridget was a bright, laughing, endearing person who took responsibility for monitoring Dorothy's students when they visited London, Coventry and Birmingham that year.

The upshot was that Mrs. Heathcote duly arrived at Aycliffe Approved School, with a two-week-old baby in a basket, accompanied by her mother, who nursed Marianne while Dorothy taught a class of adolescent boys. The boys were a group of young offenders who had been placed that week in the security establishment by Leeds Law Courts. To many they would be young toughs; others might see them as severely disadvantaged, if not victims of society. To Dorothy they were a group of young people embarked on making up their own drama. As the first example of Dorothy's teaching that was to reach a wide public, it is worth examining in some detail for, to those who had some know-ledge of her work it appeared to confirm the unorthodox Heathcote approach and to those who were seeing it for the first time, it appeared to offer a startling new way of doing drama.

As with all filming, the work was severely edited, some three hours of teaching being reduced to seven minutes. Thus what the viewer sees is a misleadingly crisp, smooth and coherent representation. The essence of the drama experience is powerfully and poignantly captured by director Ron Smedley and his photo-grapher Phil Meyer, but the raw, sometimes sluggish, sometimes tedious, some-times unproductive interaction between teacher and class is not. For instance, I can recall when the boys were getting tired, bored and unsupportive of each other, towards the end of their first long day saying to Ron Smedley, 'Oh dear, she's losing them now ... ' And she certainly was. But the next morning, she retrieved the work brilliantly, bringing it to an unforgettable resolution. But the floundering, unproductive episode, which would have been so useful for teachers to see, is edited out for the television public, so that viewers miss the struggle and her clever, inspired recovery. What they get is a seamless switch from one successful playing to another. And yet to understand the way Dorothy works, one should see how she as a teacher copes when the work is not going anywhere because they are misbehaving or being unresponsive. She eases them through a bad time so that they don't lose face nor faith in themselves and then, perhaps her greatest skill of all, she nearly always finds the arresting image that challenges them anew, changing the focus and the energy level.

The edited episodes, however, are informative. The initial dialogue of the film between teacher and class goes like this:

Now a play is just a problem for a lot of people.

There are 30 of us, so all we have to do is find a problem for 30 people.

Let's first decide whether we live today or a long time ago.

Who wants it to be a long time ago ... hands up? [One hand goes up]

And today ... ? [Rest of hands] It looks as if it wins.

Do you mind if we do it this way first ... ? [addressing the disappointed one]

Are we men or women ... ? ['Men!' ... and one boy adds: 'We could have women if we need them.']

Fair enough ... we'll bring women in if we want 'em.

Shall we be in the town or shall we live in the country? [Chorus of 'town!']

We've got to find a problem then for a group of men living in a town in modern times ... Can you talk among yourselves ... find someone you can talk to easily.

A voice-over (a different Mrs. Heathcote with a carefully modulated, somewhat posh voice with southern vowels, a voice she now finds intensely embarrassing) explains that 'this is just one of my ways' of starting to work on drama. For Dorothy it was but one of a number of ways of introducing drama, but it became a rule-of-thumb recipe to would-be followers. It appeared to follow a pattern of theatre law to do with people sharing a common dilemma, reading their social health, narrowing the focus, and agreeing on the first brick in a fictional edifice. Such an evident pattern could be transformed into a procedure for those who were looking for a system. Perhaps the more perceptive noticed how she always acknowledged the possible rejection felt by those who were in a minority and how she reinforced any suggestions from individuals, echoing their words but perhaps subtly changing them, as in the instance, the boy's 'we could have women if we need them' to the more colloquial, more immediate, more 'action-poised': 'we can bring women in if we want 'em'.

We are not shown the boys' interactions nor how teacher and class settle on 'Death of the President'. We hear the posh voice explaining: 'I have accepted the boys' ideas and it is my job to make them work dramatically' ... and she proceeds to instruct them to close their eyes while she narrates in a solemn, emphatic tone, painting images connected with a warehouse context they have obviously discussed earlier. She concludes with:

' ... and behind this packing case is another door ... which is where we meet.'

Then we are offered a glimpse of the whole class playing the game of being a gang in a secret room – enough to recognise that it is a shallow game, while the voice-over tells us: 'it is important that as soon as possible the class must make their own decisions and put their own ideas into their own words'. But then there is an extraordinary change of gear when we see Dorothy in some kind of neutral interrogatory role, interviewing the man who has been elected by the gang to carry out the shooting 'in ten days' time'. Teacher and pupil feed each other with their profound commitment to their roles. Asking about the plan of action, the interrogator throws in 'Are you married?' Unfazed, the boy talks about his little daughter, aged five, for whom he will buy a flag to wave at the President.

As audience to this, the rest of the class are given their first taste of dramatic truth, a quality they try to emulate in the whole class scenes that follow. One is of the gang waiting for the news of the shooting on the warehouse radio; in a second scene, the police carried out a search for the chequered jacket. Each of the scenes has been carefully focused by Dorothy who, while following the directions in which the boys appear to want to take it, knows that their ideas will only work for them if she supplies the tight structure for each scene. As long as the form is dramatically sound, these boys who are inexperienced in drama are freed into finding the truth of the scene, a basic principle many teachers failed to grasp. Notice that Dorothy has typically avoided a scene involving murder or any kind of aggression. She explains this to me more fully:

> This is the constant dilemma isn't it – I support a lot of antisocial decisions regarding nasty mischief . (I've planned a lot of murders and bank robberies in my time) and yet my morality forbids me to set up circumstances where one person enacts an aggressive act upon another. I therefore had to woo them to a radio enactment in their own heads which felt more tense than a gun or a president. *Now* I have lots of other ways to do it.

Individual leaders among the group achieve an authenticity rarely seen in improvisational work. One boy, bringing a dignity and authority to his role as detective, prompts Dorothy's voice-over to instruct the viewers: 'Watch this boy ... without any production in the conventional sense from me ... notice his dramatic power ... his sense of timing.'

I have asked Dorothy about this comment. She agrees that she probably never again directed the observer's attention to a child's acting ability. This was 1966 and she was fully aware of her viewers' theatre backgrounds. But in its way it represents her final concession to the popular notion at that time that truth of acting was the single, satisfying goal and arbiter of effective improvisational drama. She was to spend the next thirty years directing the observer's attention to what was going on in people's heads – what they are beginning to 'see', 'understand', 'grasp', 'be surprised by', 'intrigued by' or 'bemused by' or even 'awed by'. Achievement in acting was rarely to feature as an educational priority.

> *At this point in the interview, Dorothy and I are interrupted by the cat. Now I think about it, nearly every interview has been so interrupted.*

The film finishes with a moving scene, after the news comes that the President, thought to be 'only winged', had died. The assassin, now in prison, is given his last breakfast. He asks for a breakfast to outdo all breakfasts, but on his way back to his cell he is pulled up short by Dorothy's ironic: 'Enjoy your breakfast Mr. Bradshaw' Its effect is spellbinding.

> Why am I having a special breakfast?
> Well **you know** the President died ... Yes.
> And **you know** who killed him ... Yes.
> And **you know** the penalty.

> The silence is profound, the camera registering the prisoner's stunned expression.
> 'Not the chair ... it can't be the chair ... I was sentenced to life imprisonment.'

Ron Smedley confirms the power of this moment:

> Now remember, we've not rehearsed this. The boy is looking at the tray in his hands ... he waits for just the right moment of time before he slowly looks up at the warder. His words are ordinary – the perfect timing before he speaks them is not. It's called acting, and it's not easy. Dorothy didn't choose the boys to play the roles, the other boys did. Whether the boys ever acted again I don't know. [Dorothy confirms they did – a lot] I do know that it was one of the things that made the series.

And then the voice-over adds puzzlingly: '*... and as far as I am concerned, our play has begun!*' We've just witnessed a resolution any playwright could be satisfied with, and she is talking about beginning! Thus she knocks on the head any normal notion of dramatic climax. She's on a different plane from the rest of us. It's not that she fails to see that the experience has reached its peak – one of her favourite expressions in those days was 'a moment of awe'. But Dorothy never wants her classes to stay satisfied with a tidy ending for she wants them to understand life, in which new problems emerge as old ones are solved. Dorothy came to regard climaxes as educationally cheap. In fact, to the chagrin of some of her students, she spent the rest of her career avoiding them.

Whatever topic Dorothy's classes chose, she tried to make connection with their own lives, not at an obvious level of factual similarity or even conceptual overlap, but at a level of cultural identification with the material. It is because she can 'read' a group at this level that, she is able to create the dramatic symbols that will resonate for that group. The 'Death of the President' is a case in point. After the class reached the low point. Dorothy planned the final session overnight. The school hall was divided into prison cells, each prisoner on his bed listening to the slopping out sounds as a bucket and mop are dragged along the floor outside the cells, though this was not shown in the final edition of the film. The class, themselves resident in a detention establishment, were united by their communal response to what was to them an emotive stimulus. However fed up they had become with the hard work the day before, they were suddenly energised by the shared meaning that slopping out had for them. Her selection of a sound to unite them was a deliberate choice from her ever-ready palette of six theatre elements: sound/silence; movement/stillness; light/darkness.

Finding the right symbol to turn disenchantment into enchantment has been a mark of Dorothy's skill. Sometimes she has had to make a sudden, instinctive decision to retrieve a failing situation. She recalls an incident when her students working in London with a group of adolescents with severe behavioural problems were too wrapped up in their own idea for a play. She found herself retrieving a difficult situation: a class generally considered disruptive was beginning to feel fed-up with drama. She chose the sound of a dog howling for its owner, a blind girl who had gone missing in a bog where the bog people had been trapped for centuries, and at once reversed her students' intentions to set up a scientifically planned search for the bog people. Dorothy has this ability to think herself inside the fiction and the cultural core of the group she is working with.

The effective, resonating symbol taps meanings beyond the immediate and invites ownership of the material. Connections spread in many directions. For these London adolescents, 'Why can't someone shut up that bloody dog!' spurred them into action. For the detainees in *Death of a President*, isolated by their cell spaces but united by the sounds of bucket and mop, connections are made to a man facing the electric chair and to their own circumstances. She puts herself through a process of selection and rejection, feeling her way until she knows it is right. This is not an intellectual, rational, logical working out of things; this is the artist's instinct, the same instinct that would guide her design of a set if she were directing a play or selecting a piece of jewellery for playing Cleopatra or a vocal chant as background to *The Trojan Women*. At this aesthetic level Dorothy does not make a distinction between working in the classroom and in the theatre.

Bringing up her daughter

While the President was meeting an untimely end in the school hall, Dorothy's new baby was being looked after by her mother in the room next door. Some of the boys, especially those with younger siblings, were aware of the baby's presence and clearly wanted to nurse her. Dorothy would feed, change or just gaze at her in precious moments at every interval and lunch break. That her responsibilities were to be divided, was something for which she had been preparing herself for some time. She had discussed whether she ought to give up work once the baby arrived with Raymond and others. Everyone who was close to Dorothy knew that she was perfectly capable of being (Dorothy really wanted me to change 'being' to 'trying to be') a mother and a teacher. Their domestic set-up meant that Mary Earl, who had begun by supporting Dorothy during her mother-in-law's illness, would readily be there for Marianne should Dorothy's mother return to Yorkshire – which she did nine months later. When Marianne started her first school, Mary was happy to meet Marianne at the school gate and take her to her home until Dorothy could collect her. And May Spooner, a close neighbour, who 'joined the family', is still helping Dorothy today. Until Dorothy became pregnant May didn't know Dorothy very well. May had this image of a heavily pregnant Mrs. Heathcote pushing a wheel-barrow at 7 a.m. and thought of her only as 'the lady gardener next door' who, she had heard, might be a teacher of some sort. May was pleased to help out when Marianne was old enough to start school.

Dorothy's boss, Brian Stanley said, 'If a University Department of Education can't handle a baby, what do we think we are doing?' Dorothy did not deceive herself into thinking it would be easy – there's 'always a price', she agrees. She tried to minimise the conflicting interests of work and motherhood. Whereas students got used to having the baby in class, conference delegates were sometimes taken aback to find that their key-note speaker popped a baby basket on the microphone table. I can recall being told by a lady of some standing in the Society of Teachers of Speech and Drama that 'Mrs. Heeethcote actually – would you believe it! – actually *changed* the baby's napkin while she was addressing us'. But most people including the classes of children she taught, found it endearing and Dorothy quickly discovered that the presence of a baby is not without its uses in getting a difficult class on your side.

Dorothy describes the joy in Raymond's face when the baby was born: 'He was thrilled and delighted to have a little girl. His face was like the sun coming out.' Mother and child were in excellent health. Although her doctor had been worried about Dorothy having a first child at 40, he found her to be the fittest 40 year old he had ever come across.

But it wasn't all sunshine at home. Raymond's father, nine months a widower, was slowly beginning to slip into a form of senility that made him uncharacteristically querulous. When they brought the new baby home, he expressed resentment that my wife and I had visited Dorothy in the maternity hospital and seen the baby before he had (Cynthia and I, along with Raymond's closest friend, John, were to become Marianne's legal guardians). But he was delighted to learn from them that his granddaughter was to be called Marianne, after his wife.

I was connected with an unfortunate incident three months later. Dorothy and Raymond, Cynthia, our son Andrew and I had sometimes been on holiday together in the summer. This was the first time we had had a baby with us. It was very hot, and I was climbing down the cliff slopes with Marianne bundled in my arms – no doubt it was my idea – to the Abersoch beach in North Wales. Dorothy carefully laid out a blanket on the sands and Marianne, the delicate shawl covering her completely, slept peacefully. The next morning a wailing from the bedroom next door awaked Cynthia and me. Dorothy had discovered that the baby's face was badly burned. The sun's rays had pierced through the protective garment onto Marianne's fair skin – she still has to keep out of direct sunlight today. We all felt guilty, but Dorothy was overwhelmed with a sense of failure as a mother. 'What have I done to you?' she keened dramatically. As it turned out, a quick visit to the local doctor established that the raw burn was superficial.

On yet another occasion, I created a dilemma for mother and baby. I was driving Dorothy from Newcastle to Bristol with Marianne in a carry-cot on the back seat of the Mini, wide awake for much of the journey. It was late evening by the time we arrived. We were to join her students who were working with Veronica Sherbourne, the movement expert whose work Dorothy had long admired. We were running late and hungry, but we felt we could not stop off to eat because the arrangement was that we were to join her students in their digs early evening. We eventually found the Bed and Breakfast establishment, but were told by an irate landlady that the students had taken one look at the accommodation and left. She had no room for us, not even for Dorothy and the baby in her arms. No, she did not know where they had gone. We returned to the car and drove round looking for accommodation. Marianne went to sleep and we were desperately hungry. No doubt on my insistence, we left the car parked in a quiet street with the sleeping baby on the back seat, while we ate a hurried snack in a nearby café. Dorothy, years later, shudders as she recalls this: 'How *could* I take such a risk!' The three of us then proceeded, like victims of a melodrama, to try other B. and B. places until we found rooms for the night. As Dorothy says, this was an image 'worthy of the Brontes or *Cold Comfort Farm*'.

Dorothy and Raymond took a risk of a more lasting kind at home as Raymond's Dad's behaviour became more bizarre. Soon after Marianne was born he even advertised for his wife in *The Guardian* and as he grew worse he did not recognise Dorothy, accusing her of taking 'his Dorothy's' place: 'I don't know why Raymond's brought you in', he would say, 'If my Dorothy knew you were here she'd have you out.' He also kept trying to run away. They learnt to watch what he was up to but sometimes they had to leave him on his own in the house during the late afternoon. Dorothy and Raymond didn't worry too much as his mildly sedating medication meant he usually slept through the afternoon. But on one winter's afternoon, Dorothy, arrived home after collecting Marianne, now a toddler, from Mary's house, to find a big bundle in the middle of High Heworth Lane. She thought at first it was a dog, but it was Dad. He had smashed all the bay windows at the front of the house, climbed through and collapsed in the centre of the road. While trying to distract Marianne by leaving her with something interesting to do in the car, Dorothy got out, leaving Old Sarah's headlights full on to warn other traffic, and managed to heave Dad, in spite of his vigorous resistance, through the front gate, by which time he was sufficiently recovered to stand up and be walked into the house. When Raymond came home, he dealt with Dad very calmly and, in a lovely moment of lucidity, Dad realised what he had done and apologised profusely. Raymond said: 'We're going to clean up every piece of glass and board the windows'. They completed the job together and Dad was peaceful for a while. It didn't occur to either of them to put him into Community Care. This was the 1960s when that was not an obvious alternative to home care.

Nothing could take away Dorothy's sense of joy and of privilege at being a mother. All the little routines of nursing were captivating. Just watching Marianne was absorbing, noticing, for instance, that as a baby she never grasped but delicately fingered things, just as granddaughter Anna does today. All the time Dorothy was alert to what her baby might be ready to do next, as though the teacher played an instinctive part in being a mother. So right through to adolescence, she observed and gently challenged her, urging her towards a next step. And she talked a lot to her baby, using a variety of language, sometimes absurdly abstract or philosophical and certainly historical as she named things and what you do with things. So 'let's put your socks on' might be followed with 'and they do say that before people had socks ... ' Dorothy had a taste for onomatopoeic poetry, and rendered recitals to Marianne of *The Ancient Mariner* and *St Agnes Eve*. Her favourite was Cargoes and Dorothy could be heard majestically booming 'Quinquerine of Ninevah from distant Ophir' and rapping out 'Dirty British coaster with its saltcaked smoke stack'. As Marianne learnt to talk, Dorothy worked at extending her vocabulary, selectively dropping in a new word, enjoying watching how her attention was arrested by its sound even when she was in the middle of playing. And she consciously sought to help Marianne read an image and trained her to look for what is underneath things. Particularly useful was the regular Saturday evening radio play. She would check that Marianne heard and interpreted the sound effects, wanting her to learn how to make meanings from these signs. At High School, if there was a text Marianne could not make sense of or found boring, Dorothy would read it after Marianne had gone to bed and slip in a note drawing attention to what was underneath the surface meaning.

As Marianne became old enough to have friends in the street, the house became a play centre for the local kids and Dorothy would find herself in free moments sitting sewing clothes for their dolls out of bits and pieces, as her mother had done forty years earlier in Steeton. Marianne fondly recalls the garden and sand pile they all played in and, if it wasn't being lived in by a student guest, the caravan behind the house that became their playroom. Dorothy saw that Marianne had every chance also to play privately and freely. At Halloween there were parties in the cellar. Her mother always made masks of carved turnips, on which she painted witch-faces with stage make-up. After telling stories in low voices in the cellar, they flew about their big, safe, walled garden, returning to the house in time for toffee and buns iced with black cloaks. Before Marianne was born, Dorothy and Raymond invited friends and colleagues to a Guy Fawkes party each Bonfire Night. Raymond was in charge of the fire and the liberal supply of fireworks provided by a friend who manufactured them. Sparklers were passed round among the children, including our son, and good refreshments followed. Sadly, such entertainment, indeed most socialising, was gradually squeezed out of Dorothy and Raymond's lives as Marianne grew older and professional schedules expanded.

Marianne was brought up to think of her home as open house to her friends. She recalls an occasion when she called on her way home from school on her friend's mother to ask if Alison could come over to tea. She was met with an anxious response: 'Are you sure it's all right with your mother, Marianne?' It had not occurred to Marianne that other families did not enjoy this degree of casual neighbourliness. Since she was a baby Marianne had witnessed a stream of non-family members making themselves at home. Students and visiting professors sat round that meal-table and disappeared into the spare bedrooms, rooms always rigorously cleaned and liberally laid out with dust-sheets as soon as a visitor left.

An unspoken rule was that visitors were not to join Dorothy in the kitchen and Marianne learnt that this was sacred time between her and her mother. As a toddler, she would make herself a den under the kitchen table. As an adolescent schoolgirl she would loiter in the kitchen, knowing that Dorothy at the Aga was all ears, ready for her daughter's school-tale of the day and alert for anything in it that could really be a question. As Dorothy puts it, 'When a mother's eyes are on stirring the gravy, that is the time when mother and teenager can really talk'. Of course Marianne was sharp enough to be aware of Dorothy's divided loyalties. She tells of an occasion when an 'important' visitor on a brief visit from abroad shared their evening meal. Having missed her chance of a pre-dinner kitchen chat, Marianne was determined to use the opportunity offered by the meal to share her story of the day with her mother, only to discover that the guest, short of time, saw the meal as her only chance of pressing Dorothy on serious drama questions. Suddenly Marianne became aware that her mother was fielding each of these competing attention seekers in turn, giving beaming responses to each.

Early on in her school days Marianne realised that whereas other families went on shopping trips at the week-end into Newcastle, the very concept of shopping as an outing was anathema to her mother, who would confine such trips to the greengrocer's round the corner, the warehouse for large orders and the flea market for the odd garment and anything interesting that caught her eye. In recent years Raymond and Dorothy befriended two ladies, Verena and Marion, who kept a *bric a brac* stall in the Saturday market at Chester-le-Street. Verena has written to me expressing her fondness for them both and her admiration for Dorothy's sharp eye for the unusual in the way of pictures, embroidery or books. 'It gave me great pleasure finding little treasures to keep for her'.

Dorothy would usually buy material for making their clothes from quality fabric shop or mill shops. Occasionally, she would visit a bookshop, always in a rush, and buy a pile of books at one go, darting from shelf to shelf. I can remember Anne Thurman of Evanston telling me about accompanying Dorothy round a bookstore. Dorothy proceeded to pile books, mostly connected with education, into Anne's open arms and when her own arms were also full, she took them to the salesperson, saying she would like them mailed to England please – and went back to the shelves for more. Anne, bemused, managed to splutter: 'But Dorothy, many of these texts are published in England and are much cheaper there'. 'Oh', says Dorothy, justifying such rashness to herself on the grounds that it was a specialist 'Jungian' shop, 'I don't have time to shop in England'.

So for Marianne Saturday is associated not with shopping trips but with planned outings that cost her mother precious time, she came to realise, to a stately home, art gallery or museum. The Shipley Gallery, ten minutes drive from home, be-came a favourite place and some of the paintings on the Highburn House walls

– with its pictures at all levels – were purchased from the Shipley. There was always a planned destination.They never went walking, unless it was along a beach gathering shells. Early in their marriage, Raymond had bought Dorothy a life membership of the National Trust, setting up the same privilege for Marianne when she was seven, and it was his first Christmas present to grand-daughter Anna. Raymond was a great planner. Whenever they were in, say, America for part of the summer, Raymond would prepare carefully designed ex-cursions each day for Marianne and her friend, even if he was unfamiliar with the territory, using map and travel books.

Holidays in England were spent in their caravan parked at the farm of their York-shire friends, Joyce and Alfred Simpson. Marianne recalls full cooked breakfasts, something they didn't have for the rest of the year. Most days she and her friend would play on the banks of or even on the nearby River Aire, for Raymond provided a blow-up dinghy. Her parents relaxed with books and they all found exploring the farm entrancing, especially at lambing time. They never ate out, not even when they visited local National Trust properties. 'My parents', Marianne explains to me 'are incredibly frugal.' Not wasting money on restaurants would be part of this ethic, except in America, where she thought they probably ate out most of the time. She emphasises that such frugality should not be mistaken for meanness. Whereas her mother would save money by bulk buying of food, by making her own and Marianne's clothes or buying them at the flea market, she would splash out on quality paintings, books and fabrics. She was unthinkingly generous in her offer of free board to most of her students, and some of her students, arriving, say, from South Africa with more determination than financial resources, were sometimes helped out by Dorothy who with her impecunious background recognised both their hardship and their pride.

Joyce and Alfred Simpson were Dorothy and Raymond's closest friends, a friendship that started just before Marianne was born. Joyce was lecturing in English with Drama at Margaret Macmillan College in Leeds, when she and Dorothy met for the first time. Having heard about Mrs. Heathcote's work, she had invited Dorothy to talk to her students. When a further visit was mooted, Dorothy said she wasn't sure, because she was three months pregnant. Joyce had responded: 'So am I'. That was the start of a closeness between the two women that was to last until Joyce died in 1995. The offer had come for Raymond to leave his caravan at Alfred's farm, and so the four of them spent a great deal of time together. Raymond and Alfred got on very well. Alfred would make Ray-mond laugh, even though Raymond was not a laughing kind of man. When Joyce moved to Ilkley College of Domestic Science, a two-week visit by Dorothy's students became part of the diploma course. Joyce visited Dorothy's course in Newcastle whenever she could and as she became seriously disabled with rheumatoid arthritis, a bedroom was specially prepared for her downstairs at Highburn House. Alfred died first and Joyce ten months later. Dorothy gave an address to the mourners at both occasions.

Dorothy had told me in an interview that 'Part of the joy of being a parent was being a teaching parent, but not an interferer' and then she mused: 'Well ... who knows?' A week later, I interviewed Marianne and, on summing up her relationship with her mother, she said immediately: 'She never interfered with my life.' Marianne offered an example from her final school year when she was to take her A-level exams. Marianne discovered that the American evangelist Billy Graham was to appear at the stadium in Sunderland each evening for ten days immediately before the exams started , a time when students generally have their heads down for final revision. But Marianne had other ideas; she wanted to be in the Billy Graham choir for all ten nights. She asked her parents and they replied: 'If that's what you want to do'. Marianne's persistence automatically involved her parents, who, as Dorothy explains: 'solemnly sat through each evening's 'do'.' What Dorothy did not realise until after the last evening was that Raymond had sat fretting every evening about the fire hazard of the stadium, which had wrappers, cigarette packets etc ankle deep beneath the ranked wooden seats. 'Each visit Raymond selected seats according to his growing awareness of this hazard, but he didn't tell me till the last visit was over and Marianne was in bed'.

There were times when Dorothy feared for Marianne. She noticed that strangers were drawn to her. Nothing untoward ever happened but that fear, competing with an awareness that her daughter's attractive personality in the eyes of others was in most contexts quite safe and indeed enriching, remained with her throughout Marianne's school life. One or two incidents shook her, especially the time Marianne and her friend spent a week-end of camping with the guides. On the Friday they had driven her the few miles to the field that was to be the camping site and helped set up the tents. When Dorothy and Raymond returned on the Sunday evening at dusk to collect them at the arranged time, they discovered Marianne and her chum alone in the field, all the leaders and campers having left early. Similarly, after ballet class in Gateshead one dark Monday evening, the teacher had simply shut the door on Marianne, assuring her her parents 'wouldn't be long'. Dorothy found her alone outside the building, just waiting and apparently not bothered. Even when Marianne was older Dorothy still felt uneasy when Marianne had to return from her school, Dame Allan's Girls' School in Newcastle, by metro in the early evening, having left her bike at the deserted premises where Dorothy worked during the day.

An interesting divergence developed between Marianne and her parents in respect of religious practice. Dorothy had attended Anglican church, singing in the choir from early childhood until she started Theatre School. After arriving in Newcastle she did not join any local place of worship. She and Raymond were married in church but did not attend on a regular basis afterwards. When Marianne was born they were faced with a decision about a christening and decided against it, wanting Marianne to make her own choice. However, from seven years of age Marianne seemed to be attracted to the local church communities, attending Sunday School and church services, accompanied by any of Dorothy's students, especially those who were nuns, who wanted to attend. By her early teens she knew she wanted to be confirmed, but first it was necessary for her to be christened. Dorothy gave her full support and threw a party following Marianne's formal baptism at the age of eleven. From this time Marianne became an ardent follower of the Anglican evangelical movement, took theology in her degree, married a fellow Christian and is now professionally engaged in working on training teachers in multi-faith religious education.

Marianne's life-story is marked for its independence, in this respect, from her own parents' life-style. Dorothy gave support and encouragement to a commitment she herself could not share, or at least, not as a practice, not as a church-goer nor as a believer, nor as an adherent to a particular faith. And yet at a deeper level Dorothy and her daughter meet, for Dorothy is a profoundly spiritual person. She has always had a strong sense of otherness, of significance outside the immediate, outside the present, out of time. Marianne says that: 'The spiritual oozes out of Mother all the time'. Those of us who know her probably see it expressed in different ways. For me it is to do with the expanse of her perception; it lies in her capacity to see beyond, to feel beyond, and to know beyond. She remains awed by her own perceptions, but has no wish to know more. She goes on living, accepting that insights will come to her and that, she acknowledges, is a privilege not a challenge. She just, to use her phrase, 'gets on'. Such far-reaching perception feeds into her work and takes her to places others can only wonder at.

Perhaps the nearest one can get to defining Dorothy's deeply spiritual sense is to recognise the link she makes with the notion of Gaia, a philosophy derived from the name of the Greek Earth-Goddess, the mother of gods and men. At its broadest it represents a merging of two kinds of faith: (1) Gaia as a catalyst for scientific enquiry, giving birth to a sense of wonder at everything scientific and (2) Gaia as a sense of mystery and a reverence for a wholeness of which science is but a part. At its narrowest it stands for a moral compulsion to protect the single living organism that is our planet.

Being in touch with the mystical has always been part of Dorothy's life – there was the benign ghost in Silsden and the aunt who foretold the future. From an early age she sensed the possibility of, as she puts it, 'many possible lives and possibly parallel lives/times'. She pursued these kinds of thoughts through her reading. Her vision of otherness has little place for one religion claiming authority over other doctrines. The Creed that she was brought up on can have little meaning for her. She writes: 'Perhaps I think that all thoughts stay around somehow and we need the wise ones (Christ, Mohammed, Krishna – though he's too mischievous for me) to occasionally catch them and personify their truths'. In her recent grieving for Raymond, she talks to him and knows he is there to hear her.

She will sometimes attend church with Marianne, Kevin and Anna, their baby daughter, when she visits Nottingham. She can enjoy what is going on but cannot believe in its message. It became a custom for Dorothy to go with Marianne to Mid-Night Mass on Christmas Eve in a church near their home in Gateshead. Although Marianne was used to aspects of Dorothy's family and professional life overlapping, there was one occasion during the Midnight service when both of them were taken aback. Along the row, they heard an exclamation, something like 'Oh ... Mrs. Heathcote!'. They looked to where a woman a few places along had delved into her handbag and produced an envelope with Dorothy's handwriting on. After the service, this woman introduced herself. She explained to Dorothy that she had kept this letter in her bag since she was seven, a letter Dorothy had written to her. As a child attending a drama class, she had asked Mrs. Heathcote what made her hair curly. Dorothy had said, 'I'll write to you about it' – and she had. The child, not from a family that was used to receiving letters, had been so awed by this that she had kept it, undisturbed, among all the clutter she had passed from one handbag to the next over the thirty intervening years.

From the early years of their marriage, Dorothy and Raymond always had a cat, sometimes more than one. Dorothy's grannie always had cats for there were mice in the cellars in those days. All the Highburn House cats adopted Raymond: 'I fed them, but they related to Raymond mainly. Tabitha followed him like a dog can ... I wonder if she is still looking for him'.

> One day when I was interviewing Dorothy about this book, Tabitha went into the hall and started to howl, a long crying with alarm and pain. Dorothy explained that that occurred only when Tabitha went into that part of the hall: 'She sees Raymond, I'm sure'.

Marianne writes feelingly: 'Remember anyone that's met my mother professionally at Highburn House will know about her love of her cats. They were her

Dorothy, aged two 1928

Dorothy, aged six 1932

Dorothy, the loyal Girl Guide 1938

*Dorothy and her mother with cousin in
push-chair 1940*

Dorothy 'cap and gowned' for elocution ALCM

Dorothy, glamorous in her first dance dress

Dorothy with Raymond's parents 1956

Raymond and Dorothy on their Wedding Day 1956

children! Have you any idea the number of times we have to stop what we're doing to open a door for a cat? They're a major part of her life'. To impress upon me the extent of this attachment, Marianne offered the following anecdote of an incident about ten years ago. Dorothy and Raymond and Joshua the cat were staying with Marianne in Nottingham. They travelled down from Gateshead in their caravan and parked it in the garden behind Marianne's house, where they slept during the week's stay. On their first day there the cat disappeared. Each day they made desperate searches and Raymond put a notice in a local shop. Marianne had never seen her mother so upset. She was bereft. She would stand at the sink washing dishes, silent tears rolling down her cheeks. 'That week lasted for ever,' Marianne tells me. And the strain became greater as the day of their departure drew nearer, a day when they were obliged to leave because of professional commitments. Marianne longed for the week to end yet dreaded its ending. When she got up at 7 that final morning, she discovered her parents had been fully packed and ready to leave since 4 a.m. Her mother excitedly explained that the cat had suddenly turned up in the middle of the night. Waving goodbye to Marianne, they drove home!

Marianne was very aware of being an only child with no close relatives, for neither of her parents had brothers or sisters. The death of a school friend's father brought home to her how vulnerable she was, especially as the suddenness of his death drew attention to an over-casual arrangement in that family that allowed her friend to sleep over without the parents knowing the address at which the girl was staying. The shock of these two things together caused Marianne to evolve compensating schemes of communication whenever she went away. She explains:

> I never went anywhere overnight without them having contact details. This is a very significant aspect of my relationship with my mother; she knew (and still knows) to expect extremely short telephone calls (matters of seconds) in which I announce an address and telephone number and the number of days of my stay, which she writes down. Can you imagine a month's inter-rail trip consisting of lots of brief calls to give emergency contact details in case one of them dies?

> I still do it now whenever I travel away for an overnight stay for a course, staff meeting, weekend away etc. You should see the photocopies she gets of flight tickets, holiday bookings, insurance cover etc when we go away.

> As an only child with no other immediate family, aunts, uncles, grandparents, this runs very deep.

There was another aspect of this that impressed itself on Marianne as a school-girl. Her friend confessed that she had only one photo of her father, 'a poor shot with his head half turned away'. This startled Marianne into taking family photographs. The thought of not having even a good picture of her parents was unbearable. But she had always lived under the gaze of a traditional means of capturing memories – the four Heathcote family portraits in the landing upstairs, which 'I'd shot past going to bed all through my childhood'. So in 1996 she commissioned a portrait of Raymond and Dorothy, taking on Margaret Robinson to do the job, and Margaret was delighted. It is interesting to see their marriage through her eyes. She writes:

> When I painted the double portrait, it was important to get the relationship right. Raymond so quiet and unassuming; Dorothy with the capacity for dominance (not used). I saw Raymond as a protector, so placed him high on the canvas. He was easy to paint, a private, uncomplicated man: I painted what I saw. Dorothy was not so easy to capture: a powerful personality, but hemming a duster! To get the shell right was not enough, so the likeness came and went during the week, while I tried to get under the skin and say something.

Dorothy the constant traveller

When Dorothy and Raymond decided that she should carry on working, they cannot have anticipated the extent to which the professional demands on her would expand. When I first met her in the early '60s, she was hardly known outside the North-East and Cumberland. I would often lead her unwillingly to drama conferences in other parts of the country, so that people would at least get to know her face, though, being Dorothy in that kind of social/educational/ego-fanning context she tended to keep a low profile. I recall a southern Drama Adviser saying to me: 'Oh, so *that's* Dorothy Heethcote ... she hangs back doesn't she!' I replied: 'Just you wait'. He did, but she never came forward.

It was a great opportunity for me to learn more from her, because I would do the driving. On long distances we would talk about principles of teaching. One of her favourite investigations was to see how people's minds worked, so she would name an image – cat or clock or door – and ask me to think aloud about the connections I immediately made with these objects. She examined my response in terms of quantity, variety, levels etc. It was when it became her turn to do the same that I realised how rapidly and unexpectedly her mind worked. On one of these journeys, twisting through the many villages from Gateshead to London before the days of motorways, I suddenly realised I could see the shadow of my car in front of the car. Dorothy was in full flow. 'Dorothy, sorry to interrupt, but the shadows are the wrong way round', I exclaimed. We'd been talking so much that in negotiating a one-way system in one small town, I had set us for travelling north – going home. When I visited South Africa a few weeks later, I sent her a postcard saying 'And the shadows are the wrong way round here, too!'

Mostly she travelled on her own, usually by public transport. It seemed to me that if she could be given a lift even locally with a colleague or one of her students, she would prefer that to driving, although driving herself in Old Sarah was later to feature in *Three Looms Waiting*.

As people borrowed or bought copies of *Death of a President*, as more and more local education drama advisers and training college lecturers[1] invited Dorothy to work with or address their teachers or students, demands on her time grew in different parts of the country. Whereas she had been used to some travelling around to visit her full-time students' schools, she was now to become 'honoured guest' in prestigious establishments such as Church of England colleges for women teachers, where afternoon tea, with delicate sandwiches and cakes served by maids in uniform, was still a feature of the staff-room ritual. For the first time Dorothy found herself working alongside drama specialists whose daily responsibilities were parallel to her own. Now people whose normal professional work was with teachers and students were watching her work with those teachers and students. It was a significant shift, for she had not before been required to see her recommendations for classroom practice through the eyes of those who trained others for the classroom. She often strongly disapproved of what she picked up about, for example, a college's priorities for teacher-training, but she knew she had to keep it to herself during those brief visits.

Time became ever more precious. Her persistent dilemma was to fulfil the demands of parenthood and take on more and more professional engagements up and down the country and eventually abroad. She made strict rules for herself never to stay anywhere after the work had finished; Raymond and Marianne must be able to trust that mother will come home at the earliest the transport system will allow. This self-imposed guideline led to some peculiar travelling times. She would often set off on the first train of the day and find herself on the last train, arriving in Newcastle in the early hours. She soon learnt to demand First Class travel from the people who engaged her and insisted on travelling by air if there was a suitable flight. Never did she let these freelance engagements take priority over her Newcastle responsibilities. There were occasions when she had to leave her full time students with a task, but this was never merely a convenient way of keeping students occupied. She ensured that the task was always integral to the course. Her diary was a network of strands, none of which must get out of kilter. But not surprisingly her meticulous time-tabling did not always work. Kathy Joyce, the adviser in drama at the Abraham Moss Art Centre, re-members this vividly:

> Dorothy was coming to do a one-day course for me in Manchester based at the centre. I had around 100 teachers and a class of children ready for the demonstration. D. asked if she could fly down and I persuaded the LEA to agree to this.
>
> On the appointed day I drove to M/c airport to meet her plane. It duly arrived, but no Dorothy! I thought I must have missed her and rushed round all the Ladies' toilets in search, but to no avail. I approached the airline per-sonnel but they would not disclose names of those who had been on the flight. I had a tannoy announcement made, but still no D. At this stage I thought I must have made a mistake with the date. I drove back to the centre, the opposite end of the City, in the rush hour.
>
> I phoned D's home and the plot thickened because the lady I spoke to said she had left by taxi early that day to catch a flight to M/c. I returned to the Studio wondering what to do with all these teachers when suddenly there was a commotion from the theatre, next to the studio, and Dorothy entered from the top of the steps and swept down towards me, very flustered.
>
> She quickly explained that she had gone to the airport as planned and been told that it was too foggy and the plane would not be flying. In desperation she had asked the taxi driver to drive on to Manchester as fast as he could.
>
> Back in Newcastle, the fog had suddenly lifted – and the plane had taken off!

Accommodating Dorothy was sometimes quite a problem for employing authorities that did not want to splash out on a hotel room. Pam Bowell found she was faced with a catering dilemma. She writes:

> When I was one of the Newham Drama Advisory Team in the late seventies and early eighties, we invited Dorothy down to work with our teachers over several days. At that time, I had the only spare bedroom amongst us, so it fell to me to host her in our family home. I remember spending days baking and cooking (people tell me that I'm a pretty good cook) trying to ensure that she would feel welcome. When I got her home, to my amazement she declined anything to eat, declaring that 'on occasions like these I like to take the opportunity to purge my stomach'. She just took a little toast for break-fasts and little else. David, Nicholas and I were eating up the leftovers for weeks. However, about two years later she came again and, having learnt my lesson the last time, I did not bother to prepare anything. To my consterna-

tion she arrived with a ravenous appetite and I found myself scrabbling around like a chicken with its head off trying to conjure a meal out of thin air!

Three Looms Waiting – and many more

Six years after filming *Death of a President*, Ron Smedley seized his chance to make what turned out to be a seminal programme. He was in charge of a series of documentaries by the BBC called Omnibus, a programme that went out at peak viewing time on a Sunday. It was sold to countries round the world and won an Italian award for the best documentary of the year. Its effect was phenomenal. Ron Smedley writes that when he visited Boston, USA 'they almost kissed the hem of my garment' when they learned that he was the man who had directed *Three Looms Waiting*. Ron Smedley, a gifted and modest man, wants us to understand that he and Dorothy were very fortunate in the camera man, Phil Meheux, who went onto a distinguished career in Hollywood, and in the film editor, Anna Benson-Giles, who had the task of cutting 80 hours of filming to the 58 minutes of an Omnibus programme. He describes the work as follows:

> Tom Stabler's children broke though the screen again with a Bible story retold in Hartlepool accents. Dorothy worked with another group of in-carcerated boys and some older adolescents from a Wallsend Youth Theatre (and therefore a harder nut to crack) and, unforgettably, at a residential mental hospital with a group of damaged, disturbed, handicapped children who, in spite of their severe limitations could still react to Dorothy's magic.

> I also interviewed Dorothy, on camera, at some length, at her home and in her final sentence she gave the programme its title – *Three Looms Waiting*, a reminder to her of what her old boss had said to her when she decided to go to theatre school. She'd always find a place waiting for her back at the mill if things didn't work out.

One can imagine the effect of this film on drama teachers world-wide, and newspapers from all over wrote rave reviews, including *The Yorkshire Post* and, even nearer to her old stamping ground, *The Keighley News*. People who knew her from childhood also saw it, and she received letters from people she had not seen for years. One is from one of the amateur drama people she taught immediately after theatre school:

> Dear Mrs. Heathcote
> I watched with great interest the Omnibus programme on Sunday last. Long before the programme started I was certain that you were the Dorothy Shutt that we all knew in the fifties. Perhaps you have forgotten [of course she

hadn't!] Kettlewell and the players you produced all those years ago? We never forgot you and *Great Day* was a play that will always be remembered...

From the 1970s, sitting in front of cameras became almost part of the job and one can recall visitors keen to audio-tape Dorothy's every word. Most of Dorothy's work was recorded by one or more camera, sometimes held by an amateur delighted to be given permission to make the recording and, at other times, for a production by the University of Newcastle or of Central England, the BBC or university departments all over the world. More formally, she started to have a long series of lectures recorded at Newcastle University's Audio Visual Centre in the Medical School. The technicians learnt to skip from surgical operations in one kind of theatre to film Dorothy's observations on another.

On her retirement, Roger Burgess, a freelance film director with the BBC, gave his time and expertise to produce the celebratory *Pieces of Dorothy,* which contains brief excerpts from a whole range of her past teaching. *Pieces of Dorothy* included excerpts from earlier filming, one of them with an A-level English class studying *Pilgrim's Progress*. Highfield Comprehensive School, round the corner from Highburn House. This school became a spider's web for attracting ambitious and distinguished young drama teachers. A list of English department staff in the 1970s reads like a *Who's Who* of top fliers: John O'Toole, now Professor at the University of Brisbane, John Grundy, BBC television presenter, David Davis, Professor at University of Central England, Mike Fleming, senior lecturer at University of Durham, Val McClane, actress and lecturer in drama at University of Sunderland and Geoff Gillham, writer and director. One wonders whether the proximity of Highburn House had something to do with this success story – not that Dorothy actually visited it a great deal, but one suspects that her energy and artistry spread across the space from house to school, from Highburn to Highfield.

John O'Toole was the first to invite Dorothy to work there. She evoked wonders with the students – the film is still available. But John offers an entertaining account of what it was like to suffer behind the scenes:

> I do remember with both admiration and embarrassment one very significant set of visits to Highfield – her first, I think – to teach Bunyan's *Pilgrim's Progress* to my sixth form. You probably know the video that was made of this sequence, *Making Progress.* It nearly didn't happen, through my stupidity. She'd offered to come and teach at Highfield, and I was so eager and self-important to have her, both for the benefits to the students and what it would do for us (and me!) to have this famous person in the school, that I didn't think it through.

We agreed on the dates, the class, and the subject matter – I'd confessed myself stumped at having to teach *Pilgrim's Progress*, which the students were dreading, too.

I did remember to check the room and rearrange other classes to free it. On the day, she arrived bang on time with her retinue of auxiliaries and miles of butchers paper for large walls charts ... only, I'd forgotten to organise the class for her – so there were no students for her to teach.

As she and her students stood in the draughty hallway more and more balefully discussing this dickhead and his stupid invitation that they'd wasted so much time preparing for, I ran around like a demented hare. Firstly to the Headmaster's office – kind man that he was, wonderful Walter Cook took pity and agreed on the spot to students being released from their other subjects for the two or three days even though it was getting perilously close to their A-levels. Then round the other classrooms I went, hauling startled students out of history, English and maths lessons to come and do drama on a book they'd not even read.

The students rose magnificently and generously to the task, the drama work was marvellous (and immortalised on video), and I spent the whole time trying to pretend I was invisible and hadn't stuffed up bigtime.

There was a curious sequel to this episode a few years later. A man from the Prudential Insurance called Dorothy on the phone. Having checked that she was indeed Mrs. Heathcote, he informed her that 'her policy was ready'. Mystified, she explained that she had had nothing to do with such a company. He then said, 'Don't I know you? Aren't you the drama teacher that did *Pilgrim's Progress* with us years ago?' The outcome was that he asked if the class of that year could reassemble and see the video. And so it was arranged for a lunch-hour, with the lads she remembered transformed into white-collar workers. They enjoyed seeing it and confessed, 'You know, we all thought you were mad!' And the insurance policy? It turned out there was another Dorothy Heathcote (pronounced Heethcote) in the area, also in teaching. The two namesakes once met professionally, 'only ...' says our Dorothy, 'the other Dorothy Heathcote looked like I would like to have looked'!

During these months of interviewing Dorothy, the Audio Visual Centre of the University of Newcastle is also filming her biographical recollections.

Note

1   A rapid growth in the appointment of Drama Advisers in local authorities and courses offering drama in Teacher Training Colleges took place in the 1960s. Teachers in schools, newly promoted to positions of adviser or college lecturer, sought help from recognised pioneers in the field. It became possible to identify the character of their work according to whether they were Slade, Way or Heathcote/Bolton followers.

6

A sea-change

Learning by attending

'A woman is rocking a cradle with her foot.' That is how one of Dorothy's dramas started in 1971.

This chapter, differs in its content from the preceding ones. It is about a seminal change in Dorothy's work. There is no continuation of her life story in this chapter, so if that's what you want, may I suggest you skip it. On second thoughts, this attempt to explain a fundamental change in her work may well be a critical point in that story.

An attempt to identify what Dorothy changed to implies that we can put into words what she changed from. 'Who are we going to be?' Dorothy typically asks at the beginning of, say, *Death of a President.* From that question everyone recognises that she is doing drama. And what does that entail? 'Putting yourself in other people's shoes' is one answer favoured by Dorothy, the idea being that one learns about other people by fictionally standing in their shoes. She does not mean this in the sense of becoming another person but simply as trying on someone else's shoes. This qualified degree of identification with how someone else thinks, acts and sees provides a fresh angle from which to view that person, her culture and her problems. To try on someone else's shoes in order to view that person is to be doing drama.

There are other ways of viewing her – one could look at a picture of her or read about her, or be told about her or even observe her. The quality of one's understanding after following these customary practices, we argue, may be less rich than if you attempt to stand in her shoes. And if you try her shoes on, you can walk them in an amazing variety of directions, so that the angle of your viewing is vastly extended. So drama offers optimal scope. Additionally, it is interactional, so that other characters, other shoe standers-in, give you feedback, thus adding to your perception of the character you are playing. More than that, we claim that you will experience a sense of making or creating something: making a play. And like the potter looking at the finished pot, you can be proud of what has been made, for you are its creator. This acknowledgement of ownership stimulates, so we claim, a critical interest in re-examining what you have done and, perhaps depending on the kind of teacher one has, seeing new things in it and enhancing your understanding. We note that just as the potter, even as he works, is aware of what he has just done, so the new things in the drama can be absorbed as they occur. Thus reflection can take place during the creating as well as after, two opportunities for enhanced understanding and if you are in a class led by Mrs. Heathcote, the potter's wheel is stopped now and again to check whether you have taken in what you have done so far. And finally, there is the sense of theatre. One engages in selectivity, in bringing meaning to time and space, in the excitement of climaxes, in the tension of fraught moments and in the satisfaction of their resolution. In summary, doing drama offers a means of identification, a range of alternative directions, interaction, a sense of creating something new, a means of reflecting on it, and an aesthetic satisfaction.

This is why we do drama in schools: we see all these possibilities for educating young people. Dorothy demonstrated over and over again that she was highly skilled in helping young people create such drama. It was exciting and rewarding and people all over the country tried to emulate her. But by the late 1960s successes of this kind were no longer satisfying Dorothy. She gradually turned herself into another kind of practitioner and experimented with another kind of drama. She switched from standing in someone else's shoes to regarding the other from a distance, from being to watching. 'Watching', however, does not seem to be the right word, for it is not the watching of an entertainment as a theatre audience might engage in when they follow the plot, and become caught up in fictional time. So 'watching' won't do, for it implies following a story-line. 'Attending' or 'contemplating' are perhaps nearer the mark, for these two words suggest arrested time, being held by something, attention riveted on one thing. 'Attention riveted by one thing' brings us as near as we may get to the nature of Dorothy's new approach to drama.

'A woman rocking a cradle with her foot' is the image the ten, severely disabled, hospitalised children are to gaze at. One of Dorothy's students is dressed as a gypsy woman, in full skirt, waist sash, bandana. She nurses a baby – a bundle of shawls that cries by means of a looped tape that the actress can control with her foot. Her actions are rigorously selective and their sequence finely and sensitively timed. She is singing softly. Each child is partnered by one of Dorothy's students. Coming into the room and sitting down with their partners – mentors – on the bench provided takes up a lot of time. One or two are awkward or frightened or out of control; one or two need to be carried or insist on being carried. The whole business of moving from one area of the hospital to the room where the drama is to be is itself a fraught and lengthy operation. Dorothy's students are aware that a child may even refuse to come in.

As they enter they encounter one image, the sound of singing, that they may or may not register. Eventually seated, the children cling to, fidget with, or demonstrate their independence from their adult partners. The interest for Dorothy is the extent to which individual children focus on the woman and what they read into what they see – it cannot be assumed that the children will see a gypsy mother, nursing a baby, rocking the cradle with her foot and peeling potatoes at the same time.

For the children the act of contemplation of this unchanging scene has, to varying degrees, begun. It is a gazing at a picture, the number of actions being sufficiently limited, so that the children have the chance both to take in the whole and to interpret each action, the rocking and the peeling. The simplicity is all, or as Dorothy would prefer me to say: 'simplicity it seems; selectivity it is.' And if learning of any kind is to take place, the children must see what is happening – never assume that an explanation will suffice as a starting point for learning. There is another kind of 'reading', some of which may be detected as the session proceeds. Are the children recognising that it is indeed fiction, that it is a pretend baby for instance?

The student mentors' responsibility is to keep up communication with the child and to press for the child to articulate what s/he is seeing, noting the clothing, the knife, and then asking questions – why peeling? why rocking? Such prompting could be clumsily handled for asking directly 'what do you see? may be the least useful way of discovering what the child sees. This act of contemplation is central to the approach. It is an exercise in reading. There are two levels of meaning here. There is the immediate one of a person carrying out an action, but there is another that may or may not be part of the child's perception. This meaning, at a more abstract level, is about caring for a baby and, further, about the baby's need for food.

For this project is to be about food and in particular about meat. The request had come from the senior psychiatrist, Iain Fraser, who asked if Dorothy could help children realise that the meat of hospital dinners comes from animals. Dorothy, in her mind, translates this into action terms: 'Meat runs about before we eat it'.

Hidden in this action statement is the need some humans have to eat meat, so it is a three-cornered action concept of animal/meat/human, and beneath that triangle lies the key abstract conception of living and dying. Whatever action terms one dresses the topic in, its underlying meaning is inescapable. This

Dorothy has to face, but she cannot start with such a raw challenge to these children. She therefore chooses to go for a linked frame, that of satisfying hunger, something the children already know about. So she is going to edge her way into 'meat runs before we eat it' through a parallel issue of the need to feed. She mustn't face the children with hunger for meat initially – they need to be led into the theme by a more comfortable image of a baby needing milk, and a mother caring. Hunger is going to be the link that will logically take them from one aspect of the topic to another. Thus there appear to be four main stages to Dorothy's planning of the experience: (1) translating a topic into an action phrase, (2) finding the central concept that will hold the work together, and (3) finding the image that the class can already identify with (4), taking the experience, if possible, to the critical universal concept they need to learn from.

This is my attempt to offer a rationale for planning. The practical steps to be taken in the classroom demand equally rigorous attention. For instance, once the children are settled and attentive to the image, a key step has to be taken: the picture must somehow embrace the children – 'us' and 'her' must be changed to 'we'. This merging of the contemplated and those who contemplate must be timed right and without complication. It would be too soon for the gypsy to talk to the children that would present too many things to be registered. At this first step towards inclusion, there must be only one extra sign to read.

So she smiles warmly at the children, her eyes going along the bench so that no child is left out. It takes time, as indeed everything the actors do will tend to be isolated in time. The baby starts crying and she rocks the cradle with some concern, but it doesn't stop. She picks up an empty bottle from the cradle and puts it down again in order resume rocking.

At this point the students ask their partners questions about what is happening. Some of the children, though not all, may be able to interpret that the the baby is crying because it is hungry and their mentors gently urge them to tell the gypsy. This is a bold leap forward. Dorothy hopes that those who recognise that the baby needs milk are capable of and motivated to speak to the gypsy, and she listens for the word 'hungry'.

In a journey that takes some time and organisation, they all go to fetch milk from the hospital kitchen, bringing it to the gypsy who has remained in her fictional space. The gypsy, assisted by any child who wants to help, fills the bottle. She feeds the baby and the crying stops. Relief all round and the gypsy – do some see her as a mother? – thanks the children. And then gypsy dancers, men and women, wearing colourful garments and necklaces of bones, enter with their tambourines. After they have danced they cautiously, perhaps squatting on the floor if they feel they need to appear unthreatening, say hello to the children. A long process begins of telling the children their names and learning the names of the children. Exchanging names is likely to be an interaction the children are most comfortable with. Then the dancers say goodbye, Dorothy dropping in that they will be back tomorrow.

And Dorothy's function in all this? She is watching the needs of individual children, prompting any student who is not operating economically or pitching enthusiasm too eagerly, or failing to build on or even understand his/her partner's responses, whether verbal or non-verbal. For the children, Mrs. Heathcote becomes the anchor person. She becomes their collective voice, wondering aloud, for example, who the gypsies are, where they have come from, where they have gone, what their names are ...

For her adult students this is also an experience in reading. Here are children who have limited resources for signalling. The student has to interpret and respond to below-the-surface signs, such as a change of tension, a shift of posture or a change in physical contact. S/he must watch particularly the direction and degree of alertness of the child's eyes, and try to fathom incoherent speech. Finally, the student must be sensitive to how s/he is being seen by the child and how the child wants her to be, and try to adjust. This relationship will change from day to day, perhaps growing in trust and affection.

Back in their own school when the year is over, it is hoped that the teachers will bring greater sensitivity to reading the signs of their own pupils or students as they go about school or in the drama classroom. They will also be more aware of the signals they emit towards their pupils, understanding better what they are reading in their teacher. Dorothy would claim that this kind of child brings to students a basic humanity and a basic way of expressing it. Could this be a fundamental, radical training that all teachers, carers and social workers could benefit from? In 1982 Newcastle University was persuaded to add the word 'therapy' to the title of its Drama Diploma so it would be seen as a viable course for professions other than teaching. They had in mind a particular occupational therapist, Jane Sallis of Bristol, whose exceptional qualities in working with the handicapped was recognised[1]. A rich Newcastle dignitary, Norman Holm, on seeing one of Dorothy's films, *Seeds of a New Life*, left a benefaction to Dorothy, which she made available to the Portway Centre. Jane Sallis ran the Centre, which had sixty adults with severe learning difficulties.

This new approach of Dorothy's, this sea-change from what was seen as the essential Heathcotian method, put her students in touch in a fundamental way with how Dorothy herself operates, whether she is meeting someone in day-today living, looking at a painting or doing drama. She 'reads' sensitively and intensely, as she has done from childhood. She sees this as the basis of her skill and wants to pass this on to her students. Susan Battye, a New Zealand teacher already very experienced when she arrived on Dorothy's course, speaks for many when she writes as follows:

> Working at the hospital was the hardest work I've ever done and it taught me a great deal about relating to people and what it meant to be a teacher.

Pam Bowell from London writes of the work at Earl's House hospital as 'so revealing, because it forced us to strip the drama bare and see the absolute essentials ... '

The experience runs through six hourly sessions over six mornings, without Dorothy ever taking on a role. It finishes with a very different type of 'resolution' from her earlier drama teaching: a well-timed smile, changing 'us' and 'them' to 'we', developed into a close bonding between all adults and children; an empty bottle slowly transformed in the later sessions into meat to eat. Its satisfying resolution is dependent on Dorothy's recognition that the bottle's 'emptiness' can eventually point to 'hunger' and 'hunger' to 'meat', and eventually a ritual of skinning a hare. This ability to find a sign that, like a seed, carries its future is the essential craft of all dramatic art in the classroom and on the stage.

The children were never in role. There is a superficial parallel here with the kind of children's theatre that Brian Way's company was doing in other parts of the country. But his actors performed characters who now and again sought help from the audience. In Dorothy's work there is no story, no fixed script; it is a series of action pictures to be read and entered.

The gypsy work took about an hour over each of six mornings. Dorothy would be in charge of the planning, building the next stage out of what had happened in the previous session. You will appreciate how much of Dorothy's planning requires her to prepare materials at home. She justifies this as follows: 'I know it was risky to take over the planning, but I felt they [her students] had enough to do just coping with the action of each session. Also in planning I could demonstrate the interior of the plan, so they followed that, not the story. I think – hope – they recognised I laboured for them because I know how tiring are the demands of such concentration.'

At the end of her notes on the work she poses the question; 'Who knows if the children are more knowledgeable?' She and her students believed that the answer is likely to be yes. But whereas in the 1970s this kind of tentative assumption about achievements was accepted as having integrity, twenty years later it was described by a few critics as complacency. It is strange that educationists who would not expect to find objective evidence of what people have learnt from a theatre experience, nevertheless pretend to themselves that such objectivity is somehow accessible in the classroom. Firm indications of different levels of learning may subsequently emerge as these children continue their hospital lives, but to expect that such evidence to lie obligingly on the surface is fanciful.

Other groups with special needs

It was not fortuitous that Dorothy began a long period of commitment each year to institutions for children and adults in need. For as long as she ran full-time courses, she sought such engagements in local hospitals for the severely disabled, institutions such as Prudhoe and Earls House. For she saw an opportunity to teach her students in a way that normal schools could not provide. For a few years of the course, Prudhoe hospital became the pivot of the whole course. An unused nursing home was offered to Dorothy for her students by the chief psychiatrist, Iain Fraser, at £3 a week. It included a lounge that could become their common room and be used by Dorothy as a seminar room. Eve Carr, a former diploma student, was appointed as assistant to Dorothy to be a kind of resident tutor, and Dorothy drove there in Old Sarah most days. Sadly, Eve, of whom we were all fond, died of cancer just a year or so later.

Their work in the hospital became extended to include adult patients, some with little knowledge of the outside world, others with many memories, but their minds not stimulated and used. These were people, mostly girls, who had many years before been taken into care and were then seen as needing protection. The recently appointed chief psychiatrist's aim was to rehabilitate such patients. He was anxious to experiment by putting them into various social contexts in the nearby town of Prudhoe.

One year it was arranged for one of the local cafés to close for a morning, so that the patients could experience 'going out for coffee'. Dorothy invited me to be part of the group. Each of us was given an adult patient for whom we were responsible for driving to the restaurant but, once there, we were to be our partners' coffee guests. I partnered a woman in her thirties, who got into my car with great excitement. I was fifth in a line of six cars, Dorothy on her own driving behind. Parked at the pavement outside the café, I helped my passenger get out of the car. She grabbed my arm and we walked into the café. Dorothy got out of her car as two local women, who obviously recognised my partner as a hospital inmate, passed by. Dorothy saw them regard me with contempt and heard one of them say: 'Aren't men swine!'

There are other contexts than residential hospitals that test the ability to read signs. Children with behaviour problems provide just that opportunity. It is no coincidence that in both *Death of a President* and *Three Looms Waiting* Dorothy is seen working with disaffected boys. A major part of her timetable involved working with emotionally disturbed, anti-social or mentally ill children. Curiously, an extraordinary, insulting distortion of her teaching of adult patients at Earl's House hospital was portrayed in a novel, first published[2] in 1973. It purported to tell the story of an adult mental patient. No specific reference is made to Earls house or to a patient from there but Dorothy is clearly identified as the visiting, unnamed 'Drama teacher'. The dramatic example David Cook, the author, gives, about a baby being caught up by a tree and requiring the patients to help with the rescue, does indeed correspond to a session Dorothy conducted. However, the picture of 'this big woman with wiry hair drawn into a bun, sitting crossed-legged on the floor, with her six disciples', and the account of what occurs in the drama, are so utterly distorted that one begins to doubt whether the author could possibly have seen Dorothy at work, and yet parts of his description make him sound convincingly present. David Cook was an actor by profession and this was his first novel. Artistic licence allows him to paint whatever picture he likes, but one wonders why he chose to vilify what appears to have been a positive experience for the patients. It makes one wonder whether casual visitors who perhaps merely caught a glimpse of Mrs. Heathcote's drama, or even the regular staff who coped with the patients when the session was over would report less adulatory versions than her students. I suspect there was some suspicion of Mrs. Heathcote's visits from the kitchen staff for example, who perhaps did not want a party of excited children and strangers invading their territory to pick up milk.

That institutions throughout the north sought Dorothy's help is evidence of the high regard in which her work was held. But not invariably. Once she attended a national conference held at Durham of staff, mostly men working in Approved Schools, as criminal institutions for the young used to be called.. They loved the work she and a group of boys were creating each morning, but two days later, she played a tape-recording of adolescent girls who swore their way through the sessions and dropped obscenities into their drama. 'There was a chill in the room' says Dorothy. They were so shocked they found it difficult even to speak to her and one man stated: 'Girls don't talk like that', as though Dorothy had somehow provoked the obscenities.

And we should remember that a few of her students did not see the relevance of her work to secondary school teachers, dismissing it as therapy, as nothing to do with real education. One of her very early full-time students wrote, 'At the time

I was not happy with our, albeit brief, skirmishes into working with the mentally handicapped children: I felt she was dabbling and treading a dubious if not dangerous path.'

I personally find her ability in this field of practice astonishingly skilful. My career has taken me into working in adult psychiatry and very occasionally I would ask Dorothy's advice. Her immediate grasp of what was needed was amazing, as though she had been trained in therapy of that kind. On an early visit to New York, she had seen Moreno conduct a session, not long before he died. She was a little upset about it, feeling that it was orchestrated and mishandled. At that time, he was *the* guru – his work was to be applauded, not questioned.

A new direction – Dorothy's 'archetypal' period

Dorothy had been intrigued by the way some of her students played their roles in a number of these projects and the effect their playing seemed to have on the children. She was aware that the persona and the physique of the person playing the role matched the role. For instance, Bill Backman, who was a week-end hunter at home in Canada, wore the gypsy role like a fitted garment so that all the verbal and especially non-verbal signals he naturally expressed daily were reflected effortlessly by the 'gypsy'. Thus there was no confusion of signals for the children but rather integrity and an enhanced opportunity for communication.

Dorothy had noticed this matching of persona and role in previous students' work and in 1970 had experimented by building a role round one of her students, that grew organically from the student's own personality. The student was another Canadian, Wayne Balanoff, and the role was that of the Wild Man, a man who lives in a very natural way with shells and other natural objects serving as his comb and bowls etc, and living in a bivouac type shelter.

Telling her students about this experiment next year, Dorothy shared with them her gift for perceiving the essential person in anyone she met. She had once told me that she could look at individuals in any audience she was addressing and cast them as a particular animal or bird. She explained to her students that what she read was a person's non-verbal system of signals, those unconscious means of communication that underlie an identity, often overriding the person's outward appearance. Donna Brandes, an American counsellor now living in Western Australia told me the following story:

> One time, Dorothy rang me and asked me if I would pick up someone at the airport for her. I lived out in Wideopen, close to the airport, and Dorothy couldn't get away. Of course, I said yes ... this was 1973.

I asked Dorothy who I was supposed to look for ... she said she wasn't at all sure. She *thought* it was a woman from a course she had taught in Colorado the previous summer. All she had was the flight details and no name or phone number. She described the woman as 'large, golden, fair and shining'. So I went uninformed to the airport, with a sign saying: 'Are you looking for Dorothy Heathcote?'

The plane landed, and I looked for a shining golden woman ... none appeared. But after a few minutes, a woman did approach me , and said 'I am looking for Dorothy Heathcote' ... I looked at her, a tall, sinuous, stunning, slim *black* woman ... and stammered 'There must be some mistake!' I was very embarrassed, and we talked it through until she convinced me that she was indeed a visitor from the USA who would join Dorothy's course for a few weeks, and that she had been invited to stay in Dorothy's trailer.

Her name was Rosa Scott. I took her to Dorothy's, and on the way I found her delightful, funny, bright, and very cluey.

I phoned Dorothy about this story. She remembered Rosa very well and immediately said 'She was a sunflower' – and this is what Dorothy saw. Indeed she subsequently used Rosa twice in that role of 'sunflower'.

Chris Lawrence, one of her students present when Dorothy described this skill, tells me this:

DH sat us all in a circle and asked if we wanted her to suggest roles that our non-verbal signals suggested to her. We of course said yes please. This is how Bill (a second student to take on the role; the first was Wayne Balanoff) took on 'Wild Man' – his non-verbal signals made that suggestion to DH and she reflected it back to Bill. The seed was sown. Another student (she felt) would make a good Unhappy Princess, and another one a Teller of Fortunes. When she came to me she mused somewhat and then sowed the seed of Derelict into my imagination. (Chris later gave the Derelict the name Albert, for a role that was to stay with him for many years).

The essential and vital process here was that it was derived out of Geste, or Non verbal Signals. She made this very clear at the time and it is etched into my awareness (and has since proved to be a vital element in the witnessing of my own life). As she explained to us, these were the signals that we gave off most naturally to the children . That is, we did not always know we were doing them but the children did at all times, so we could harness the energy of these signals to our advantage through the role, rather than having them work against us.

On reading this account, Dorothy is anxious that it might be misunderstood. She writes a note to me as follows: 'In no way am I asking people to be characters like themselves. I'm only reading a sort of 'indicator' sign which I then clothe into a person *in situ*, not a character in situations. The 'indicator' breeds the situation they would inhabit.'

Dorothy's concern in using what became known as a Person-in-Role, was to deepen the contemplating or attending behaviours required by the kind of gypsy presentation I've described. Dorothy's aims in any work she has done have always been multi-layered. It was easy to tease out from the work her interest in, for instance, developing the concept that meat comes from live animals, but wherever possible she would also try to bring the children closer to what she calls 'ancient wisdom' by the use of rituals. Wherever possible she would try to put her classes in touch with something beyond surface information and knowledge, ancient wisdom being but one example of many possible penetrations.

Part of the excitement of working in the art form of drama is that in purposefully, and often necessarily, arresting attention in one direction, one can unwittingly close or half close the door on another direction intended for later. We have seen that in order to alert the hospitalised children, they were invited to watch a gypsy nursing a baby and encouraged to work out that the baby was hungry. There was a problem to be solved, one that the class could help with. This is worthwhile, straightforwardly and productively focusing. Is its very efficiency and sufficiency also limiting?

Supposing you wanted the children to do more than identify and solve a problem; supposing you wanted them to understand something of the life-styles of those gypsies, to understand, say, their closeness to natural things or how they see the world, and how they value the world? If this were one's teaching priority, then trying to get a class to take in and read a group of characters at this level would be unrealistic. But if there were only *one* ...

'Albert' was among the earliest of a line of characters Dorothy was to evolve over many years. Chris Lawrence describes[3] one of the early experiments:

> It is a school hall with a very shiny floor. There is very little to pick it out as an ESN [Educationally subnormal] school. I am lying on the floor, my cheek resting on the cold, polished wood. My whole body is covered over with newspapers, which crackle softly as I move. My feet, wrapped in rags tied with rough string, are just poking out. I wear an old pair of baggy trousers, an old shirt and an old, cold, black buttonless PVC coat with a string belt and large pockets. In one of the pockets is a small, battered lozenge tin with

a (very old) boiled sweet in. I am clutching a small dolly made out of newspapers and sellotape ...

Footsteps! Children's voices, cries, clopping feet, a teacher's voice ... It occurs to me how much at the mercy of feet I am. Their names come in excited voices, some very indistinct, but all repeated, made clear, by the gentle Yorkshire voice of the teacher leading the session, Dorothy Heathcote.

The children, grouped round Dorothy to share their names with her, are attracted by what they see as a pile of newspapers in the corner of their hall, especially when one of the papers twitches, at first gently, and then slightly more vigorously.

Thus the dramatic episode has started with a mystery, prompting much talk from Dorothy and class, Dorothy reinforcing whatever line the children appear to take. A brave child removes one of the newspapers, exposing Albert underneath. 'Gerrup' says another child, helpfully, and they all, a little scared, back away as they see a tramp looking equally frightened, sit up.

There is no inviting smile here from the 'role', no kind-faced mother feeding her baby, working at turning an 'us and them' into a 'we'. What is on offer here is a cowering figure, straining for separateness, not inclusion. Thus if the children are to be beguiled – to use one of Dorothy's favourite words – it will not be because the role is inviting but because it is withholding. Dorothy's function is a very delicate one. Indeed, she sees it as 'very risky – we don't want children drawn to strangers'. She wants the children to be sufficiently intrigued to take the initiative and yet during this early hiaitus, she senses that they may need a gentle nudge. She finds herself saying things like: 'I wonder what he's got in his tin?' thus initiating the first 'what has he got?' stage, preparing for the 'what does he need?' stage, and on to the 'what does his doll *mean* to him?' stage, to 'what can we do for him?', and 'does he have a story to tell?' and to the final 'what is his way of life?' And, moment to moment, she must sustain the mystery. If any aspect of Albert that they are considering becomes unfruitful or boring, she must find a way of leaving a little of the mystery in it by turning to something new.

In practice, how far Dorothy takes a class will depend on the children themselves. The children differed notably in the extent to which they chose to become intimate with Albert, one or two holding his hands or even cuddling, while others kept their distance. Variation in that kind of individual response certainly affected how far a teacher's objectives could be met. Throughout the sessions – and he successfully played this role many times for the ESN and infant schools

– Chris was guided by Dorothy's leadership and above all by his in-depth sense of the person he was being. This surely epitomised Stanislavski's 'search for a character', for the only way it could work was for the person playing the role to know the character from the inside. But having achieved this, the actor still has to maintain his 'teacher' ear, alert for how the children need him to respond. Dorothy used many such roles, each of them open to broad, archetypal or stereotypical interpretation.

There are two questions, not unlinked, that one might ask about this kind of work.

(1) To what extent could this be regarded as drama? Neither the children nor Dorothy were in role, although Dorothy adopted a specific function of trying to be the voice of the class. This was a pure experience of attending intensely to a picture and allowing the picture to let the children see themselves. Dorothy was fond of saying that she wasn't interested in drama for itself, that she was first and foremost an educationist. Few believed her, but this approach may support her claim.

(2) To what extend should it have been made clear that the role is fiction? I wonder what those children told their parents at the end of the school day? A tramp in the school hall – and cuddled by some of the children?

Dorothy was not unaware of these questions and must have recognised that there was some danger in children being taken in by the role. We shall see in Chapter 8 that she sometimes misjudged this. She occasionally adopted the simple routine of introducing the actor and having him or her dress up in the garments of the role in front of the children. This took away the original mystery but as long as the role was sufficiently arresting many of the classes seemed temporarily to forget that the character was fictional.

Whereas at first the use of Person-in-Role seemed to be a ready-made source of stimulation for slow learners, Dorothy gradually realised that it could also challenge the brightest students. The person in role could be framed as a portrait of someone who was well-informed in an area of knowledge required by the students – a playwright, monarch, scientist, explorer etc. The task for the class was to prepare and then formulate the questions they were to ask when the portrait stepped out of the frame. This sometimes involved the students themselves being in role as, say, researchers, trainees or even examinees. Perhaps the most well-known and much referred to example of this is *The Treatment of Dr. Lister*[4], in which the primary school children are medical students presented with the opportunity to engage Dr. Lister in conversation. The pupils are invited to knock at Dr. Lister's office door and wait for permission to enter into the past.

As the 1970s progressed, those of us who continued to revel in teacher-in-role wondered what had happened to this central feature of 'drama in education', as the work of the North-East was now indelibly labelled. Although Dorothy would occasionally take on a role, even with Albert – of a policeman or some authority figure who wanted to question the children about the tramp – such a modest re-positioning lacked the dramatic intensity of Dorothy's previous roles. Dorothy moved away from her dramatically and educationally successful use of making up a play to being a creator of pictures in which she becomes a fellow reader along with the class.

There was to be yet another sea-change – and a distinctly different order of teacher-in-role took central position once more. And the word 'task' was to claim a dominant place in Dorothy's drama vocabulary.

A communication disaster

Central to both forms of the sea-change described in this chapter are the semiotic concepts of signing and reading sign. Her adult students, in both the gypsy and Albert presentations described, had to be trained by Dorothy to sign their roles and fictional situations selectively, economically, effectively and, most important, evocatively. Dorothy was rightly excited by the educational potential of getting classes of children to learn to read and then respond to the signing. She saw it as part of her professional mission to pass on this conception to fellow drama teachers. She saw how her own students were enthralled by the experience, although she didn't rely on their approbation for she recognised that she was drawing on what she felt she had been learning all her life, that signing was at the centre of theatre.

A splendid opportunity to pursue this work arose in 1978. Gerald Chapman of the Royal Court's Young People's Theatre Scheme initiated a joint conference at the Riverside Studios in London of professional theatre personnel and drama teachers, to determine the common ground of working in the theatre and in the classroom. Three of us were to demonstrate workshops, Bill Gaskill of the Royal Court, a fellow student of Dorothy's at the Northern Theatre School in Bradford whom she had not seen since then, who would work with his own professional actors, and Dorothy and I who would work with a class of local school pupils. As a bonus, Dorothy was invited to do an extra session with Royal Court actors.

Actors! Just what Dorothy needed to (a) demonstrate subtlety of signing to some hypothetical class of children and (b) expose significant differences between how the actor needs to prepare himself for having his role interrogated by children and the actor's normal preparation for performing in a play. She also had ready a theoretical backing for her exposition, drawn from Goffman's concept of framing. Dorothy began her session by asking her group of actors to accept the notion that they had just performed a play in a school using the theme of Jason and the Argonauts and that they had been invited by the head teacher – her role – to discuss ways of following up the work.

In her session she begins a long, slow process of turning one or two of the actors into a statue of Jason, Medea etc. A mixture of speaking in role as the school headteacher and addressing the large audience of teachers, directors and actors combined to help everyone understand her educational thinking – or so Dorothy intended. The actors became but a small part of her exposition of the theory and practice of using a person-in-role. She delivered with conviction and passion. But the audience, mystified, grew more and more tense and restless as they watched Dorothy ignore her actors during long periods of philosophical exposition. Those of the actor group who were set up as statues were not sure whether they were still in that role or whether Dorothy's addressing the audience was a signal that they could relax. They grew more and more embarrassed and the audience, feeling for them, focused on what they read as the growing humiliation of the neglected actors, and could not take in what Dorothy was talking about.

Dorothy was in her way making it very clear to everyone, actors and audience, what she was doing and why, but still they could not read the overall meaning of the event itself. She knew that she was sharing her latest educational mission; but the audience and actors thought they were witnessing an illustration of how a well-known drama teacher works with actors. I had spoken to one or two of the actors before the session. They were excited and nervous, not knowing quite what to expect but certain that in the hands of this talented woman they were going to be given a wonderful experience. They assumed, as did the audience – apart from Dorothy's own students who were present – that Dorothy would create a quality drama and that the audience would see themselves as privileged spectators. Privileged they were, but they were wearing the wrong hats. It was as if Dorothy and the audience were at two different events. There was an angry public discussion that evening. Perhaps this occasion was the worst event of Dorothy's career. Fortunately, in the book Ken Robinson edited soon after, *Exploring Theatre and Education*[5], Dorothy was given a chance to explain what she had been trying to do.

The furore was over the way that the actors were left idling with their engines running or, in the Argonaut context, with their sails slack. Curiously, this image offers a powerful metaphor for drawing a distinction between acting in a play and acting in a role. In a play, sails are full blown; the actor is part of a fleet in full sail. In role, however, the actor, in a solitary vessel as Jason was, is waiting for a wind to fill the sails, waiting for a class of children to set the degree of power and direction so that a journey might begin. Dorothy, with hindsight, concedes that on that day she did not provide for even the slightest stirring of those sails. If there really had been a class of children, instead of an imaginary group, the actors would have indeed set sail.

Notes

1   The word 'therapy' was removed from the title one year later, once Jane Sallis had completed the course. It was not a word that Dorothy was ever comfortable with.

2   The most recent reprint was in 1978: *Walter* by David Cook (Secker and Warburg). Channel Four television made an award-winning film called *Walter*, with Ian McKellan playing the lead.

3   From an article Chris wrote for *2D journal*, 1982 – but the drama he described took place ten years earlier.

4   John Carroll, a distinguished Australian lecturer, registered with Newcastle University three times during his career, to take the Advanced Diploma course in Drama in Education 1976-7, the M.Ed course 1979-80, during which he recorded and published *The Treatment of Dr. Lister* and finally registered to do a doctoral study supervised by Dorothy, completed in 1987. At the time of the IDEA conference July, 2001, while he was sailing up a Norwegian fjord a passenger joined him at the rail and said 'Dr. Lister, I presume'.

5   Kenneth Robinson (Ed) 1980 *Exploring Theatre and Education* London Heinemann

7
Travelling abroad

The first invitation to USA

It seems remarkable that the first detailed analysis of Dorothy Heathcote's work should come from America. She herself had not published in book form and no one in England had shown any inclination to do so[1]. Dorothy had been teaching in Newcastle for 25 years when the American publication appeared, only seven years after her first visit to America in November, 1969. Its perceptive author was Betty Jane Wagner who writes in her *Acknowledgements*:

> When I first found myself in a class of Heathcote's, I knew I was in the presence of a genius, but I didn't know how important she would become.[2]

B.J.'s book, revised in 1999, for B.J. continued to monitor Dorothy's work in both USA and the UK, remains the most illuminating text about Dorothy's classroom practice that we have. Her recollection of first attending one of Dorothy's lectures is vivid:

> She stirred in me something that has bubbled up ever since, splashing into my ordered thinking with a left-handed paddle. Her boat was not headed merely toward a new teaching gimmick, but rather toward a truth beyond mere facts where the waters stirred are deep within. I wondered where I had been before I met her and saw what teaching could be.

For Dorothy, being invited to America was an uncomfortable mixture of excitement, apprehension and worry about leaving her young daughter. She had been doing one of her flying visits to Manchester, this time to speak at a meeting of the National Association of Teachers of English. An American in the audience, Dr. Wallace Douglas, of Northwestern University, offered to drive her to the airport when it was over. On the way, he asked her if she would be willing to take part in a two-day National Council of Teachers of English conference on reading and literacy to be held in Washington D.C. – he was to be in the chair. She had doubts on two grounds: one, that she was not trained in the subject and two, that as it was to be during her term time, the University may not give permission for her absence. Her driver waived the first of these, saying that she had given the clearest exposition of English teaching he had ever heard. And with regard to the second obstacle, he would write to Professor Stanley himself and make the necessary request. Dorothy returned home, leaving all thoughts of teaching abroad behind her in Manchester, for she had a job to get on with in Newcastle. A few weeks later, however, Professor Stanley, now having received a glowing account of her presentation in Manchester, gave his blessing and a three-week itinerary was arranged for the Fall.

In the meantime, *Death of a President* was finding its way across the Atlantic, so that leaders in the field of creative dramatics were beginning to have their attention drawn to a powerful woman doing strange things in the name of drama. Professor Barbara McIntyre, in her office at Northwestern University, Evanston, Illinois, received a note from Dr. Wallace Douglas. The note said that he had acquired a tape of a film he thought she should see. It goes on: 'It has to do with creative dramatics but it isn't the way you work. It's different and I'd like you to see it and tell me what it is about. Her name is Dorothy Heathcote'. This was a name Barbara McIntyre had never heard of, even though she had been a regular visitor to educational drama activities in England. She watched it and phoned her friend Anne Thurman who supervised drama in schools for District 65. They watched it together over and over again, deciding they must attend the Heathcote lecture Wally Douglas was to stage in Evanston after Dorothy had spoken at the Washington conference.

Family arrangements

Dorothy's domestic preparations for her visit to America were considerable. Meals for Raymond for twenty-one days had to be prepared and deep-frozen, complete with labels and instructions. Her greatest anxiety was Marianne. May Spooner, a neighbour with a toddler a year older than Marianne, was invited to support Raymond and look after Marianne during the day while Raymond was at work. Marianne's travelling bed, a huge black box made by Dorothy for use in the car, was carried over to Mary's for Marianne to sleep in at night Monday to Thursday. When Raymond got home, he was to join them at Mary's and play one of the twenty-one taped stories Dorothy had prepared, so that Marianne could hear her mammy's voice before going to sleep. She had selected a second story for Raymond to read. Marianne always slept with her teddy, its ears well-chewed, so Dorothy prepared 21 new pairs of safety-pinned ears, one pair to be attached to teddy each day – until mammy comes home. And Raymond himself made a model of the USA with a flight map, so that Marianne, who still has it today, could fly mammy's plane around the map.

According to May Spooner, Raymond was 'brilliant' with Marianne, but inevitably there were times when Marianne would not settle when he put her to bed at the week-ends and he would come over to May for help. He never told Dorothy about such times. He always assured her that everything had been just fine.

When she was seven, Marianne accompanied her mother abroad, the longest period covering a three months' visit to Singapore and Australia. That visit co-incided with the tidal wave that had struck Northern Territories so that as Dorothy went from school to school round Australia, she was asked to do 'disaster' dramas, the most difficult topic of all. Once Marianne was old enough to attend infant school, it became a summer routine for Raymond, Marianne and her friend to join Dorothy wherever she was in the world. Raymond would some-times organise daily outings for the two children, or Dorothy would have them in her class if the children she was working with were not too much older. As Marianne and her friend became adolescents, they did much exploring on their own and on one occasion they came across a Macdonald's, which they insisted on taking Dorothy to that very evening. Juliana Saxton tells the story:

> A tandem bicycle (ridden by Marianne and her friend), DH pacing sedately along beside. In the bicycle basket: linen table napkin, silver fork, knife and spoon, a glass and a china cup and saucer lent by the college cafeteria. The destination: Macdonald's. The context: the girls (who were left to their own devices while DH was teaching) had found a Macdonalds and thought it was wonderful. They wanted to take DH there for supper. Dorothy who knew from her previous visits to North America, just what Macdonalds was like, laid down her conditions: she would go with them but only if she could eat in a civilized manner: no plastics or paper for her!

Organising leaving an empty house in England for the whole of a summer vacation was not without its worries. Highburn House, a distinctive abode that no doubt appeared mansion-like to local inhabitants in a traditionally working class area, was an attraction to burglars, especially with its contents of valuable artefacts collected over the years or inherited from Raymond's family. A security system and a routine of putting silver-ware in the bank, and the daily visits by Mary and May eased Raymond's mind somewhat, but the anxiety never entirely left him. May became 'the guardian of the telephone', never divulging that the family were actually away. On one occasion, when Dorothy and Raymond were away in Portugal, the telephone dialogue went something like this:

> 'Dorothy's not in at the moment ... '
> 'I need to get in touch with her ... when will she be in?'
> 'Oh, not for a while yet ... I'll tell her you called.'

First visit to America

'Are you buying new clothes?' I had asked her. 'Clothe', replied Dorothy. She arrived in New York with her modest hand-lugguge, with her one dress and a toothbrush, but bulky with books. Those who met her at airports round the world over her twenty years of traveling alone learnt that she would be one of the first passengers to appear because she had only hand-luggage. They would also be ready with the necessary purchases of washing powder and hand soap etc that Dorothy had ordered, for she adopted a routine of washing, drying and ironing her dress each evening. This avoidance of carrying any other luggage was not just a matter of weight but part of a deep feeling of needing to get home. When Marianne travelled with her, as for instance, for three months in Australia, both confined themselves to hand-luggage.

New York was the first stop in a work itinerary that included Harlem, Tallahassie, Washington and Evanston. Her memory is of opulent hotel bed-rooms, an embarrassing cornucopia of food on display in hotel coffee shops and a heart-warming courtesy from her hosts in each city. This was the beginning of long strands of employment when, thousands of miles from home, she would exist in the limbo of an impersonal, albeit luxurious bedroom, waiting to be called to the lobby. 'Don't wait there on your own!' she was warned in New York. She would then be transported by an affable stranger to the convention centre, the university, the school or the studio. The work over, she would be safely re-turned – along the carpeted corridor on the umpteenth floor to her room with its king-size bed, its telephone, her photographs of Raymond and Marianne and her books. She recalls on this first visit sitting in her hotel room gazing at a bowl of fruit left by her kind hosts with a star-fruit in it, wondering what is it? is it decoration? do you eat it? Everything seems unreal; she is a stranger to the room, to the country; to the people. She wonders what Marianne is doing; there are hours ahead before the next spell of work; and here she is gazing at this fruit-like object. She pulls off a bit ... nibbles dubiously ... it's sort of bland ... perhaps it wasn't meant for eating ... better leave it. And she picks up her book.

One hotel that had character was in Evanston where she was to meet Barbara McIntyre and Anne Thurman for the first time. Called The Homestead, it was an early hotel with dignified, elderly black waiters and Quaker furniture. She recalls a notice over the bed that read: 'We have a fleet of Rolls Royce to take you whither you would go'. Her first visit to America coincided with Thanks-giving celebrations. She shared them in Washington with Geoffrey Somerfield, a fellow Englishman and friend from York University. They drove out in Geoffrey's hired car to a dark, weirdly ornate restaurant in Georgetown, the doorman of their hotel insisting that their car be brought to the main entrance rather than have them risk going to the car park themselves.

The drama Dorothy remembers doing in New York and Washington seems also to have had a sinister element. In Harlem, her first visit to a school in the States, in response to asking 'what would they like to make a play about?', she found herself helping to plan a racial murder in the subway and learning from these streetwise students which station would be the most suitable for such an event. In Washington, she was asked – curiously, for the itinerary of a visiting English woman – to do drama with a group of young men with severe behaviour problems who were being given a 'last chance' to pursue their education in a conventional school. The floor of the room she was to work in was covered with cushions – for sleeping off drugs or punching, no doubt.

> *Even as she describes meeting this class to me, Dorothy says 'I'm trembling now', for she is appalled at the way she would say – and still does -'yes' to anything, even though, as on this occasion, they gave her the chance to opt out. She can hear Marianne, in later life, saying to her: 'You just don't stop to think, Mother!'*

So she got rid of the cushions and brought in long bamboo canes from a nearby carpet factory for spears, and she started five sessions on the Trojan War. 'I should warn you ... my name is Odysseus ... and I run a fleet that never loses ... but I am the 'Wily One' ... guard your back!' And so Dorothy Heathcote, at her most powerful when she so chooses, mesmerises the youths into taking part.

Laying herself open to criticism

Dorothy Heathcote's approach to drama teaching inevitably challenged whatever was the customary practice in the countries she visited. One has only to think of Australia with its post World War Two 'elocution' tradition. In the USA, polished school productions were part of the educational culture and there was the wonderfully innovative 'Creative Dramatics' of Winifred Ward at Northwestern University in Evanston. In Canada, Brian Way, strongly supported by the influential Richard Courtney, was successfully laying the foundations for what became known as 'Creative Drama'. Such were the rapturous receptions with which Dorothy was received that opposition to her work was rarely voiced. Indeed teachers who were uncomfortable with or critical of her work found it difficult to raise points of criticism. Dorothy's constant assertion in the 1970s that she was not interested in drama made it extremely difficult for, say, theatre specialists or creative dramatics exponents in her audience to know what the ground rules were supposed to be. Anne Thurman, who was responsible for bringing Dorothy over for her first and many subsequent full summer schools in the States, regretted that she had not widened the range of invitations to include language arts and social studies exponents, as she came to understand the breadth of Dorothy's vision. Most newcomers to her work were so overwhelmed by her charisma that any uncertainty about identifying what it was supposed to be if it wasn't drama was held in abeyance.

The very settings of Dorothy's demonstration classes made voiced criticism seem out of place. Dorothy's teaching tended to be observed by audiences that outnumbered the young students in her class, so when her class departed and she smilingly invited questions, it was not easy in a room often of people who were strangers to each other, to articulate their doubts, especially when most of them were agog with admiration. And Dorothy herself did not always help.

I recall an occasion in 1974 when she and I were both running summer courses for Anne Thurman at Northwestern. I was teaching at a different time of the day, so I was free to watch one of her demonstrations with a large group of senior high students. It didn't seem to be going anywhere and Dorothy was having a struggle to hold their attention at a point where it was necessary to get their decision on the next step. And when the decision came, it appeared to express the choice of the few in the class who were still with it, rather than general consensus. After the class left the audience chatted among themselves. I heard several comment on the students' loss of interest and wondered whether splitting the class into small groups at an earlier point would have eased the group through a sticky impasse. Foolishly, when the open discussion, soothingly uncritical, had been going for quite a while, I voiced this opinion as if it were my own, for I felt there was some sense in it. I must have touched Dorothy on a raw spot, for she turned on me, saying: 'If you think that small group work is the answer, you'd better have another think!' I was too taken aback to respond. There were no more criticisms from the audience after that. A leading Canadian teacher suffered a similar experience in California, when Dorothy answered her question: 'If you do not know then you shouldn't be teaching drama.'

Interestingly, a lone voice of criticism did appear in print two years before B.J. Wagner's 1976 publication about Dorothy. Margaret Faulkes, a British colleague, co-founder and co-director with Brian Way of Theatre Centre, London, had been Associate Professor of Drama at Alberta University since 1967. She wrote a scathing account of Dorothy's teaching. It was distributed among members of CCYDA, a Canadian Drama Association and published a few months later in the American journal, *Children's Theatre Review*. Professor Faulkes felt, as did many, that Brian Way's approach to child development through drama was being challenged by this fellow Brit, who appeared to be turning up in North America at regular intervals. In 1974 she and Dorothy were invited to share the teaching of a week's course to be held in Minnesota. Dorothy asked that her contribution should include having two classes of children for one hour in the morning and afternoon for each of the five days. This was Ms Faulkes' chance to see Dorothy at work for the first time. She remained un-impressed and indeed hostile. Although she didn't say anything to Dorothy at the time, she sent her article to the publishers as soon as the conference was over.

In her article she gives a detailed account of Dorothy's sessions with 6-9 year olds, where the topic was 'medical science research into a cure for cancer'. Faulkes split her attack into three sections, asking 'Is this Drama?'; 'Is this Creativity?'; 'Is this Education?' And, coolly, reasonably, eloquently, she argues that it is none of these, that Dorothy's teaching is seriously flawed. In fact, she makes Dorothy sound stubborn, inconsiderate, self-indulgent, bullying, not understanding young children and lacking in any kind of artistry.

Professor Faulkes' first complaint was that the theme of cancer had been Dorothy's choice, not that of class. I wasn't there, so I don't know the truth of this. Manipulation by a teacher is sometimes justifiable. If Dorothy had insisted on this subject she would have had a good reason for it. If she pushed the topic of cancer without checking whether that was a genuine majority choice, it would be because she saw in it something that would challenge this particular class. Nevertheless we should accept that there have been times when she felt she had to override her own intention of following the class consensus. Sometimes the very structure she chose to use, such as whole class decision-making, could land her with a cumbersome, shallow level of operating which she had to find a quick way out of. Sometimes she may have allowed herself to be too influenced by the requirements of a demonstration. She occasionally tried to demonstrate a strategy she was anxious for her adult audience to see in action, but which failed to make much sense either to her class or to the adults watching because the time ran out. And the opposite could happen. Once in Vancouver when she was asked why she had persisted when the class were clearly becoming more and more tired during the final hour of the session, her terse reply, according to Margaret Burke who was present, was: 'I was being paid to demonstrate for three hours. I wouldn't go on like this if it were left to me to decide.'

The very notion of a demonstration class can sometimes bring a public dimen-sion to the work that may distort. Juliana Saxton of the University of Victoria, British Columbia, and formerly of Toronto University, recalls the first time she saw Dorothy teach a class of students – Grade 10s. Unbeknown to anybody, their teacher, worried that her students wouldn't behave in front of all these visitors, strategically placed eight Grade 12s among them to keep an eye on them. The curious effect seemed to be that the class left feeling deservedly pleased with themselves, but that Dorothy's input had been disappointingly modest. Unless, you knew about the humiliation of the Grade 10s, you couldn't possibly read what was going on. But Dorothy, who didn't know what the problem was, nevertheless sensed that the class was somehow losing face and set out to make sure they felt good; this had to be her priority at the risk of her as a teacher appearing less dynamic and less ambitious in her aims than people expected.

Dorothy Heathcote and Margaret Faulkes, as they smiled at each other in Minnesota, were philosophically miles apart. Because of their distant starting points they would necessarily have disapproved of, if not despised, each other's work. Though despise is too strong a word for Dorothy, for she always acknowledges quality in others' way of working even if she thinks their approach to be misguided, but the hostility in Ms Faulkes' article is unmistakable.

Quite by chance I was supplied with evidence of just how biased Margaret Faulkes' perception had been. For her, the final curtain to Dorothy's disastrous teaching came towards the end of the final cure for cancer session when the scientists were ordered to board the plane for Washington, leaving their dying plants behind – a failed mission. Each child had been partnered by an adult who represented the plant. One girl refused to leave, steadily continuing to water her dying plant, as the rest of the class left the room, waving her goodbye. Tears sprang to the girl's eyes. Margaret Faulkes confessed that she had been so upset for the poor girl that she 'broke all the rules, went over to her and took her out into the fresh air'. Reading in Ms Faulkes' published article about her protectiveness, I was prompted a year later to give a paper to the 1975 Children's Theatre Association convention in Washington on 'Drama and Emotion', in which I discussed, among other matters, the importance of protecting children *into* rather than *from* distressful subjects, and I referred specifically to Margaret Faulkes' article, suggesting that her gesture of sympathy for the child may have been misplaced.

The paper was well received by the large audience, and when it was over, a young teacher hovered by the dais on which I was standing. She told me: 'I am so glad you mentioned Dorothy Heathcote's cancer lesson ... I was there and I was the 'plant', partnering the little girl who remained behind.' She continued with an account that turned Margaret Faulkes' rendering upside down: 'The girl wasn't upset at all. When she arrived for the last session, she came up to me all excited, saying that she'd had a super idea: she would like me [me, as a plant, that is!] to die and then when all the others had to go back to Washington, she would like to be the one who refuses to go with them – did I think that would be okay? I mentioned this idea to Dorothy before the session began, and it all worked out as the child wanted it – she thoroughly enjoyed being left to water her dying plant.' The scientists' departure to Washington had been more rushed than Dorothy had planned, for when Dorothy arrived that morning, she was asked to finish her session early so that everyone could watch President Nixon's resignation announcement on television. Real life is more powerful than fiction, after all.

This story surely confirms that we often see what we want to see, or at least fail to appreciate the complexity of a classroom situation. And when I say *we*, I don't mean Professor Faulkes only – I mean me, and all of us who work in this medium, including Dorothy. It sometimes needs the overstated criticisms of a Malcolm Ross, a Peter Abbs, a David Hornbrook, a Margaret Faulkes to make us pause and reappraise what we do.

The question of whether it is appropriate to engage children in unpleasant or disturbing subject-matter – or in the USA, religious subject-matter – was raised many times in Dorothy's visits abroad. Most people realised that Dorothy has such astonishing skill to bring a dignity and seriousness to an unpleasant topic, that very deep understanding can be evoked. Juliana Saxton has given me an illustration of this ability, that took place in Fairview, Alberta, Margaret Faulkes' home State. Juliana, who along with Margaret Burke of Brock University, were sharing the teaching with Dorothy, writes:

> DH never refused to deal with what 'nice' people might consider the darker sides of life. There had recently been a plane crash in the north that was on everyone's lips, including the children's who proceeded to insist on that topic. The crash became the area for investigation for the five drama sessions. One of the final strategies was to create a wax museum to commemorate the crash and to educate 'the visitors'. The children – upper elementary – were deeply engaged because it was a topic of such relevance to them. The teachers – Dorothy's own class – had to create the artefacts that would be in the museum and also represent [as statues] the people who had lost their lives. The idea was that any 'visitor' who had a question could press a button and the 'statue' would 'come to life' and tell part of the story. The teachers were horrified at this and wondered how they would be able to do such things. The children, who were equally engaged in the design and layout, had a fine time working to make sure that everything would look authentic.

> There have been many times when I have seen DH go where others fear to tread and the results have always been wonderful learning. She knows how to use the power of tragedy to build deep commitment and engagement, and the quality of the reflection that occurs is a testament to the learning that is happening.

Not surprisingly, observers are impressed with the depth of Dorothy's approach in particular examples of her teaching, but when one considers the whole picture of her work abroad, one is struck by the breadth of topics, dramatic genres and educational contexts. There seems to have been no theme too difficult for her to handle, no theatrical style outside her range of skills, no abnormality of human kind with which she could not empathise. Dr. Norah Morgan of Brock University, one of the most astute observers of her work other than Dorothy's own students was struck with Dorothy's use of drama for learning. Norah, originally a teacher of Math before moving on to Drama, welcomed Dorothy's deliberate creation of opportunities for reflection. Norah writes that the fashionable, experimental drama in Ontario in the 1970s seemed to be about 'lying on my back listening to the sound of my own breathing or wandering round the room with my eyes shut, thinking and wondering where was the learning'. She contrasts this lack of clear purpose with a lesson of Dorothy's she observed in St. Catharines:

> Dorothy was guest of honour at a conference in Brock University, Ontario where she gave a wonderful keynote followed by a workshop with twenty-five 7/8yr.olds. They decided to do medieval times. Dorothy took on the role of a guard armed only with a spear against a mob of people demanding to see the King. It was a remarkable example of Learning through Drama. All but one child was actively participating. The one looked on biting his nails until he sat on my lap as the only white-haired person there! He was involved and Dorothy checked on us occasionally in role never breaking from the learning within the drama. I was fortunate to see some of the reflective work done by the students on the Monday following the experience. One thing sticks in my mind, 'It was better when we were reasonable and not shouting'.

Dorothy caught up in political events

Political issues often offered themselves as material for drama. Perhaps the most uncomfortable for Dorothy – that also happened in Alberta – concerned what would happen if Prime Minister Trudeau were killed at a banquet. What had prompted this was the anger of the Albertians at being deprived of their oil revenue.

Dorothy recalls being in North Carolina at the time of the bi-centenary. Prickly topics such as Watergate or the freeing of slaves required delicate handling, especially the latter subject with a mixed class of black students and white. A neat, analogous transfer to a villa in Roman times with the Greek slaves working the vineyards allowed pertinent questions to be faced and the Greek slaves –

arbitrarily chosen for their roles – found themselves, once freed, asking the questions that all newly freed peoples have asked: 'Where do we go now?'

On another occasion in Evanston, this time coinciding with July 4[3], the War of Independence became a literal battleground between Dorothy as a governor representative of King George and a politically informed over-zealous nine-year old as rabble-rouser. As B.J. Wagner puts it: ' ... he is quite prepared to start the war and end it in the next ten minutes'. Dorothy working day after day with this class – Marianne was part of it – subtly changed the role of this active youngster from thoughtless knower of all the answers to thoughtful collector and collator of evidence against this tax-cheating governor.

The work in Israel, preparing adolescents to perform with actors from the Habimah Theatre, Tel Aviv, was related to sub-text exercises on a script – a bitter remembrance of the Nazi attempt to destroy Poland's Jewish population – to be performed by the joint cast of young people and State actors at the end of the week. It became for Dorothy a different kind of reminder. When she attended the performance the evening before she left, she found herself sitting in a packed auditorium, engulfed by an expression of grief from the audience that she could not be part of. We all know that when in drama or any other art form we try to capture the pain of another's political situation, we can never get inside, however much we may think we empathise with the problem. And here was Dorothy, as members of the audience stood with tears running down their cheeks at the end of the performance, an intruder, an outsider. Her commitment had been to technical excellence; she did not, could never, belong to that communal expression of remembered pain.

There was one country where politics nearly became a barrier to her visits. This was South Africa in the 1980s, during apartheid. The British left-wing organisation, SCYPT [The Standing Conference of Young People's Theatre] wrote her a rude letter saying that she should know they disapproved of her recent visit to that outlawed country and that she should not go again. She replied that as her visit was the result of a meeting with three educationists – a black, an Afrikaner and an ex-Brit – from South Africa at her own dining room table and as it was always a condition of her visits that she taught or addressed a multiracial audience, she would be going again.

The black educationist was surely one of the most remarkable of Dorothy's students, whose own life story shows her as a determined fighter of apartheid: Bernadette Mosala, a South African teacher caught up in but not beaten by its political régime. She had somehow persuaded the authorities years earlier to let her attend Dorothy's Advanced Diploma course. Having queued for three days to get a passport, Bernadette eventually arrived in London without much money and little sense of where Newcastle University was. In Dorothy she found a friend, teacher and mentor. She says of Dorothy: 'I learned from her that life is a gift from God, not to hold for ourselves, but to do something for others.' Dorothy and other students, particularly Dorothy Loftus, a teacher of exceptional skill in teaching Shakespeare, kept in touch with Bernadette when she returned to South Africa – and then Bernadette just disappeared. Enquiries by Dorothy Loftus failed to uncover anything. Eventually, after many months of silence, Bishop Tutu took up the search and found her in a prison. He left a Bible for her, but she was never given it. Eventually she was released, having been subjected for long periods to water torture on her head. Free again, she found ways to return to England to study further with Dorothy, even though on one of her return flights she had to pretend to be a 'sick' maid of a white passenger – another of Dorothy's students, Paddy Terry, who is now active in post-apartheid South African education. And here Bernadette was, back at Dorothy's dining table, helping to plan Dorothy's return to South Africa. How small the wisdom of an organisation like SCYPT appears to be at first sight in the light of Bernadette's first-hand understanding of what South Africans needed – they needed Dorothy to return. Yet, looked at in the broader political perspective, it could be argued that any visit at that time by the British appeared to give support to a régime that was merely papering over the cracks by making a few token concessions to the 'coloured' and black people.

The formation of the South African Association for Drama and Youth in 1979, embracing all nationalities, with Esther von Ryswick of Capetwon one of its great pioneers, allowed drama teachers from England to visit and work with mixed audiences. Dorothy's teaching in South African schools in 1985 caused much excitement among the teaching profession but also headaches for teachers whose timetables bound them to just one hour a week for their drama classes. Doreen Feitelberg, then a leading member of the South African Guild of Speech and Drama, explains:

> She had an amazing ability to take any idea that was offered to her and to build a whole series of lessons from that stimulus. In her intuitive way she added layer upon layer, dissecting, extending and defining until the main focus of the lesson was totally clear. When she prepared a specific lesson we were impressed with the letters, documents, diaries, maps and articles she used to add authenticity and truth to her investigation. She said of herself, 'If you had to write anything on my tombstone, you'd say: She broke everything up into little bits.' She took her time to incorporate those 'little bits' but some teachers found that method too laborious. They wanted the lessons

to develop more briskly and were not used to spending so much time on one theme. We could see how, in a school environment, one could take weeks and even an entire term over one lesson. Some teachers, who met their classes for only an hour a week, were not entirely convinced that they could sustain their students' interest over such an extended period. It was clear that we all needed to reconsider our goals and the validity of what we were teaching.

The enfranchisement of all citizens in South Africa in 1994 brought a new sense of hope to people such as Bernadette Mosala, who made an ecstatic phone call to Dorothy the very day she voted for the first time.

Further anecdotes of Dorothy abroad

For another destination, the School for Officers' Children in Hongkong, Dorothy had to be given the honorary rank of Lieutenant Colonel – not, Raymond pointed out deflatingly, the highest of ranks! – in order to qualify for residence in the mansion for officers. She enjoyed her two weeks work, one session with the school's pupils and later in the day with the teachers. With a past student who dropped in each day, she would visit local markets where there was an abundance of fabrics. She could not fail to notice that each afternoon when she returned to her room in the mansion she would meet a somewhat inebriated officer who would stare at her with a mixture of quizzicality and befuddlement as he made a calculated descent of the stairs. She even coped with an officers' get-together, nibbles of cheese with wine not being her scene, even without her embroidery to hide behind! It was in polite conversation at this party with two army psychologists that she asked whether there was a special unit provided for slower learning children. 'We don't have any', they replied, 'we send such families home'.

Everyone who employed Dorothy was impressed with her sheer hard work and how normal course timetables were stretched or even ignored. Anne Thurman describes the arrangements for Dorothy's first six-week course in Evanston. A working day would include: a workshop session with thirty-six drama teachers, 8.00-11.30 in Washington School; a dash to Northwestern University to lecture students from 12.00 to 1.00, while others had a lunch break; a whisk back to the drama teachers to give a 1.30-4.00 session. And either side were tutorials before 8.00 a.m. and after 4.30 p.m. – and meticulous preparation work in the evenings for the next day. Some years later when she was running a similarly patterned course, she was staying with the Wagners. Anne goes on:

At a party one evening, someone asked B.J.'s husband, Durrett, where Dorothy was dong her teaching that summer, meaning was it at National-Louis University where B.J. taught or at Northwestern where Anne taught. Durrett quipped: 'At breakfast, lunch and supper!' She was constantly 'on', sharing her wisdom and her stories to the delight of everyone who was privileged to be with her over a meal.

Always appearing to be fit, people expected Dorothy to cope with strenuous timetables and exhausting travel. There was one time she recalls, however, when she was to work with young children in Evanston for four days – coinciding with half-term at home. Sitting eating grapefruit in Anne Thurman's house on the first morning, she announced that the sides of her neck were swollen and she thought she had mumps. Off to Anne's doctor, they both knew the impossibility of can-celling a whole programme of teachers who had been given leave of absence and classes of children arriving to be taught by the lady from England. 'She's leaving on Tuesday,' offers Anne, hoping the doctor would read her sub-textual instruc-tion as he felt Dorothy's offending glands. 'I think you'd better ... see your doctor when you get back', responded the obliging doctor. And the planned programme was carried out – no adolescent boys in her classes! The mumps turned out to be mild and Dorothy, armoured with a daily aspirin, gave her all.

Whatever classes she taught abroad for a programme of several mornings or afternoons, she would provide each child with a gift, at the end of the series, usually one she could make at night and which was relevant to the theme of the week's drama – an apple, or a mineral or a related message, a souvenir to take away. Selecting gifts as reminders of a shared experience has always been Dorothy's way of marking her appreciation. In my own house there are all sorts of mementos, carefully chosen, that are delightful echoes, sometimes amazingly apt, of some work we have done together. She always gives thought and time to gestures of this kind.

On one occasion on her travels she herself was given a memorable gift of an un-usual kind. One of the lecturers at Northwestern University was an expert in Inuit culture and she had asked him, because he wanted to repay her for some extra lectures she had done for him with his students, if sometime, he would recite some Eskimo poetry for her. Unexpectedly, at the end of one of her public lectures, he asked her to stay seated on the stage and he proceeded to deliver, pumping out the words at a pitch that was nearer to singing than reciting, his eyes riveted on hers, a whole programme of poetry reading. And the huge audience who remained were spellbound by his public offering of such a gift to their lecturer. She was both awed and embarrassed, but as she says today 'I wouldn't have missed it for the world'.

Not all Dorothy's work abroad included demonstration classes. Occasionally she would do a one-off lecture. Carole Tarlington still smiles when she recalls a seminar in Vancouver

> I arranged for Principals to come from near and far to listen to her talk. We filmed Dorothy on this occasion and the film begins with her audience looking bright and alert and interested. What it doesn't show is coffee arriving at 10:30 a.m. Now, there is something that is sacred to Principals and teachers in general and that is the *coffee break*. However, Dorothy just went right on, past the coffee break, talking and drawing diagrams as usual without notes of any kind and in the film you can see the audience has become at first incredulous (She's *not* stopping for coffee!) then glazed over. Sometime in hour two of her speech when we had already gone into lunch-time, Dorothy suddenly stopped, turned to her audience and said, 'Am I boring you? I hope not. I never bore myself!' and not stopping for breath, she went right on. It was very funny.

B.J. Wagner was the first educator to take Dorothy's work seriously enough to make an in depth analysis of her work, but as Dorothy became welcome in other countries, many publications appeared that acknowledged an indebtedness to her. One has only to name people such as Kathleen Warren, John Carroll, John O'Toole and Philip Taylor of Australia, and Norah Morgan, Juliana Saxton and Kathleen Berry of Canada as examples of writers abroad who have come under Heathcote's influence. Mention should be made too of the profound impact Dorothy's work made on Scandinavian countries,where a number of publications refer to and are even dedicated to Dorothy Heathcote.

Kathleen Warren is an interesting example of someone who was already an established lecturer in Early Childhood education and who virtually stumbled across Dorothy's work in 1979. When she attended a conference in Sydney she learned that there was to be a film called *Three Looms Waiting* screened that afternoon. She writes: 'I could see nothing else at the conference that attracted me at that time ... so I went.' And her professional life changed. She came over to England to study with Dorothy, wrote a highly commended doctoral thesis on drama and early childhood, published her book, received invitations to give one-off lectures and demonstrations of drama in America and Europe and now is part of the 'drama family' who visit the North-East of England whenever she and her husband can manage it. Juliana Saxton, in describing her own response to Dorothy, perhaps speaks for many who have chosen to follow her:

> Dorothy was a masterly painter of drama. The way in which she wound us into the stories we had chosen to explore was, to me, similar to the paintings

of Rioppelle: splashes of colour, covering a large canvas and full of movement and power. And yes, it looked as if anyone could do that: just throw paint about and come up with the same results. How long it took us to discover all the painterly skills she possessed, allied to her pedagogy that continues to astonish. How far she has brought us and what a huge sense of responsibility for the work she has given us all.

Notes

1   John Fines and Raymond Verrier, in *Drama and History* New University Education, 1974, acknowledge their 'embarrassingly clear' debt to Dorothy Heathcote, but the book is an account of their own team teaching, not Dorothy's. Cecily O'Neill and Liz Johnson were the first in the UK to put Dorothy into book print with their *Dorothy Heathcote: Collected Writings on education and drama* [Hutchinson] published in 1984, some 33 years after her appointment to Durham/Newcastle University

2   *Dorothy Heathcote: Drama as a Learning Medium* National Education Association, USA by Betty Jane Wagner, 1976

3   This episode on the War of Independence is described vividly by B.J. Wagner in her book on Dorothy

8

Mantle of the Expert takes centre stage

'Mantle of the Expert has been the best teaching frame I have ever come across and it keeps revolutionising my approaches to training and teaching', writes Luke Abbott, Senior Adviser for Teaching and Learning, Essex LEA.

In Chapter Six, 'A sea-change' I described how Dorothy's students were expected to spend a great deal of time in non-school environments such as hospitals for the severely handicapped or criminal institutions for boys or young men. The second part of that sea-change took her back into schools, but accompanied by a 'full role', to be gazed at, pondered on, and interacted with. What happened next moved her students along a fundamentally different route, one that will take the rest of this chapter to explain. And to do that, I find myself adopting a profoundly different style and language. You might feel that you are suddenly trapped into reading an educational textbook. 'What happened to the biography?' you might reasonably ask. I can only plead that what follows represents the very centre of Dorothy's commitment to education. Mantle of the Expert is her biography.

A cell for change

Question: Which room in a school would you say comes closest to Dorothy Heathcote's vision of education?

Answer: a science laboratory.

The character of such a room defines the activities that go on there. The room dictates behaviours to do with clustering round work-benches for the purpose of setting up trial experiments, making observations, recording the results and communicating findings. Sadly, we know that much teacher/learning time even in such a setting actually works against the laboratory's intended character – for instance, the benches become desks on which to write notes copied from the board and a teacher stands at the front and tests the pupils' knowledge of the subject. There may not be a front, but the determined teacher manufactures one, trying to turn the room into an ordinary classroom in which a teacher has high status and pupils low status. Thus a school's laboratories only partially meet her ideal. A real lab in a real commercial or university setting, on the other hand, fulfils the image better, for when you enter such a lab you bring in your knowledge and training with you and take on the mantle of responsibility that goes with the character of the setting. Above all, you know that the result of what you do there will matter to someone other than yourself. Such settings are cells effecting change in society. And this, according to Dorothy, is what an educational establishment should be, an institution contributing to the welfare of the local community and the environment.

Dorothy points out that children in the 18th and 19th centuries were exploited and put to work down coalmines. This misuse of children's ability nevertheless established their usefulness to society, a function that has been removed from them since laws rightly prevented such employment. We have replaced this abuse with an education system that requires children over many years to be content with an absence of status, to feel useless, to exist in a limbo of learning which relies solely on the de-functioning maxim that 'one day, you'll be good enough to really do it' but never today.

Ever since she started to think seriously about the nature of education, Dorothy has been exasperated by the cultural disenfranchisement of school pupils and students. And the older she gets the more exasperated she becomes. She sees our educational system as based on a false premise, that education is to be a waiting room, not a laboratory. She has set herself passionately to erode this sterile functioning. This is her life's mission. That she happens to be a drama teacher becomes almost irrelevant in the light of this greater crusade. This is why she finds herself driven to claim to a group of teacher observers that she is not teaching drama, that it is children she is interested in, a remark that sounds silly and pretentious to the audience who have just witnessed some wonderful drama. Even those of us who knew her well could not fathom why she was being coy about her artistry. We were not ready to take in that she was setting about challenging the accepted educational code.

In the mid 1970s, she tentatively took a direct step towards undermining the established educational culture, using her own specialism to do so. She wanted all teachers to experiment with her ideas, whatever their subject areas. She tried to find a way of opening doors for children to make some link with the community and to take a degree of responsibility for their own learning. She hoped that Science teachers, Geography teachers and Language teachers would also find their way, using their subjects to do this. Hers was a drama way, and she labelled it 'Mantle of the Expert'.

Arriving at this new approach was instinctive and uncertain at first. Being Dorothy, she had to find herself doing it in order to find out what she was doing, and then she had to articulate it for others as well as for herself – never her strongest point. Her first question to a class had most often been 'who shall we be?' and the fiction that followed was generated by whatever roles were chosen. Her first sea-change switched to 'read this picture' and the fiction became generated by a small group of adult actors who invited a class of severely disabled people to join in their rituals. A further change required the fiction to be generated by one adult in role and the question to the class became: 'what initiative do we have to take to understand this person?'

The most significant change in Dorothy's approach came when she pondered on whether the fiction could be generated not by stepping into someone else's shoes, not by attending to a still picture, not by awakening an adult in role, but by the setting. Supposing this classroom takes on a role. Supposing it were to become a laboratory, or a factory or an advice bureau or a travel agency or any place that implies: 'people in here are committed to carrying out tasks'. Such a fictional labelling of the setting dictates the function of those in it, teacher and pupils alike: 'we are the people who work in this laboratory, factory etc.' And Dorothy has thus found a fictional setting that, at least partially, matches her vision of education, that automatically redirects pupils along channels of purposefulness, responsibility and industry. What these pupils do in their classroom will not be just getting ready for one day; they will be working now, honouring a contract to whatever clients the fictional setting generates. And they are barely in role; it is the setting that carries the role and defines how they are to function. They have to agree to go along with this, treating each other as colleagues in an enterprise, not as characters in a play.

For example ...

Let us look at some examples of this Mantle of the Expert approach. Eileen Pennington, a Northumberland drama leader of considerable expertise and experience was intrigued by the potential of Mantle of the Expert that Dorothy had been promoting for some years. The two of them set up a teaching programme, five days of four hours a day, with Middle School students at an educational centre in Morpeth, where Eileen worked. Present were also a small group of teachers for whom it was a training course. It was planned from the beginning as a Mantle of the Expert project so that a great deal of thought beforehand could be put into choosing the 'enterprise', the setting to generate the fiction, that would be appropriate for the educational objectives.

In this instance, only one overall focus for learning was chosen for the exercise – the significance of ritual in people's lives. Often, in Mantle of the Expert, a range of objectives covering many aspects of the curriculum may be catered for and indeed if the work had been over a longer period, perhaps half a term, a whole term, or even – Dorothy's ideal – a full school year, the whole curriculum could be met. The only project in which Dorothy reached that ideal was with the 'Shoe Factory' in Broadwood Primary School, but this, of course, was done by her as a visitor with the help of staff. We do not know of any regular teacher who has managed to conduct a full scale M of E in her own school.

If the Morpeth project was to be about 'ritual', then the young people's activities should be concerned with processes that might become ritualised or at least have ritual connections. Thus it had to be an enterprise where key actions are repeated. For this reason such settings as an advisory service, a support group, an agency or a training school do not seem to fit. It has to be a setting where some product is made ... where the making processes are few and clearly identifiable – and shared. And it had to be not just any old product but something valued, something that could have the kind of resonance one would want to hold rituals about. And if the meaning of the rituals is to be examined by the class, then the product must lend itself to the exotic, the unusual, something not readily understood and taken for granted for, as Eileen suggests, the mere repetition of a ritual action will not necessarily reveal its meaning. The actions themselves must be sufficiently mystifying for the children to seek an explanation.

What kind of product, Dorothy and Eileen asked themselves, lends itself to a need for interpretation? Something remote from their own culture, something with a history. Ah yes, says Dorothy, Taoist followers burn paper money as an offering to the dead. And if this is to be the rich source for pondering on the meaning of ritual, what should the setting be? The logical answer appeared to be a factory making hand-made paper, in Britain but with Chinese contacts. A British firm will be supplier to this religious sect.

Dorothy and Eileen settle for this and their first step now is to devise the setting that will become the fiction. The drama space in which the teaching is to take place is to become – take on the role of – the *PaperKraft Factory*. Eileen set to making all the signs that would say to the class: (1) we are working here today and there are tasks of many different kinds related to hand-made paper awaiting our attention (2) we are carrying on a tradition of a firm that goes back two generations (3) we have a wide variety of customers to satisfy, including many from abroad. Thus three visual aspects of the setting – evidence of tasks; evidence of firm's history; evidence of customers – create the behaviour of the participants. The space itself, with its newly labelled areas of 'Manager's Office'

[Mrs. Heathcote] and 'Secretary's Office' [Mrs. Pennington] and tables set out for the workers with all the paraphernalia of pens, crayons, rulers and paper needed for today's task, a large drawn coffee urn on the wall of 'the canteen' and coat/car key pegs in the 'entrance hall' and so on, help to carry the burden of the fiction. And other signs, mostly made for the children, accumulate as the mornings go by: working rosters, holiday plans, canteen menus, rules and regulations, business documents and tax forms etc, all prepared by the Secretary, combine with the workers' own designs for a bird-watchers certificate, doily edgings for plates at funeral teas; bookmarks suitable for books given as birthday presents; wedding invitations and 18th birthday invitations; announcement of birth of a baby and announcement of a death; new board game called *Rituals of the Cave Planet* etc. Together, the visible preparations of the Secretary and evidence of half-completed or completed tasks by the employees create the signs of an ongoing *PaperKraft Factory*.

The children are not in role in any obvious sense, but the leaders of Mantle of the Expert, Eileen and Dorothy, provide a model of factory behaviour, thus extending the fiction initiated by the setting. They write[1]: 'We (secretary and manager) spent a lot of time demonstrating our *in*expertness while sustaining the energy and power of the children to solve the various problems the business generated. Eileen as secretary could 'lay her hands on old records, files and orders' but as they had been used 'before she came here' she could not quite know what they meant! As manager Dorothy had a weak memory and not too firm a grasp of the technical details of the machinery.' Thus their modelling is deliberately flawed; Eileen and Dorothy must not become a source for answers.

The children are to function as adults in a world of employment and they are subjected by Dorothy and Eileen to 'colleague', not 'teacher', language. However, that does not guarantee that all children automatically submit to the fiction; there will always be uncomfortable times until the class is won over. They are not required to be in role in the usual dramatic sense, but must tacitly accede to the taking on of the expert mantle. Depending on the social health of the class and the appeal of the fiction, this will take time and may even fluctuate in commitment from day to day. Their commitment is built through carefully arranged group tasks, such as the designing of young birdwatcher's certificates to be carried out at their workbenches.

But this particular kind of M of E demands a further step from the class, one that takes them much nearer to the dangerous line of pretending. This is a factory that makes paper by hand and part of their work became, during the week, designing machines for the job, so they need to experience that central activity of paper-making. The moment they start trying to make paper, their lack of expertise will manifest itself. So, in keeping with ritual as a stated objective, it has to be a representation of the papermaking processes. Thus they have to learn about the making of paper *outside* the fiction. They can't be taught this within the fiction, for they are the experts, but it is something they can pick up sufficiently to behave as though they have been doing it all their working lives. This suspension of the fiction is a necessary convention so that matters can be discussed. For instance, in the first session, the class were able to put in their own ideas about how they wanted parts of their factory arranged. And so, within the fiction of being in the factory, they *perform* a created customary ritual of making high quality paper.

I have deliberately chosen words belonging to the dramatic art form such as 'representation', 'create', 'perform', for I am trying to convey a mode of behaving that the workers adopted as a historical/spiritual/product-making celebration. Such a shift into the art form was only appropriate because of the educational objectives. In another context, with different learning objectives, it would have been out of place.

For instance, in some work Dorothy did in New Zealand with a class of lower secondary pupils, they too had to replace skilled work with simulation, in that case not as a ritualistic representation but by genuine actions. Bamboo shoots were to be planted – the young people were, in fiction, taking on the responsibility of building a bamboo shield to protect the garden they were designing and creating. Up to this point in the sessions with Dorothy, they had been, as in most M of E activity, carrying out planning tasks on paper or interviewing people or reading up gardening manuals, all of which required them to employ skills they already possessed. But now they are to use 'pretend skills'. The very word pretend would make Dorothy cringe, but whatever it is to be called, this class are required to change from designing on paper to behaving as if they are planting. And in starting this action they visibly switched from doing thoughtful work motivated by the fiction of devising a sanctuary garden to being students in a 'drama class' putting on an act of dramatic behaviour. They obligingly get down on their knees to plant their shoots, giving their best performance of hard work. Dorothy knows that if she doesn't scotch this immediately, the honest endeavour achieved so far would quickly sink into spurious imitation. She chooses to give them her toughest Yorkshire accent, but, importantly, retains the 'we', as if she is being a tough member of the team who've got to get this done well. She is not Mrs. Heathcote, their teacher:

> **Don't** waste energy puffing and blowing
> That's all ... [with a dismissive wave of her hand] **dramatics**
> **Real** farmers don't

> They never waste energy on showing how well they're doing it
> We're not doing a miming exercise!
> **We ... are ... planting ... fields of bamboo!!!**

And the quality of their actions changes – they are *working* again, miming purposefully, with energy and without show. And integrity is re-established.

The length of time allocated to Mantle of the Expert is an important factor, the first session or two being used to lay down the chief features of the enterprise and give the students some opportunity to carry out tasks, both relevant to the factory work and to their ability. The timing of introducing the work that will directly lead to the major objective is critical. In the *PaperKraft Factory* it was towards the end of the second session that the letter from China 'arrived', thus beginning the part of the project that would lead to the study of Tao ritual. Just as in an entirely different M of E, a 'letter to the Monks from their Bishop about the designing of scriptorium for the execution of fine pen work', introduced in the third session, lead directly to a scientific study of light.

A critical aspect of M of E is that the work the students do must matter to someone, so there is always to be some kind of reporting or showing work in progress: in the paper factory they had a visit from an adult in role as Wing Tsit-Chan; in the sanctuary the students made their presentations of work to a Nun.

Sometimes Dorothy found herself trying to demonstrate the value of M of E in a reduced time, so that for instance the establishing of an enterprise with its own history would be overlooked in favour of moving on to the key curriculum area. In the early days when we realised Dorothy was switching drama styles, many of us thought that all she was doing was asking kids to play an expert role. This certainly appealed as less stressful and less risky than trying to reach moments of awe! All over the country one could find lessons beginning with a teacher inviting a class of 'detectives', 'psychologists', 'social workers', 'architects', 'councillors' or 'counsellors' to solve a problem. This work often had quality, but it only partially met Dorothy's conception of Mantle of the Expert. But B.J. Wagner has sent me an interesting example from her own writing workshops of how even this partial usage can release students into unexpected creativity. She learnt to invite her students to write in role. Cloaked in the mantle of expertise, they search for a wisdom within themselves and believe that there is a large audience of readers eager to read their newly wrought words. And B.J. makes sure that they read each other's work so that the writing class becomes 'as social and interpersonally cohesive as a drama class can be'.

Anne Thurman nicely captures the feel of Dorothy's Mantle of the Expert teaching. She quotes Dorothy's expert-endowing dialogue:

'So you are zoologists from New York zoo, the Cincinnati zoo and the St. Louis zoo; some of you know more about primates; others know more about nutrition.' They were to go to another country to deal with infestation. 'I have been called to tell you ... ', she would say in the middle role following orders from a higher authority. And so the kids, cast into an expertise they didn't know they had, are ready to get started.

Confident now of how effective M of E could be educationally, Dorothy might still begin a session with a group she did not know by asking 'what would you like to make a play about?', aware of the possibility of accepting their choice, but gradually channelling it towards an M of E genre. For instance, in Australia, one class insisted on a Western film-style shoot-out, only to discover that Dorothy, insisting as always that they face the consequences of their actions, turned them into morticians who had to bury their dead.

Sanctuary as mentioned above is another example of a drama undergoing its own sea-change. It started with a group of pre-adolescent pupils hammering on the door of an old house fronted with a high wall and a large iron gate in the middle of the night. 'Who's there?' from Dorothy could have been the start of a melodramatic, 'living through' drama, as she used to call it, especially if she had adopted her witch's cackle. But this 'who's there?' followed by an unemotional 'just a minute ... ' as she unlocks the door, is the voice of someone who is anxious about the unusual hour for sanctuary seekers although her vast experience as warden gives that voice a ring of professional authority. It does not come as a surprise that this warden speaks of sanctuary finances and problems of state subsidy for the homeless. And somehow, before they know it, a Mantle of the Expert experience is launched in which the youngsters demonstrate their skill, intelligence and ingenuity in devising a plan so that the sanctuary land could become productive. Over a week's sessions this somewhat giggly class become totally committed to tasks involving maths, science, technology and presentation skills.

In a New Zealand school, leading an extremely reluctant class of adolescents into choosing a topic for their play, Dorothy eventually asks: 'Do you want to decide how it should start or do you want me to start something for you?' and they nod their agreement that she should do their thinking for them. But then she adds: 'Shall I start *technically* or *philosophically*?' They have no answer to this one and within seconds they hear the first line of Dorothy's dialogue: 'Please gather round the radar screen'.

Dorothy would agree that drama is a matter of human affairs, but here, with her 'shall I start technically?' she is bringing a frame of mind to the making of drama that most of us would think of as the least productive. She is seeing human affairs as primarily dealing with *things*: how many? how big? how made? how monitored? how protected? how preserved? how controlled? and how treasured? When M of E is at its best, the students are researching, designing, categorising, conferring and reporting. They are sitting at tables, kneeling at the edge of some map, chart or plan, or sellotaping a display to the wall. And the deepest problems of humanity, ethical, cultural, political and spiritual, underlie these activities. Her sea-change is for better education.

Her enthusiasm for purposeful activity appeared on one occasion to blind her to a possible negative side effect. She had been asked by John Fines and Ray Verrier of Chichester to use drama to interest primary school pupils in Elizabethan architecture.

They had received an offer from the owner of a house built in that period who was prepared to let the children explore the house under supervision. Dorothy had not previously met the children and she asked John and Ray to provide a wheel-chair for her. They all met outside the house and the first glimpse the children had of Dorothy was of her being helped out of a car, placed in the wheel-chair and being lifted – John said it nearly broke his back – up the steps of the house. She had already written them a letter saying that she was thinking of purchasing this house but needed their advice in their role as experts on how it needed adapting for her and her wheel-chair. The children enthusiastically examined the house with an eye to its new owner and worked hard to make their recommendations before her departure. They learnt a good deal about architecture, but the trouble was they had been conned into accepting Mrs. Heathcote as a genuine invalid and buyer, for no-one had made it clear to them that they were all role-playing. John explained to me afterwards that when they learnt that it was only role-play, the children were very angry and didn't want to trust John and Ray again.

I began this chapter by quoting from an ex-student's of Dorothy's, Luke Abbott, an LEA adviser. When he was following Dorothy's course as a drama teacher at Stantonbury Campus Comprehensive School, Milton Keynes, he discovered the astonishing effect that a M of E approach to textual studies could have on examination results.

He gives me two examples in which 'an investigation' had to be conducted:

LORD OF THE FLIES
INVESTIGATORS INTO THE DEATH OF A BOY NAMED PIGGY AFTER A DEATH BED CONFESSION BY A MAN CALLED JACK, INSTIGATE CONTACTS WITH ALL JACK'S ISLAND ACQUAINTANCES, IN ORDER TO PUT THE RECORDS STRAIGHT (6th form in role as characters from *Lord of the Flies*)

LORCA'S BLOOD WEDDING.
BONES OF TWO MEN AND TWO KNIVES DISCOVERED UNDER AN OLIVE TREE PROVOKE A DOCUMENTARY TV COMPANY TO INVESTIGATE THE PAST (6th form Theatre Studies group and Yr 11s in role as characters from play)

Luke goes on to say that this teaching was often done by three teachers collaborating in the areas of Humanities, Drama and English. A huge leap in examination results of all three subject areas ensued. They discovered too just how important it was to have an audience to whom findings could be presented. Valuing the students' work is an integral part of Mantle of the Expert, as indeed it should be of all education.

A thin screen

The above heading became the title of a video made by Roger Burgess and Sandra Hesten of a course led by Dorothy and undertaken by Volkswagen Audi middle-managers, high-flyers in the industry. *A thin screen* became a metaphor for the role exercise that, in terms of the problems they had to face was only a shade different from their own work. That difference provided the key to the learning process.

Norman Morrison, in charge of personnel, which included organising their training, had chanced to see a BBC programme showing Dorothy at work with the primary school children in their shoe factory. One of the things he says he admires Dorothy for is her risk-taking, a feature not far removed from his own temperament when he invited her to work with top managers. At the time he was employed by the Northern Gas Board, who were facing a management crisis over the complex transformation to North Sea supply. I would love to know what these ambitious young men thought on being presented with Dorothy as someone who was to work with them each Friday evening for several weeks. It was some years later that Norman, having moved on to be head of personnel for all English-speaking regions of Volkswagen Audi, persuaded Dorothy, just retired, to be part of a three week course to be held in Germany, attending for two of the three weeks. It was felt by the firm that its product's success had led to a degree of complacency among the service staff of the industry and that the future would make more demands on management skills. Dorothy was given a clear remit: 'Can you get these selected middle-managers to look at themselves, and identify their own and other people's strengths and shortcomings?'

Having spent some years devising fictional enterprises for children of all ages, Dorothy was faced with people whose job was to run a factory and who knew far more about it than she did. Replication of their own industry would simply have rehearsed their day-to-day problems, but to move a shade away, or, better, a 'thin screen' away, they could carry out tasks in a fictional enterprise yet be aware of their own enterprise on the other side of that thin screen. Thus the Northern Gas managers found themselves advising the leader of an invented third world country about its economic resources and the managers of Volkswagen became business consultants, one of their tasks being to update the image of an old established [fictional] tarpaulin company.

Dorothy's preparation for both of these was meticulous. The tasks had to honour their professionalism. The video *The Thin Screen* shows the managers taking up the first set tasks with long-faced earnestness, until Dorothy, pricks that bubble of endeavour by deliberately showing her ignorance of some matter and adding, 'To think, I've been a bloody university lecturer all these years!' and they all laugh. She confirms that she's glad to see them laughing and that the work 'needs seriousness, not gloom'. After that they start to trust the work – and her. It is astonishing to observe the rapport she builds up with them over the two weeks. Norman Morrison writes to me in a letter:

> When the students arrived back at Heathrow after week two in Germany I was through customs first. I took the opportunity to find a place to watch them meeting their family and friends and I have no hesitation in saying DH had caused in every one of them change you could visually see.

> These managers who had left two weeks previous were different people on their return. I know that following the programme many changed their lives either jobwise or in relationships. Some I know wrote to her after the event and still, to-day, after many years, would still mention her as a conversation piece like Paul's conversion on the road to Damascus.

> Introducing her into Senior Management Training was always a problem from a programme perspective. When a programme is first proposed it is usually very carefully scrutinised with questions asked particularly regarding outside trainers. I have to say I always 'hid' DH. Looking from the outside it is/was difficult for Senior Management to see the relevance of DH. How do you explain her? Even after the courses, I found it difficult to explain and justify. However I was always rescued by the zeal of those who had had the experience. Literally last week I met a fellow guest on some of our programmes. He is an ADC to the Queen, held the rank of Col. of the Regiment, a keen educationalist etc., and almost his first words on meeting me were 'do you still see that Mad Mata Hari ?' He saw her in operation with others and never forgot it.

It is noticeable that Norman Morrison is using the language of psychological change, rather than improvement of skills or identifiable learning. He is claiming that people were 'different'. In his commentary for the video he speaks of Dorothy's finding a context for amalgamating the popular therapeutic systems of transactional analysis, neurolinguistics and gestalt. He claims that she has discovered a new paradigm for helping people to change. It is always of interest when professionals from outside our school or university education institutions offer an opinion about Dorothy's work. Norman has no vested interest either in promoting Dorothy or in advocating a particular educational policy. There is no hidden agenda in his expression of admiration for Dorothy's work. It is an outsider's honest reaction. That same degree of respect and admiration has also been expressed from time to time during her career by other professionals outside education, such as doctors, nurses, and the police.

So what is it about Dorothy's perpetual planning of tasks that attracts these people? Dorothy has the answer herself. The tasks are and must be fictional. At a visible, concrete level they demand normal intellectual application from whoever is carrying out the task, but at a subsidiary level there is a 'no penalty' awareness felt by the doer, a sense of freeing the individual, so that they may find themselves 'caught off guard' into identifying skills they did not know they had, into seeing some aspect of themselves in a different light, into revising the way they habitually think about themselves. They learn these new things privately, safely. This is the essence of drama as a tool for education. It releases new capacities. Thus the science teacher, the history teacher, or the teacher of any subject may see a pupil take a leap forward in understanding; the English teacher may observe the acquisition of a new skill; and the therapist may observe a new level of self-awareness. All these shifts occur because the context is dramatic fiction.

What Dorothy was offering those Volkswagen managers was a chance to take a look at themselves, but importantly this was manifestly not a public self-examination, an invitation to confess, or a touchy-feely trust exercise. Dorothy demonstrated over and over again that she had no interest in probing their inner selves. The result was that because she and the fiction made it so safe, many of the group found themselves sharing with each other and Dorothy some of the new insights that the work had evoked. This was work that had to be tackled, not therapy to be indulged in. This is the opposite of that other system that uses theatre – psychodrama. Dorothy requires her classes to apply their intelligence to reading signs and finding that the signs read them. 'Look at the signs', says Dorothy, whereas pyschodrama says: 'Look at me.'

Norman Morrison recognises the potential in this 'no penalty' way of helping people change. He writes as follows:

Finally, I appreciate that in her field she is well regarded though I have to say she could have had a greater impact if she had a) come out of Education and moved into Business and b) tried to 'package' the product so that it was more easily understood and was able to be taught to others in a structured way. When thinking of the DH product I am always reminded of the story of the process analyst asking the furnace foreman how did he know when the molten glass was 'ready' to which the foreman replied 'I just spit into it and depending on the sizzle I know whether it's ready or not'. That's DH! However as time proved eventually they were able to replace the foreman with a machine. I am not advocating replacing DH but I wish someone had the time and inclination to 'package' the product and then sell it because it is a unique product which would benefit many businesses and people.

It's a bit late now for Dorothy to move out of education into business, even supposing that she would ever wish to. Let's hope it's not too late for educationists and their political bosses, and those whose concern is to help people develop, to recognise that dramatic fiction releases new capacities. This should be the slogan for the 21st century. In the meantime, Norman Morrison has introduced into his enterprise a new paradigm for management training.

Chamber Theatre

Not that Dorothy single-mindedly pursues only one genre of drama education. While she was developing Mantle of the Expert, her attention had been caught by Reader's Theater in America. She subsequently introduced Breen's *Chamber Theatre*[2] to her M.Ed class and from there developed her own approach. Thus while moving along her non-theatrical enterprise path, she was also experimenting with the theatricalisation of literary texts.

I have not really been able to get a grip on Chamber Theatre, perhaps because I've never tried it or seen it in action. The structure is that a narrator speaks the text and others synchronise the actions. But that doesn't take me inside the genre. So today's interview turns into a tutorial around the dining room table. Dorothy begins with the reason for using Chamber Theatre, a deep study of life encounters. It may be because the class are literature students for whom the text appears off-putting or because they want to do drama with an immediate taste of success. The class begin as detectives – who is the narrator(s) and what vested interest does the narrator have for telling the tale? Nothing is ever changed of the author's words, but for the class those words have changed their position from arid stones on a page to become alive in the mouth of a person they have invented. The detectives now become directors, bringing their own understanding of the world to build the action pictures that those words appear to stand for.

Thus the 'reading game' has changed its focus, which is especially appealing to a disenchanted class.

The acting rules, too, have changed. Sitting on chairs until needed, the actors – it can be the whole class – rise and demonstrate the actions, and as they rehearse the timing needed to fit in with the narration, they inevitably bring an appropriate quality to their actions. They are not required to become the characters, to signal their feelings, to express the unspoken. Costumes and supporting props are important, for both the actors and the narrator(s). And sound effects and brief dialogue may be appropriate. But the actor's responsibilities in respect of bondings, motivations, thought processes and personalities are already given, carried by the author's text. More than one actor may represent the same character at different stages in a life or in a different place or as a mere memory. The game for the class is to invent and try out visual ideas to support this 'sacrosanct' text.

Obviously, the teacher's careful selection from the text has some bearing. Chamber Theatre in a school classroom – unlike Reader's Theatre in which whole novels may be presented – will deal in selected excerpts, perhaps from different points in the novel or poem or diary or essay to be studied.

Chamber Theatre may be utilised as part of M of E, since the experts could prepare some Chamber Theatre to illustrate certain points to the client. But the two genres are in important ways wide apart. In Mantle of the Expert the class are carrying out the responsibility they have to an outside client. They have a prescribed function. They are in a prescribed place, some place of work. The place, and their function in it, tells them who they are – and they don't have a teacher. In Chamber Theatre, the students are 'students doing Chamber Theatre – with their teacher'. In other words the two genres are expressions of two fundamentally different conceptions of education – unless you put them together, as Dorothy has done many times.

Nevertheless, Chamber Theatre is a godsend to the drama teacher or English teacher who merely wants to find an opening into a difficult text. Within her drama/English classroom, she can move along with this novel approach, without feeling she has to justify an innovatory philosophy of education to her head-teacher, her colleagues, herself or her students. Chamber Theatre looks like drama; Mantle of the Expert doesn't. This latter sea-change of Dorothy's requires teachers to undergo such a fundamental change of conception in respect of pupil/teacher power, such a high degree of planning and preparation, such a degree of confidence from the students, that one wonders how many teachers will risk it.

1 A detailed account of this work may be found in the Spring 1989 edition of the Australian, NADIE Journal
2 Breen, Robert S. 1986 *Chamber Theatre* Evanston Illinois William Caxton

9

An authentic University Tutor

'I always felt I was in the presence of a genius'. This is not over-the-top flattery from a wide-eyed sycophant. It comes from Kathleen Berry, a gifted Canadian teacher who, by the time she took Mrs. Heathcote's summer school course in Evanston in 1983, was a lecturer and academic of some standing. Steeped as she was in theories of phenomenology, she was astonished to find that the teaching of this woman from England somehow brought the printed page of *avant-guarde* academic knowledge into physical existence. Dorothy seemed to offer, in Kathy's words, 'deep structures of experiences that came through the way she organised and processed a drama experience for students'. It was as if phenomenology was made alive. Many people who have had the privilege of working with Dorothy have found in her work a practical manifestation of educational ideals. This chapter looks at the work of this esteemed visionary and genius as a tutor at the University of Newcastle until her retirement in 1986.

An erudite scholar

I use the word 'scholar' in the proper sense of someone who is seeking knowledge. Dorothy's capacity for delving into and absorbing writings on education and disciplines impinging on education has been immense. She is a searcher for ideas and many of the giants of educational literature, such as Dewey, Hall, Freire, Bruner and Polanyi, along with ground-breakers in related disciplines such as Freud, Mead, Buber, Richards, Jung, Rugg, Bales, De Bono and Hudson have provided her with ideas from which she has drawn selectively and sometimes idiosyncratically. How she uses these authorities is itself of interest. For one thing, she treats them not as authorities but as searchers like herself. Rarely does she lean on their writings for some self-authenticating quote, but rather uses them for pondering on and developing from. Very occasionally, she has fallen into an academic trap of inserting a quotation that is not going anywhere. For instance she tells us in one article that she is '...using the principle of *ostranie* defined by Viktor Shlovsky as being that of making strange' – but *ostranie* never appears again. Any reliance she has on these big names in education tends to be temporary. She needs them in so far as they offer her a way of saying what she herself is feeling but has not yet found her own way of articulating. She does not use these writers in isolation. They may well provide her with a handle with which to try out her latest thinking but she has a deeper, broader source of inspiration. To literary geniuses from William Blake to Doris Lessing she turns for wisdom; from visionaries such as Robert Pirsig and Alvin Toffler she seeks inspiration; and from the theatre, Stanislavski, Brecht, Growtowski, Tynan and Brook she gains references for her analysis of practice. Her knowledge of literature is vast but she has a line of interest that doesn't fit any of these categories: she will read books on science, engineering, archaeology and anthropology. Dorothy says:

> I exploit books. I have never revered them or stood in awe of them, or in their shadow. I use them as some use alcohol or dope – to get high on, to argue with, to be excited by. Some must be almost shouted into one's mind, others whispered with, in corners. I have that kind of imagination which gives words vocal texture as I read.

When she enters a classroom she brings a wealth of knowledge from many fields that she will patiently help her students pave the way to: she will never 'give' it, 'present' it, 'tell' it or ask 'teacher' questions about it – her way is to provide stepping stones.

> *When I turned up to interview Dorothy today she had started to pack her books into huge cases for collecting by a local second-hand book shop-owner or for transporting to the Dorothy Heathcote Archives, now based at Manchester Metropolitan University. Her library is extensive, for she would rather buy a book than borrow from a public or university library, a corner of academe where she never felt entirely comfortable. Letting all her books go is a sad but necessary step towards moving house. Some books she is keeping. Included in these is a massive collection of books for children that will be housed on the attic shelves Raymond built at their cottage in Steeton for granddaughter Anna to use in the future.*

When Dorothy puts pen to paper she has a wide range of authors from whom she enjoys quoting, so her articles are filled with a surprising number of references to other writers. Yet she openly scorns 'those detailed references so beloved of academics'. Indeed, a contradictory streak in her sometimes prompts her to adopt a false posture of apologetic regret that she fails to live up to standards expected of academia and yet at other times she relishes her separateness, her independence from its narrow strictures. Roger Barnes, an ex-colleague and friend, writes: 'If I had a complaint to make about Dorothy, it would be her residual self-denigration – I'm just a mill-girl whilst you are so well educated –

this strangely married to a disconcerting ability to detect low standards where-ever they may be concealed'. She knows in her heart that her strengths lie in her refusal to play the academic game. And this was one of the attractions of her courses. She wanted her students to be artists, not pedants. Heaven help any visitor to her course who attempted to pitch a discussion at the wrong level. David Davis, of the University of Central England writes:

> I took my students to work with her and her students once a year in the heady days when there was money for field trips ... I remember on one occasion she did something like use the words 'idea' and 'theory' as synonyms and I had the temerity (foolish in retrospect) to ask her if they did mean the same thing. Her reply was something like 'Oh you academics! We don't need to waste our time on that!'

Dorothy occasionally even struck an apologetic note about herself as a teacher. In Ken Robinson's *Exploring Theatre and Education* she writes:

> For a long time I have known that I am an amateur in educational circles. By this I mean that I always feel that, besides other people's thinking and talk, I stick out like a sore thumb. I read another book recently, however, and was immediately heartened by the realisation that my amateurishness comes from never having learned the language of depersonalisation.

It is also of interest to note what Dorothy does *not* read. Of the academic texts appealing to educationists in the 1960s and 70s, Jean Piaget's vast publications became the received wisdom of the time and a popular source for drama lecturers in teacher training who quoted from his work on play and intellectual development to gain academic approval. Dorothy, while liberally referring to other works in psychology, seemed to eschew Piaget. Did she know something we didn't? And as the trend began to favour the Russian psychologist, Lev Vygotski rather than Piaget, she also avoided quoting from him, although, curiously, she had Vygotski thrust upon her by left-wing theatre educationists who saw Dorothy's teaching as epitomising Marxist values. And there is a sense in which they were right, for they recognised that among her deepest passions is the need for justice in society. Leading left-wing figures in theatre and drama education such as David Davis, Warwick Dobson, and Geoff Gillham remained devotees of her work, although kinship with their political stance is not some-thing she ever acknowledged.

Unlike her fellow drama lecturers and advisers, Dorothy rarely read drama teaching books or articles – other than those of her own students. Among the many references she made in her own writings, one would be unlikely to find 'as Peter Slade says' or 'as Richard Courtney says'. She was not interested in the kind of packaging that such writers offer, even if, as in my case, I was often trying to give voice to her methodology without reducing it to a recipe. Following the occasion of my key-note address in Washington – referred to in Chapter Seven – I was amused when I tried to defend Dorothy's position over the cancer drama in Minnesota. A few months later, when my speech had been published, I called at Dorothy's house about some other matter. Oliver Fiala from Australia, opened the door to me, Dorothy standing behind his shoulder. Dorothy said she was so grateful for my Washington speech as she had been rather hurt that no-one present on the Minnesota course had responded to Margaret Faulkes' criticism. The editor of the Canadian journal to whom Margaret had sent her article had given Dorothy the chance to reply but Dorothy had preferred to leave that to others who had been there to defend her. Nothing had happened, so she was particularly grateful to me for taking up the cudgels. I was pleased with her response but its shine was diminished when later in our conversation I referred to some point in my speech and she looked at me blankly and then exclaimed: 'Oh, I haven't actually *read* it – Oliver has told me about it'.

While resisting the academic packaging of drama colleagues she paradoxically offers her own. She has always sought a vocabulary for her brand of drama teaching in the form of two distinct kinds of language: she resorts liberally to labels and charts. Her students find themselves trying to digest labels: brotherhoods, dramatic elements, frame distance, keying, sign, ritual, segmenting, twilight role, role conventions, domain, breeding, collage, anagnorisis, blurred genres, induction, the grace element, internal coherence, moment of awe, depicted time, bonding, productive tension, dramatic focus, cool strip, dropping to the universal. Listed like this, these labels look absurd. One can be sure that each one of them, at some point in Dorothy's career, has grown out of something real.

Nevertheless, there was a danger that students, faced in lecture or tutorial sessions with Dorothy's usage of such terms, felt that if only they could start using such vocabulary themselves, they would somehow gain an approximation to the philosophy and practice behind them. By sounding like Dorothy Heathcote, they would become her – I noticed that some even adopted her Yorkshire accent in the classroom! Dorothy was aware that her language caused problems. In an interview with Sandra Hesten, she confirms this: 'People often think I should be able to call things what other people call them. But I often think I've located something I don't have a name for. Then it gets systematised, and I hear it coming back as jargon, and I'm sorry'. I have not listed the above concepts in chronological order of usage, but in fact very few of her terms stuck with her. She would change her vocabulary as and when a new angle cropped up. Sandra Hesten, who took Dorothy's diploma course in 1972-3, writes: 'When I returned ten years later to write a dissertation on Dorothy, for my M.A. with Lancaster University, 1982-3, I was puzzled and frustrated to learn that I understood very little of her new terminology and what at first appears to be her very different approach to drama in education.' Her colleague Roger Barnes would sometimes sit in at Dorothy's sessions, but feeling at sea with her vocabulary, would rely on a student on the next chair to translate.

Dorothy also resorted to charts and diagrams as a way of helping herself think. Whenever she plans anything, her classifications of choices sprawl diagrammatically across a blank page, bold, precise and alive. Headings and subheadings terminate angled tracks, competing for prominence in a circle of possibilities. In a tutorial her talk is accompanied by these pencilled formulations so that the student both listens to Dorothy's talking and stares at a rapidly filling page. This has the additional advantage of creating a shared focus, breaking away from the usual hierarchical apprentice/master postures.

Mapping, planning, diagramming and charting her thoughts as they occur provide Dorothy with a visual classification of possible routes, but she goes further than this. She gradually started to use these same devices for encapsulating her whole rationale. There is a seeming contradiction here. Dependent on intuition, inspiration, the creative moment, the language of images, an inner sense of coherence, all the elusive components of artistry, she nevertheless develops a fondness for intellectualising her artistic integrity into circles of classification and flow charts. She is desperate to find a vivid explanation of how she works. That is the responsibility she has taken on. She must teach others. And this is where her wide reading is reflected, for the categories she uses to classify her methods are borrowed, often modified, from such authorities as Edward T. Hall, Erving Goffman or Michael Polanyi. She builds on others' theories. Kathy Berry says: 'I read Polanyi before I met Dorothy, but not until she converted his thoughts to a workable framework was I able to see the implications of his work for teaching drama'.

Dorothy likes best the kind of diagram that indicates relationships, that flows from one zone to another, giving differing weight to variables. One such chart, dealing with work/play relationship and teacher intervention, was created by her colleague Lesley Webb. Another, derived from Goffman, labels stages of involvement in a fictional event, 'Frame Distance', as she calls it. It is Goffman's conceptualisation that stands out as the principal basis for Dorothy's practice. Framing has stayed with her consistently throughout her academic career. It is never out of her mind when she is required to make decisions in the classroom. However, there are also 'brotherhoods', 'segments', 'modes of exposition', 'Laban's efforts', 'styles of teaching', 'Kuhn's paradigms'; 'Bales' interaction process categories', 'chart of enabling' and plenty of managerial charts from industry.

No student has complained to me of over-feeding with such categorisation of Dorothy's practice. It has probably worked out that the different years of the course favoured a fashionable few for study. For instance, one ex-student wrote that she found 'brotherhoods' very useful, and another said: 'She doesn't use 'brotherhoods' so much now – thank God!' Occasionally at large public lectures, Dorothy would get carried away with these visual presentations, projecting one after another onto conference centre screens for the benefit of delegates. It was as if she were saying: 'Well, if you insist on the absurd, unproductive formality of a key-note address, then I will thrust these at you and you can deceive yourselves into thinking that you are learning something'.

Nevertheless, some of these charts, studied separately and in context on her own course, have provided a practical, focused way of representing complex issues. She has found a visual language that can give the reader a firmer grasp than words would do of complex concepts – it's not a language with which some of her more insecure academic colleagues in the university could cope.

Putting together articles describing her methodology did not come easily to her. She always finished up feeling that words on paper somehow distorted the art and spirit of her work. Such was her frustration that when she was asked by R. Baird Shuman to write an article for *Educational Drama for Today's Schools*[1] she used a loose verse form, explaining to the editor that the manuscript 'is in this form because I'm tired of trying to take my language of metaphor (my natural tongue) and twist it up for right-handed people.' Her poetry began with:

> Someone said, 'Write me some words,'
> I said 'Yes, if I can.'
> 'By a certain date,' said that someone.
> 'Yes, if I can,' said I.
> The date is come. I am not ready, yet must fulfil the promise made.
> It has always been thus in writing myself down into print

And the environment for Dorothy's penning of the above? A hotel bedroom in Louisville, Kentucky. Baird's request had hung round her neck like an albatross. Suddenly having the idea of writing it as verse, Dorothy had searched for pen and paper. All she could find was a bundle of laundry lists you put outside the hotel room door for service and a thick black pen, thick enough to write over the print of the laundry instructions. By the time she got through a whole block of such stationery, her poem was finished.

She even manages to describe some actual lessons in verse. One of these essentially captures her artistry. The setting, in Jarrow, is a small group of young men, offenders on probation, suspicious of each other let alone Mrs. Heathcote, who is presented to them as their teacher for the afternoon. She describes it as follows

The action of the work – the outer form made manifest	The intention of the work. The matter of the action
The choice of place is a casino,	In the slow companionship
The game roulette	Of no pressure to act beyond
They sit around a large table resting on	The pushing of money forward;
their elbows and invent	All the men can slowly relax and test the
Outrageous amounts of cash to place upon	atmosphere,
the black and red	Like rats who swiftly hide in hole and hurry
Nothing ever moves, except their own	out of sight.
rough, red hard hands	If their security can be found for them,
Pushing imaginary amounts of money	They will stay 'to the next place'
Forward to the centre.	And I may earn the right to ask them
They share no eye contact, for they are	'What do you really do here in this casino?'
Not yet able to make such frank exchange	Not because I need an answer – that is not
In the presence of a 'teacher'.	my right –
The only words spoken are teacher's	But because I have the teacher's right to let
'Gentlemen, place your bets' in TV style	them ask themselves.
Never, in two hours	After this times comes (as each bet is
Does anyone move other than their hands,	placed)
Yet each man gradually declares	A tallying of their values and their ways of
Who brought him to this place,	life
And soon declares his hopes in winning	'invented' into the fabric of the 'play'
And the purpose in his life of what he wins	And in this manifestation some small
These words are as rough hewn	beginnings of reflection occur,
As the hands and faces in the room	Well hidden in the action and the exchange,
And no moral judgement clouds the view.	I hear 'loneliness' and 'no family' and 'needs
	of men' come into the space.

Dorothy was under pressure to write articles for journals worldwide. Editors of drama magazines got used to receiving wads of foolscap pages, penned with distinctive handwriting, crafted while fellow passengers slept or drank their wine on some flight across seas and continents. Her articles became precious sources for those who knew they had no chance of studying with her. Cecily O'Neill and Liz Johnson had the foresight to collect some of her writings into a book.[2] It became evident that she was not going to publish anything more ambitious – until her retirement, that is.

But where and how should Dorothy be placed philosophically? Kathleen Berry has come to my rescue, but even with her help I am not sure I can find a useful way of positioning Dorothy's genius. Dorothy's background, drawing as she does on a received cultural inheritance, is seemingly traditional and positivistic, but her spontaneous, open-ended practice leans towards postmodernism. She does not pursue feminine issues yet her identification with Gaian ideology is in part political. It seems we could go on listing conflicting tendencies. To today's generation, however, her work may seem politically conservative, in the sense that she does not explicitly attempt to change society. So is there a conceptual common ground? Kathy suggests it lies within the notion of 'contextualising'. Dorothy's work is about contextualising knowledge. She overrides subject distinctions, teacher specialisms and the limitations of curriculum objectives. In contextualising knowledge she re-orders the traditional teacher/learner relationship. Dorothy further gives emphasis to the common tool of all learners, the reading of sign. Her brush with the terminology of semiotics goes well beyond an analysis of theatre; she knows how reading sign and symbol is the very basis of our ability to make connections. I suggest, therefore that Dorothy's overall theory may be summed up as **being open to connections**, a phrase that I hope hints at an inherent contradiction.

Dorothy Heathcote, member of staff in the School of Education, University of Newcastle-upon-Tyne

There was in the 1970s an uneasy merging of two departments. The Institute of Education, with its handful of staff tutors responsible for in-service training, was absorbed by the much larger Department of Education whose staff ran Post Graduate Certificate in Education [PGCE] courses for graduates who had already followed three years of study in a specialist subject, usually a subject that was part of a secondary school curriculum. The combined departments were given the new title of School of Education. It was not a happy marriage. As Professor Tony Edwards, Dorothy's boss from 1979 put it: 'There was, both literally and metaphorically, an upstairs-downstairs structure. Upstairs, on the second floor, were the real academics, and below, on the first floor, were the trainers, teaching the Advanced Diploma and related courses'. He continues: 'My guess is that Dorothy was seen from above as the prime embodiment of the non-academic'. It caused some, not always stifled, indignation when Dorothy invaded their higher degree territory by changing her course from Advanced Diploma to a Master's degree [M.Ed.] or for those that did not have an initial degree, a B.Phil. But they were on their guard, these 'grey men' as Dorothy called them. Weapons at the ready, they were prepared to fire, for instance, at her examination questions, ridiculing their lack of academic integrity. No doubt they eyed the qualifications of her chosen examiners with suspicious diligence, but with names like John Fines and John West, they could find no weakness there.

When her first degree course was about to be launched, Dorothy anticipated the extra investigation to which her work would be subjected. She spent hours in the library reading past examination questions and then in her free time in Evanston where she was teaching during the summer, she drafted out some fifty questions which Anne Thurman typed out for her. Sure enough, on her return to the department, a rather sheepish request came from a man who was to hold the higher degree committee chair for that year: 'Would Dorothy, sometime, let him see her examination questions?' He had clearly been put up to this by other members of the committee and was feeling embarrassed. 'When?' asks Dorothy. 'Oh, whenever you can get them ready ... ' 'They are already done' says Dorothy – and they arrived in his office next day, models of scholarship.

Opposition to Dorothy became entrenched, but the grey men generally failed in their battle, for there was usually someone present at examination meetings who was prepared to back her. This was often the philosopher lecturer, Roger Barnes, who sometimes felt cross because he found himself defending her in her absence. Much as she tried to attend, it was not always possible. The meetings were always lengthy, but she knew she ought to attend for the sake of her students. When she did manage to be there her questions were always kept to the last. She recalls one question being condemned as 'not up to higher degree standards'. It was a short piece of literary text that the examinees were required to translate into theatre form, step by detailed step exposing the fundamental differences between the two genres. As fellow committee men carefully re-scrutinized the offending question and began to shake their heads at what they assumed was its undemanding character, a woman's voice broke in with 'I've listened to three hundred questions this morning and this one is harder than any of them. Anyone who thinks this is not up to M.Ed standard wants his head seen to'. Dorothy was grateful and enjoyed the discomfort of the grey men.

Had they known, the grey men involved in checking questions included in Dorothy's later courses were in fact staring at what they would have seen as a flagrant disregard of examination regulations. The evidence of rule-breaking was there in front of them. What they did not know and Dorothy was going to make sure they never did was that the questions had been prepared by the candidates themselves. To those of you who work in progressive educational institutions this will seem to be common sense, but to Newcastle University this would have been a horrendous flouting of the foundations of traditional scholarship, indulgent, unethical and almost criminal. Dorothy had a special reason for allowing this, one that she knew the department would not have understood. Her students were mostly professional people, experts in their field, from varied vocations and cultural contrasts. The course for which they were giving up so much time and money must satisfy the professional and personal needs of each one. Whereas the choice of dissertation could cater for their work-related interests, there was a serious danger that the traditional examination format could fail to make connections.

So Dorothy asked students to draft out a number of questions of relevance to their professional specialities and then she would adjust the wording to the expected style of the examination. The students, grateful that the examination paper connected with their professional work, knew without it ever being stated that this was something that had to be kept to themselves. It nevertheless provided Dorothy with a niggling worry that one day she might have to justify this to the grey men, although according to Roger Barnes, they more and more kept their scepticism about her academic ability to themselves as they realised she was a huge money earner for the University, bringing in a flood of foreign students. As Roger puts it: 'Latterly, the attitude of colleagues changed. This was not because they acquired a new regard for her work. No way! But they had to admit she brought in the cash'.

One of the academic problems was having to guide her students in the writing of dissertations. Some of them were better at it than she was and she gave them her blessing, but some needed help and she was not herself always sure of what kind of writing would meet regulations. On the other hand she was often determinedly confident in guiding them towards a topic. Derek Stevens writes:

> Typically the area of my dissertation was decided unilaterally by her, as she baked, while I sat on the kitchen steps at Highburn House [in fact, the site of many far-reaching moves in my life since 1969]. 'I know that I'm bull-dozing you, but I know I'm right' was her concluding sentence in this tutorial. I've learnt to surrender to this kind of vision that appals me at the time but comes out sure and firm and proper in praxis.

But Dorothy was sometimes at a loss when it came to translating into the icy language and format of academia. Her great friend and soul-mate Oliver Fiala came to the rescue. He read some of her students' drafts of dissertations and helped her see how the personal element could be retained while still satisfying academic requirements. Oliver, an emigrant Czech, was Professor of Drama in the University of New South Wales. He had never heard of Dorothy until he picked up an old magazine during a long flight from Perth to Sydney and tried reading an article, torn in half, about an English woman who taught drama. Even with half the page (longways!) missing, he knew he wanted to meet her, seeing her as a 'Brecht' of education. Indeed he published an article on that subject. He is one of the two friends who have been able to inspire Dorothy professionally.

Dorothy, her mother and Old Sarah 1966

Dorothy with Marianne, aged five, at Highburn House 1971

Dorothy, entertained by her five year old daughter 1971

Summer 1981

In their garden at Highburn House 1991

How's this for a likeness? Dorothy and Marianne 1993

Dorothy and Raymond 1998

Life is full of surprises at Highburn House 2000

The other was John Fines, whose imaginative telling of stories from History, she recognised, matched her own combination of artistry and scholarship. With both men she experienced an affinity in their shared field of expertise. With Oliver, this was accompanied by a warm companionship that Dorothy valued.

Even before her Master's courses started Dorothy experienced suspicion and put-downs from certain colleagues. For instance John Crompton of the old department of education, a man who should have seen her as a potential ally for his speciality was 'English with responsibility for Drama' simply dismissed her work. Indeed, in his own M.Ed thesis on drama education he cynically gives a chapter the title of 'Drama as Mrs. Heathcote' and concludes it with perhaps the most absurd statement ever to appear in a higher degree dissertation: 'What she does differs little from Slade's practice'. At staff meetings he would make snide remarks such as 'Even I don't understand what Dorothy's talking about'.

And there was opposition that Dorothy did not know about, that went on out of her hearing. According to close colleague Lesley Webb, a distinguished expert in the education of young children, even one or two of the original Institute staff were jealous of Dorothy's reputation and consequent travelling. Behind her back the mandarins, as Dorothy and Roger Barnes called them, made things difficult for her. This was relatively easy to do, for Dorothy's place of work was always some distance from the school of education. Indeed Dorothy was the only member of staff not to be given an office of her own – not that it bothered her. A largish hall or a large lecture room had to suffice. This was fine for drama workshop type activity, but here was an esteemed senior lecturer whose phone conversations, interviews and tutorials were held in the corner of a semi-public space, a space offering no shelves or lock-up desk for her books and papers. According to Roger Barnes, the room at 42 North Road 'was in a dreadful state of repair, and the teaching area was heated by one or more ancient gas stoves which put the fear of God and carbon monoxide into everyone who worked there'.

Roger went over the head of the department boss and arranged for the stoves to be repaired, for he knew Dorothy would never complain. He recognised that sticking up for her dues or her rights had no part in Dorothy's psychology. Just as she was prepared to teach drama in any kind of space in a school – assembly hall, gymnasium, corridor, school yard or under a tree – so her university tutor functions could be carried out anywhere. She did not realise that in not having an office along with other colleagues on either the lower or upper corridor, she was missing what Lesley Webb calls the inner circle of back-biters who did what they could to make trouble for her. When Lesley Webb travelled extensively round British Universities examining their courses, she would often be told:

'Aren't you lucky having Dorothy Heathcote as a colleague'. She kept to herself that some of Dorothy's own colleagues did not feel that way.

In a curious way Dorothy picked up the feel of the department, even though she was not given an official place in it: Roger Barnes writes of her all-seeing crow's nest:

> Whilst those of us who caught the 8.30 train into work never saw Dorothy in the department, this didn't mean she hadn't been in. Anyone who had dealings with her knew of her irritating habit of returning their letter, with the reply scribbled on it. I must assume that she arrived at 6.30 with the cleaners, sorted her mail, wrote the answers and then photocopied the result, along with other items to be photocopied for her files. The photocopier wasn't always in the same place, but it tended to be somewhere where the copier saw more of the world passing by than the world passing by saw of the copier. As a result, Dorothy, presiding over the copier, got to know all sorts of things about the school of education that escaped the rest of us.

Because Dorothy's video tapes earned money for the University, an arrangement was made with Professor Tony Edwards that she could have unlimited access to photocopying, and so she was able to undertake her students' photocopying chores, for which they would normally have had to pay. Dorothy explains: 'So I arrived at 6.30 with the cleaners, who used to have it switched on for me and was done by 8.30 when I went over to 42 North Road'.

This access to free photocopying coincided with us all getting our own letters to Dorothy returned. I was puzzled at first, as were many people, and indeed thought it mildly discourteous, until I appreciated how time-saving, paper-saving and labour-saving it was. And it promoted clarity. Handwritten comments of 'Good!', 'Cor!', 'Yes', 'I agree', 'I've made a note' plus ticks of approval etc., with numbered elaborations at the top or bottom of one's own letter, made for precise communication. All photocopied and filed. I cannot see that money-saving came into this, but Dorothy's custom of re-cycling her Christmas cards, saving both rainforests and cash, suggests it would not be out of character.

Dorothy's own students thrived on having a space apart. 42 North Road became a refuge of enlightenment, safety, companionship, trust and laughter, all generated by Dorothy at the centre of their world. It raised a wry smile from Dorothy when on retirement she offered a list of the furniture at 42 North Road to one of the Department secretaries. The Secretary showed little interest, suggesting that the room would be of no interest to the department any more as 'No students are going to want to trail over there, are they'.

Dorothy was always given support by her heads of department. Indeed Tony Edwards often popped in to see her at work, both at 42 North Road and in local schools. University registrars, perhaps unexpectedly, supported this eminent maverick. Edwards puts this down to loyalty, as they happened to come from Education originally. And Vice-Chancellors seemed always to back Dorothy. The strangest coincidence allowed Dorothy to meet one of them even before he took up his appointment. She was doing some work in Evanston for Betty Jane Wagner and found herself caught up in a crazy drama with an elementary class about language and mathematics in which in her role as a 'word witch' – under instruction from the young mathematicians – she was not allowed to speak any words connected with number. The sheer impossibility and improbability of this drove her into a corner of laughing defensiveness. When it was over, Dorothy, while gathering her things together, happened to be standing near B.J. who was in conversation with a man Dorothy didn't know. B.J. was asking him what plans he had professionally. He replied: 'As a matter of fact I'm about to leave for England; I'm going to be Vice-Chancellor of the funniest university you've ever heard of. It's called Noocastle-upon-Tyne'.

'Meet one of your lecturers,' says B.J.

Dorothy – to her students
The critics among Dorothy's colleagues had no conception of the amount of time she gave to her work – and if they did it would have only fuelled their resentment. Her planning for projects was incredibly detailed and thorough. As Dorothy had to find more and more time to help her M.Ed students with their research, she would start tutorials with those living in the house with her at 2.30 a.m. – and they would go back to bed again. And those who did not live in occasionally found themselves staying overnight so that they could have the early morning tutorial. (Dorothy, on reading this paragraph, wants readers to understand that this was no sacrifice for her – it was a necessary expedient. 'I am *never* a martyr!' she affirms.) And sometimes she would arrange to meet a student for a quick tutorial on Central Station at 7 a.m. before she boarded the 7.30 train to wherever she was heading for a few days. One wonders how her students felt about these tutorials at such unsocial hours. They would not dare complain. 'If I am prepared to do this for you, I expect you to make yourself available' would be the understanding between tutor and taught.

Rigour was the dominant feature of all aspects of the course and personal inconvenience was something to be overcome or ignored. Yes, there is a hardness here in Dorothy's character, a hardness acquired through genuine poverty and the tough régime of the mill. She knows it and in one of her interviews before

the camera (*Pieces of Dorothy*) she identifies the unsympathetic streak she recognises in herself:

> It's the sort of thing where a student would say, 'I'm hard up'. I would say,
> 'Are you still smoking? You aint hard up mate. You don't know what it's like
> to be hard up till you've stopped smoking and you don't have a half pint at
> lunch time and you don't *buy* a sandwich – then you might know.'

> So in that sense I didn't fit into the academic world because there was
> always this little hard line that I still draw.

If there is a hard streak in Dorothy, it must be set against her warmth of compassion. Sometimes her generous tolerance takes her into dangerous territory.
Because she has a soft spot for the underprivileged, the underdog, the inadequate, her judgement when it came to accepting students for her courses was
not always rational. She would visit an applicant, recognise a difficult temperament and say to that teacher: 'I don't think I can handle you in a group' – and
then proceed to accept her or him for the course. It was as though Dorothy could
not bear to add to the failures that person had already experienced in life. She
saw it as a challenge – even while recognising she might be martyring the rest
of the group. Indeed one group suffered from a racist hysteric whose presence
became intolerable for them. For some of these 'lame ducks', as one observer
called them, a year away from their own classroom with continual support from
Dorothy was just what they needed to ease them through a bad time. It should
perhaps be explained that sometimes the reason they managed to be granted
secondment by their employing authority was because it was recognised that the
rest of the school staff needed a breather. There were a few however who were
unable to adapt to being one of a group of students, and their egocentric behaviour at times tended to dominate the course. One student confirms this, telling me:

> I did get angry with some of the individuals on the course. Some seemed to
> have very severe personality difficulties and were expert attention seekers,
> which got to me at times ... The only time I ever saw Dorothy 'lose it' was
> with one of these individuals, who just seemed to leech all the energy out of
> her. One day Dorothy just blew it and told her she could help her no more:
> she had to help herself. We all felt her anger (frustration?) ourselves.

Sometimes students, collectively, would become obstreperous. Professor Nancy
Swortzell of New York University recalls in 1973 visiting Newcastle for the first
time to observe Dorothy at work in a local primary school, only to discover that
Dorothy's students were in a state of mutiny. Nancy writes:

The 'inciting action' was immediate upon arrival at the school! Twelve or so graduate students, who Dorothy had just introduced, blatantly confronted us with their grievances. (oh, dear — and in the presence of a foreign visitor!) Memories of the American 1960 student mutinies raced through my mind. To my astonishment British students were behaving exactly like self-righteous Americans! Also, I felt the irony of my traveling great distances to experience Dorothy's work first hand, only to arrive at the very moment of student mutiny. Dorothy controlled their insistence for an immediate discussion, authoritatively stating that she 'had an administrative meeting' and could not see them at this time. Therefore, an hour's recess was granted. They graciously whisked me away to a nearby pub where the issues were energetically vented.

Apparently there was a general feeling of dissatisfaction – this was still the first term – with Dorothy's priorities for the course. Nancy managed to offer neutral observations and when the next day they eventually had their discussion with Dorothy, their zeal for mutiny had been assuaged – and they apologised to her some weeks later.

Roger Barnes, however, who was continually in touch with Dorothy's students, never heard a single complaint, in marked contrast to other colleagues' students. One of the reasons he had so much contact with Dorothy's students was that when she wanted to upgrade her course to a B.Phil qualification, it was felt by the grey men that drama alone could not stand as an adequate subject. They insisted that drama students chose two more disciplines, a restriction which most of Dorothy's students resented, for they had come to study drama, not philosophy or psychology or whatever. The result was that their attention to other subjects' requirements was often half-hearted, failing to read the set books, submitting below standard written work. It was an embarrassment to him that he had to give her students such low marks – there is an apocryphal story that Dorothy 'mistook' his '30s' for '50s' when she copied from his marks list! Roger Barnes writes:

> I grew up – during Hitler's war – on the Lancashire Yorkshire border, and am familiar with the forthright down-to-earth no nonsense attitude that prevailed. The combination of such, in Dorothy, together with her physical presence compelled people, other than the School of Education, to take her seriously. I can imagine – if there were someone in this world, with the same message, but lacking the physical presence and the matter-o'-fact manner – I can imagine them failing dismally to get the message across. Sadly, one's words seldom speak for you in this world. It is the words plus the messenger. I remember doing concept analysis with her students and making the

mistake of putting on the list of concepts, 'charisma'. We never got to the others, they simply wanted to talk about Dorothy. Come to think of it, she would have made a stunning barrister, she would have the streets crowded with guilty folk, found innocent by a star-struck jury.

I wonder how much paper Dorothy's students have used up in their attempts to record, capture, or analyse the essence of Dorothy's teaching. It was interesting how students in the latter years of her teaching would arrive on the course with, as it were, a luggage-full of received Heathcote wisdom, not always recognisable by Dorothy herself. So they had to unlearn. This was in marked contrast to those early diploma days when they may have thought they'd be learning about stage falls. Now, steeped in literature about her, their expectations were high, their senses alert to artistic possibilities of role, sign and symbol. Mike Fleming, who took my place at Durham University when I retired, recalls that once when Dorothy came to Durham to teach my class – of which Mike was a student – they entered the room to find her eating an apple. They pondered on the significance of this, mentally spinning the symbol in all directions to do with cultivation, knowledge and healthy living. It turned out she was merely finishing her lunch.

These last few months I have been in touch with many of Dorothy's past students and the unqualified response is one of sheer joy as they recall their year with her. Many write that it changed their lives. They don't confine their comments to what they learnt about drama teaching; they invariably claim to have grown in wisdom, to have become more sensitive, more compassionate, more open minded. And having studied with Dorothy Heathcote was for some a means of promotion in educational circles. Perhaps Brian Edmiston is the one for whom that year wrought the most dramatic change in his circumstances. He writes: 'I studied with Dorothy 1983-4. I am not using hyperbole to say that that was a watershed year which radically revolutionised my life, both professionally and personally'. He was a Bristol teacher of English and Drama. The course was re-commended to him by David Hornbrook who became one of Dorothy's severest critics. Brian married a fellow student, Pat Enisco, an American. He moved to America with her after the course, and now they live with their two children in Ohio where they are both University lecturers. He adds: 'If I had not gone to Newcastle, I am pretty sure that I would still be a secondary teacher in England who would have settled for second best in the classroom.' Brian offers a testimonial to Dorothy that echoes many of the feelings that have been expressed to me by students:

> It was Dorothy who fostered the emergence of my 'real' teacher self. She demonstrated what a real teacher was for her — someone who brought her whole being and the best resources available into the classroom, someone

who was as authentic and respectful in her relationships with all students, with cleaners, with 'mentally handicapped' people, as with anyone else. Someone who lived excellence in her own life not just expected it from others. Someone who laughed with you as she pressed you to reflect on why you were doing what you were doing. Someone who expected all worthwhile learning to be complex, and learning to teach to be textured and lifelong. Someone who saw drama as a way to teach about life and who saw teaching and learning as happening in a crucible – where everyone in a classroom (adults as well as children) may be transformed, often slowly, but also often radically.

The students who stayed at Highburn House felt particularly privileged. In becoming part of the Heathcote family, they absorbed its joys and its paradoxes. Pamela Bowell is one, who became particularly close to seventeen year old Marianne. She recalls all sorts of incidents at Highburn House with affection. For instance, one morning when they were pushed for time, Dorothy as usual was loading the Volvo, their second car, for departing to class. Suddenly the hatchback door literally fell off its hinges. Raymond was summoned and finally succeeded in putting it back, but not without an accompaniment of a completely unexpurgated running commentary, which Dorothy explains to the awaiting students as 'his air-force language'! Pamela writes:

> The state of the Volvo was part of the paradox of the Heathcote approach to life. More welcoming and truly generous people it would be difficult to find and yet their parsimony was remarkable. I could just list a catalogue of examples – the perished rubber plug for the butler sink in the kitchen made to fit the plughole by wrapping it in corners cut from worn out flannels. The coffee percolator and the saucepan with lid and handle, respectively, attached with perfectly applied string. The rubber bands made from cross sections cut from the wrists of worn out rubber gloves. The carefully washed and re-used packets in which frozen peas had come. I could go on and on. I really want to stress that I am *not* suggesting for a moment that this is meanness, I love these people. It was just that the plug was a perfectly good plug – only shrunk a bit, and the saucepan was a perfectly good saucepan – just that the handle had come off ... a completely different way of looking at the world.

On one less happy occasion, the house was burgled. A great deal went missing, including jewellery. Raymond confessed that he had failed – and this is so out of character with his normal notorious control over matters – to have jewellery insured, an oversight that also affected the students staying in the house. Pamela tells me that 'Dorothy was thunderously faced but quiet and Raymond just 'shut down', sleeping in his favourite chair in the dining room with a tartan shawl around his shoulders and Scrap the cat on his knee'. Dorothy did her best to make sure the students were suitably compensated.

Dorothy's efforts to retire

It was winter, 1984. Dorothy was sitting in a department meeting. The topic was the PGCE. Dorothy had never been happy about this course. She was only given one hour a week for Drama, which meant the students did not have time to see her teaching in schools unless she smuggled them in in their lunch hour to make a longer session – which she did whenever possible.

At this meeting she heard the Geography lecturer say: 'The problem with these students is that they haven't done enough Geography'. Dorothy couldn't believe she was hearing this, for by definition they had just completed a three year undergraduate course studying that very subject. Dorothy came in with: 'But isn't it now that they need help, not with the subject itself, but with how to introduce children to this fascinating subject of Geography?' There was a pause. And then they did what they have done all Dorothy's professional life – they ignored her. Professor Edwards, sitting next to Dorothy, nudged her and whispered 'Try again'. A Social Science specialist confirmed the Geographer's concerns, bemoaning inadequate expertise in his field. Dorothy tried again: 'I still think it isn't a matter of how much Geography they know or the Social Science they know; it's how to help pupils love it'. Dorothy was again ignored, and they are about to resume when Tony Edwards comes in with: 'I think Dorothy's got a point ... ' And they ignored this too.

At this moment Dorothy was not fuming inwardly, for an idea had just hit her: 'I will resign; I've had enough; I can finish here; I don't have to listen to this any more; Raymond has recently taken early retirement; Marianne is in her last year at school prior to University; I too will retire'. Instead of seething, she felt newly relaxed and announced her decision to Tony Edwards in his room immediately afterwards.

His reaction was that she would not be replaced because the University, going through an economic crisis, was not replacing anyone who left. He put it to her: 'Could you not stay on a couple of years? ... you could teach any course you wanted to ... and drop any you don't want'. Dorothy found this irresistible and asked to have a two-year part time M.Ed. so that all the local teachers who had attended her Advanced Diploma course over the years and others who had been regular but casual observers whenever they could, would have the chance to do an intense study and she in turn would work once again in their schools. And she would drop that detested PGCE!

The day she did retire, she was glad to leave. In the corridor she met the woman in charge of Primary Education, who had never got round to inviting Dorothy to contribute to her courses. 'Oh, Dorothy ... I hear you're *leaving* ... I've been meaning to ask you to teach on my course ... someone has been telling me just how important drama is ... he's been explaining it all to me', says this tutor with a patronising smile. 'I've just retired', replies Dorothy with a fixed one. And another voice along that same corridor, this time from a senior member of staff: 'Oh Dorothy, we were wondering if you would do a Summer School for us – we thought it would bring in a bit of money for the department'.

> A curious reminder of Dorothy's treatment 'in her own country' occurred last week. She received by mail an award 'for outstanding lifetime achievement' from the American Alliance for Theatre and Education[3]. However, that very same week, Kathy White Webster, of Queen Elizabeth High School, Hexham, who was in the process of applying for a grant towards the Hexham Commission, received a phone call from one of the trustees who happened to be from Newcastle University School of Education. Interested in the person Kathy had named in the application as one of the initiators of the Hexham Commission, he, from the very department Dorothy had worked in, had naïvely asked: 'Who is this Dorothy Heathcote?'

Planting an orchard in the garden of Highburn House

For the last two years Dorothy worked at Newcastle University, Raymond was at home. He marked the occasion of his retirement by ordering thirty-five cordon apple trees, two espalier pear trees and seven plum trees of compatible varieties for their garden. For him it was an exciting new project, involving the careful monitoring of the harvest, the weighing of each basket of autumn pickings, the recording through graphs of each year's productivity for crop comparisons between each tree, the careful wrapping of fruit for storage – the peeling and the cooking. For her it was a lot of extra work, but she saw that he needed her to look pleased at his inspiration, for, full of anticipation, he had said, 'I've got a surprise for you ... !'

> There is a FOR SALE notice outside Highburn House. Dorothy has agreed that it would be sensible for her to leave Gateshead and live in Nottingham, near Marianne, Kevin and Anna, but she dreads finding herself in some pretty bungalow, with a pretty garden, a manicured lawn and a privet hedge. As she watches Raymond's orchard being dismantled, she is grateful that someone has been found who will really care for those trees, but it is as if part of her is being taken away.

Her part-time M.Ed course

This was partly Dorothy saying a thank-you to the many local teachers who had been loyal to her throughout her career by lending her their classes. She had built a family of followers and she would give them all she could. It surely must have been one of the most enriching courses ever run anywhere. She was at her peak; they were all very experienced in the classroom; and she was prepared to give them all the time and energy she could spare. She made them work hard and some of them were out of touch with the demands of academia. A huge adjustment she had to make was the switch from having full-time students, from whom she could demand their twenty-four hour attention, to part-time students for whom the course could not be a central focus – they had families, classes to teach, staff meetings, marking, exams to set, discipline problems and rehearsals after school etc. And some had long journeys to make – Cumbria, Ripon and Leeds, twice a week.

Eileen Pennington, whose M of E project was described in the last chapter, has furnished me with a picture of the M.Ed course. Rich as it was in many aspects, it lacked for the students the opportunities to see Dorothy teach in other schools. She often helped out in their own schools, but this could not be observed by fellow students, so that the evening class discussion about a particular student's work lacked a meaningful focus. Appreciating this, Dorothy endeavoured to draw out teaching points from these reports of 'what happened in my class to-day'. New principles and skills were thus absorbed indirectly, 'by osmosis' as Eileen puts it. They were apprentices picking up from the master.

Eileen usefully summarises what she remembers of the overall content of these sessions:

Drama strategies I had never known before
Needle-sharp analysis of what happened in a drama
Direct training in interactive skills
Direct training in role methods
Emphasis on theatre skills used in the service of education

Unfortunately, the grey men had insisted on a heavy evidence of attainment load – two papers of 10,000 words and a dissertation of 40,000, and two three-hour examinations. (My Master's Course at Durham University required a dissertation and one three-hour examination.) Sitting alongside other education department examinees, they were the only candidates who flourished coloured pens, drawing instruments etc. The need to make the answer papers visually interesting as well as academically rigorous was an inevitable expectation of Dorothy's students – one can imagine the number of diagrams, graphs and charts splashed into their answers. Dorothy, somewhat out of character, insisted on providing a coffee machine in the examination room, causing an invigilator's eyebrows to rise.

Tutorials provided an anchor for help with lesson preparation and advice on dissertations. But it was clearly expected that you came to your tutorial with your own thinking prepared, ideas sketched out, alternatives thought through ... and only *then* did Dorothy give you her full, inventive attention. As Eileen puts it:

> When you thought you had said every last thing there was to say about a subject, Dorothy would always introduce yet another tangent which would land you in research, statistical exercises with or without children, another piece of teaching or another chapter in your dissertation.

And if you were lucky enough to have Dorothy work in your classroom, such was her sure grasp on what you were attempting in your dissertation, that she simultaneously gave your class a first-rate educational experience and facilitated the enquiry you were conducting, carefully selecting her material for the lesson in a way that met both those objectives.

The atmosphere on the course was what Eileen describes as 'a culture of inter-dependence'. She explains:

> The norm in the group was that everyone was expected to help each other. If you were free and someone needed a role-playing at their school, you went and did it for them. One evening, when the session began, Dorothy said, 'So-and-so needs 36 drawings of old furniture. Can you all do some? Give them to so-and-so and when you've done it, we'll begin the session'.

Dorothy's energy could not always accommodate to her students' lack of it when they arrived at class, perhaps straight from school or on the way from collecting and feeding their children. One such student, Voula Foscolo-Avis, a dynamic teacher who eventually took over that PGCE course from Dorothy, laughs as she recalled arriving at the evening class at the end of a particularly tiring day.

> During the second year, February I think it was, when the days are short and bleak, I arrived at one of Dorothy's twice weekly evening sessions. I had not eaten since lunch time, had rehearsed for two hours after school for my next production and got to the class bleary with fatigue. One of the blackboards had Dorothy's clear and rounded script, filling it with:
>
> **The knights who owed fealty to Wrothgar waited in the night for Grendel to come**

Dorothy began, her eyes twinkling, with an introduction about 'how to begin' ... 'where to focus' ... 'what to explore'. She gave examples of choices, that is, Where would we begin the story?

(a) ... on the _k_nightness of knights?
(b) ... on the _f_ealtiness of _f_ealty?
(c) ... on the W_r_othgarness of W_r_othgar?
(d) ... on the _n_ightness of _n_ight?
(e) ... on the _Gr_endelness of _G_rendel? Etc etc.

My heart sank as I struggled to add yet another arrow to my quiver.

Fatigue, inevitably shared by most of her 25 M.Ed. students, plus the ever present 'unofficial' followers of her course, for those last two years of Dorothy's official working life, was far outweighed by their gratitude to her for running a course which was both school-based and unparalleled in its commitment to a deep study of education.

Knowing her students well, Dorothy learnt over the years of running courses to distinguish between the possible reasons for inadequate, below standard work. If it was sheer pressure from elsewhere, she learnt to give a student space; if it was a genuine lack of skill, say, in writing a dissertation, she would virtually write it with them; if it was lack of confidence, she would find encouraging, positive things to say; but if it was laziness, then Dorothy had no tolerance. Fortunately, such students were rare.

Laziness was not so easy to spot, however, when collaborating with others in the profession – colleagues, teachers, fellow drama leaders, her hosts who arranged her visits, or conference organisers. Such was Dorothy's initial gratitude to such people, on whom she relied for practical as well as moral support, that it would take her some time to appreciate that not all were as thorough, reliable, committed or knowledgeable as one might expect. Because she was always so enthusiastic, so prepared to work herself to the bone for anyone at all hours of the day, she did not always realise that they were taking advantage of her, just letting her make up for their inefficiencies, shrugging it off with: 'Dorothy would have everything covered' – which invariably she did. Occasionally however, the deliberate decision to do as little as possible in the way of helping Dorothy with the minutiae of her preparations was a way of hiding a fear of not coming up to her high standards – the less one did, the less chance was there of being exposed, a tactic that could be mistaken for laziness. Sometimes their advantage taking was totally unconscious. People did not realise that leaving it all to Dorothy was not a compliment to her but a failure to recognise that she was overburdened. Only very occasionally did Dorothy actually say 'enough is enough'; normally her way round the problem would be to edge out of working with that person without saying anything. Only once did she actually say 'I will not work with you again'.

Her M.Ed students' retirement gift

Today Dorothy has shown me her 'book of trees' – a large photograph album with tree planting ceremonies that have taken place in different parts of the world, with saplings as varied as a coconut in Fiji, a silver maple in Canada, a sycamore in Galway, a frangipani and azalia in Australia, an evergreen juniper, linden and morello in Budapest.

Dorothy had declined any official farewell celebration by the University, so the M.Ed students felt it was up to them to do something interesting. It was somehow left to Derek Stevens to come up with an idea. He'd seen an advert for a performance of *Comedy of Errors*, directed by Wendy McPhee[4], a talented past student of Dorothy's. The presentation was to be at Wallington Hall, a magnificent mansion and garden setting in Northumberland. They could arrange a pre-performance picnic.

The additional, inspired idea of an oak tree planting ceremony at Wallington came from Derek's daughter. She added: 'And how about inviting people all around the world to plant a tree in their own area, so there'll be a Heathcote forest around the world, which can be added to at any time? ... Ask them to send a photograph of the tree and details of the location to be placed in a special commemorative photo album for her to keep'. The other students thought this was a smashing idea.

Derek writes:

Secrecy was the biggest problem. Because of DH's alert 'fly's eye', getting information to and money from members of the group without arousing any suspicion in her was a taxing game to play. Dealing with the National Trust was much easier, though the estate forester was a little perplexed when he told me that the tree at Wallington would have to be an oak and that it would take two hundred years to reach its best, and I replied that was singularly appropriate for the lady to be honoured on the day.

Raymond was travelling separately to Wallington, so DH had to travel on the hired bus with us. That meant no mention of the tree could happen, and I was worried in case things didn't go right. I had no need to worry. Even if she had begun to suspect something[5], she was going to play the game.

On arrival at Wallington I announced we were going for a short walk before the picnic tea. No demur. We arrived at a small clearing to find the forester with a tree in a barrow and spade at the ready. I explained to her delighted self the whole plan of worldwide forest and book, played a special tape from John Fines, recounting her career through an allegory of a tree, and she took hold of the spade. The oak was planted with a ceremonious firming of the earth and a loud 'Now grow, you bugger!', from Dorothy. Our gale of laughter was met with a superb mock-innocent apologia of 'Well, that's what Raymond always says!'

It was a glorious occasion. She accepted our simple but significant gesture and gift, tucked in with relish to the food and enjoyed the role of 'mother-guest' with her strange family and watched the performed comedy.

It was no surprise that shortly after the course ended, I received a generous note of thanks for the occasion. All that one does for her is appreciated, acknowledged and thanked. It simply makes one want to do more for her.

Dorothy's 'strange family' know that it will take her work, as well as her oak tree, two hundred years for it to 'reach its best' – and she'll be watching!

Notes

1   R. Baird Shuman Ed. 1978 *Educational Drama for Today's Schools* Scarecrow Press Inc., New Jersey, USA

2   Liz Johnson and Cecily O'Neill 1984 *Dorothy Heathcote: Collected writing on education and drama* London Hutchinson

3   The Campton Bell Lifetime Achievement Award.

    Dorothy has received many awards and recognitions throughout her career. For example, in 1970 she was made a Fellow of the Edinburgh School of Music and Drama [she had completely forgotten about this when I reminded her]. In 1975, one of her lectures was included in the Jenning's Scholar Lectures for Outstanding Teachers, organised by the Martha Holden Foundation.

4   Wendy McPhee runs a London-based, touring Shakespeare company called 'Theatre Set-up'.

5   More than that – she knew almost from the beginning of their planning – a sheet of paper accidentally left behind on the huge table at 42 North Road.

10
Looking Forward

What a relief! It won't be a suburban bungalow for Dorothy. Marianne and family have bought a large, Georgian residence, West House, in a village outside Derby and Dorothy, when she has sold Highburn, will have her own suite of rooms there. Will there be room for an Aga?

At the time of Dorothy's retirement, there were big changes for Marianne.

Marianne away from home

Marianne had a gap year before starting University in 1985, so she could live on a kibbutz and see as much as possible of the Holy Land. She read Theology at the University of Nottingham and then followed with a teacher-training course at Durham University. After teaching in primary schools in Nottinghamshire she started working for RE Today, a Christian ecumenical charity which provides materials and training for teachers of religious education. She combines writing RE teaching materials for publication with running courses for Primary School teachers, with an emphasis on multi-faith RE. She married Kevin in July 1996 . The wedding was a delightful, happy, funny, spiritual occasion. The bride tapped her feet to the rhythm of the church songs. When the vicar asked if anyone knew of any just cause or impediment ... she turned round to give us all a raised eyebrow. Dorothy and Raymond shared giving their daughter away. When I was sitting in the congregation before the ceremony and couldn't see the mother of the bride sitting on the front row, I thought she was going to break a lifetime rule – by being late! But she and Raymond together accompanied the bride down the aisle.

The reception was held in Nottingham University Staff Club. I disciplined myself not to have a drink at the bar before the meal – mustn't overdo it – only to realise, as the courses presented themselves, that the food was to be accompanied by alcohol-free drinks. I should have known! The reception was a jolly affair. Among the guests were two of Dorothy's past students, Sandra Hesten and Pam Bowell. Dorothy, Raymond, Marianne and Kevin, as well as the best man and one of the bridesmaids, all gave speeches. Dorothy's speech had worried her for months: she felt that a straight account would sound too near preaching or reporting. So, a fairy-godmother role it had to be, a role that allowed her to offer a kind of all-seeing, timeless, wisdom with Marianne at the centre.

The happy start to Marianne and Kevin's marriage was saddened by the loss of their first baby, Ashley, who was miscarried. A blessing and naming ceremony by the hospital chaplain followed later by the dedication of an ash tree to her in Heritage Wood in Derbyshire marked the family's love and closeness to each other in this mixture of thankfulness and grieving. It was this love and closeness that would see them through Raymond's death some years later. An oak to Raymond was dedicated in the same plantation. Winter cyclamen now surround the base of both trees.

And then in May 2000, Anna Heathcote Woodbridge arrived. What a wonderful upbringing she will have, with parents and grandmother under the same roof. What a rich texture of knowledge they will be able to offer her. Kevin is a practises as an optometrist, working as a locum in other optician's practices. Uniquely he combines that profession with research studies in geology, a pursuit that takes him to Iran where he examines the effects of flooding. Marianne specialises in multi-faith work and then there is Dorothy. Anna's antennae are obviously going to be stretched in all directions. As a two year-old, she is beginning to recognise letters of the alphabet. Dorothy's reading started with *Titbits*. One suspects Anna's first texts will be more carefully chosen.

1986 onwards – has Dorothy retired?

Well, not exactly, not even remotely. In so far as she no longer has an employer she is officially retired, but her days are still heavily diaried, her kitchen table covered in reminder notes, the dining-table laid out with plans of lessons, past students coming in for tutorials, phone ringing continually, key-note addresses to be drafted, articles wanted for journals and she was also providing me with a hundred pages of hand-written notes for the books we agreed to collaborate on. 'Writing a book is not my idea of the best use of my time', Dorothy[1] had warned.

At first she had said she would give up teaching altogether and then, as work presented itself, she accepted more and more engagements. She did draw the line at travelling abroad, once she had completed her agreed commitment to South Africa immediately after her retirement. But she did agree to travel to the IDEA[2] conference in Bergen in 2001 as an honorary guest, invited by Stig Eriksson of Bergen University College, a long-time admirer of her work. His students would come over to Newcastle from Norway once a year for a session or two with Dorothy. Raymond's death in March 2001 prevented her from attending. Although she was sorry to let Stig down, she had not been looking forward to it for, as she says, she's 'not good at honours'.

Two Major launches
1. Establishing the International Centre for Studies in Drama in Education

David Davis, an ex-student of mine, and Ken Byron, an ex-student of Dorothy's shared the teacher-training in Drama at Birmingham Polytechnic, later the University of Central England (UCE). They cooperated in promoting Drama in Education, by which they meant the kind of methodology associated with the Universities of Newcastle and Durham. Ambitious to introduce Masters degrees once their institution became a University, they invited Dorothy and John Fines onto the committee drawing up a submission to the directorate. David and Ken were also prompted to consider the possibility of establishing a centre.

Outside the North-East, the one centre in England that promoted Heathcotean methodology was the Drama and Tape Centre in London, run by its Warden, Cecily O'Neill. When she left to take up a professorial post in America, however, David Hornbrook changed its name and purpose to a Centre for the Performing Arts. This gave Ken Byron and David Davis the idea for setting up an alternative centre in Birmingham. It was called 'The International Centre for Studies in Drama in Education' and Dorothy, who was teaching David's students for a week each term, as she had agreed to do since retirement, attended the launch in 1992. Its mission statement unambiguously announced that it was 'continuing to mine and develop the work of Dorothy Heathcote and Gavin Bolton'.

Ken Byron was in charge of the PGCE and David of the MA course, but they shared the teaching on each. Ken was also the respected editor of the national *2D Journal*. He was greatly missed when he suddenly left education. David carried on the full-time MA course single-handed and subsequently Ph.D tuition. Additionally, he introduced a system of annual two-week summer schools, consecutive attendance at three of which, along with a dissertation, gained students a Master's degree. The course was advertised world-wide as centring on Dorothy Heathcote's work. Indeed she would contribute to the teaching of it each summer. Teachers who thought that they had missed the chance to be taught by Dorothy in Newcastle found that they could study with her at UCE instead. The course attracted large numbers of foreign students, including some from China, Australasia, South America, India, USA, Canada, Scandinavia and Eastern and Western Europe. As it turned out, Dorothy attended only one of these because she and David Davis lost trust in one another so she stopped working with him.

David had started an archive of video material for his new centre. When Dorothy worked at the University or in Birmingham schools, she did a great deal of teaching for his Ph.D students who taught in local schools and he was there with a camera. So there is a huge unedited archival collection of Dorothy's teaching available for borrowers to study, a 'warts and all' library of raw material that Dorothy believes could be extremely valuable to researchers.

The city of Birmingham became, and indeed still is, a focus for drama in education in another important respect. One of the two major Drama teacher associations[3], NATD, currently under the excellent chairmanship of Guy Williams, has for some 30 years held its annual conference at UCE, since its Polytechnic days[4]. Dorothy has been the Association's President since 1970. This further helped to reinforce Dorothy's link with Birmingham in the minds of many teachers.

That Dorothy should have such a close link with a regular conference setting was not entirely in character for her. Such 'platformed' celebrations of egos and subsequent participation in discussion groups or workshops, with inconsequential reporting back, were never to her taste. For years she just went along with it for she concluded that that is what professionals apparently need to do. But being President of an organisation allowed her occasionally to vary the format.

She had been experimenting for some time with the ploy of drawing onlookers of her teaching in schools into the action by giving them a role, a *raison d'être* for being there, legitimising their presence to the class. If appropriate, they engaged in inter-role communication with the children. It was only one step further to organise a conference along these lines – to have the conference delegates in role all through the two or three days. This was a way of creating a sense of collective responsibility, a clear focus and a sense of a task to be completed. It had its down side, however, as participants sometimes felt inhibited by their role and the subsequent tasks. Many experienced drama teachers felt trapped by this practice called Mantle of the Expert, which for some remained uniquely Dorothy Heathcote's. They held back from full commitment because they did not want to be made to look foolish, especially as they saw others have their mistakes gently but publicly corrected. Dorothy, working logically and single-mindedly from the inside of a carefully conceived project, left some on the outside for an entire conference. Dorothy too was disappointed, for her plan was based on her belief that the various volunteer group leaders understood the Mantle of the Expert more than they really did.

2. The Dorothy Heathcote Archives

During the second year of the M.Ed course in 1985, her final year at Newcastle, Dorothy emptied filing cabinets of her notes and articles into packing cases and boxes. She'd sorted them out under abstract headings such as 'symbol' and 'ritual' – going back to early in her career. What should she do with them? Sandra Hesten, who was planning her doctoral research on Heathcote's work approached the Drama staff at Lancaster University about the possibility of saving all this material, and the idea for an archive came up. Dorothy did not like the idea at first.

It also gave Sandra an angle for her thesis, which in its final form combined an historical analysis of Heathcote practice with a classified description of the archives and an account of the measures adopted in order to set it up – a fascinating document. There are two major aspects to the archive itself, the physical library – documentary, audio and video – housed at Lancaster University and later moved to Manchester Metropolitan University, and a computerised keyword index, programmed by Sandra's husband, Bob. It was a disappointment to everyone that the finance for setting up a website of the archive material was not forthcoming, but Sandra's thesis, unique in its combination of conceptual analysis, biographical reporting and technical information, is available for downloading. John Rainer, in charge of Drama at MMU is at present generously operating as unpaid archivist. He now gets many enquiries from round the world and I am grateful to the help he has given me.

Dorothy, shedding her own vast working library from Highburn House, recently sent most of it to John who, faced with an embarrassment of riches, is waiting for the chance to add them to the website index and to develop a suite of rooms in the University to make accessibility easier. Archival material is also being collected in different parts of the world. Perhaps one day there will be an international website that makes it all available.

Lancaster conference, 1993

An opportunity to introduce the Dorothy Heathcote Archives to all the Heathcote devotees was created by Dr Hesten who undertook the organisation of a prestigious international five-day conference, celebrating Dorothy's career. Some forty countries were represented, the number of speakers from abroad far outnumbering the Brits in a carefully planned programme. One English friend greatly valued by Dorothy was Joyce Simpson, who whizzed around in her wheel chair, determined, in spite of crippling pain, to be part of the celebration. Sandra combined a vision for the event with an unerring attention to detail – she even made sure there was wholemeal bread for Raymond – 'we don't like that white dust', she had heard him say. Over the five days, 250 delegates thronged the corridors, lecture theatres, foyers and dining room at Lancaster University, purposefully and efficiently guided by route maps, large wall signs and time-table instructions, and a programme that included tutorials with Dorothy Heathcote, 7.00-9.00 a.m. each morning by appointment. The geographical centre of the conference was provided by Alice da Silva, a past student from Portugal who with her usual artistic flair made a huge world map displaying all the countries from which delegates had travelled.

Behind all the attractions of theatre presentations, key-note speeches, work-shops, another tree-planting, toasting Dorothy at a candle-lit dinner, the lighting of lanterns, the making of garlands, dining and meeting up with friends, was a quietly bustling backroom. Bob Hesten, Sandra's husband, had set up a computer laboratory into which members of the conference could retreat and under his guidance they could help test the effectiveness of the Physical Archive, the Explanatory Booklet, Keyword Index and Thesaurus of Keywords. Here was a different rhythm from the rest of the conference, a different way of searching for Dorothy. Also there, showing past videos and films of Dorothy, were Pat Morrison and Dorothy Croyden from the University of Newcastle AVA, two colleagues who had given her much support throughout the filming years.

But it is fun to think that not everything was what it seemed. Sandra Hesten tells the story of her 14 year-old daughter, Fiona who, bored with everything to do with Dorothy and the conference, persuaded Dorothy Croyden in what seemed a quiet break in the 'videos of Dorothy' room, to put on a Russian Ice skating video instead. Fiona was at first embarrassed when conference delegates came in but then became highly amused as she realised they were sitting there absorbing it, confident that the relevance to Dorothy would be revealed.

Dorothy, soon after the Lancaster conference was diagnosed as having cancer.

Hystorectomy

The year was 1995. Dr. Mike Fleming of Durham University had asked Dorothy and me to participate in a conference on 'teaching culture' to language students or, as the subsequent publication put it, a conference on *Language Learning in Intercultural Perspective: Approaches through drama and ethnography*. Dorothy was to do a day session with a class of upper secondary school pupils. She decided she would like Mike and me and Eileen Pennington to support her session with some role-play – she would tell us what was required. It was arranged for us to hold a rehearsal at my house. A day or so before the rehearsal date we each received a wad of handwritten papers outlining a detailed lesson plan, indicating the kind of thing she wanted us to prepare for our roles. I was a bit mystified in spite of the details.

At the rehearsal Dorothy talked us through part of the sequence and we felt a little wiser but not absolutely convinced of what it amounted to. Still, this was Dorothy and she would make it work. The next day I received a letter she had written on the day of the rehearsal but delivered by Raymond, whom she had instructed to drop it in at my house as soon as she had gone into hospital. It was to tell me that she had cancer of the womb. She didn't know how long the hospital would keep her and it might mean that she would not be available to do the teaching. She had not wanted to tell me before, as it would have unsettled the rehearsal but she had told Eileen, who could pay extra special attention when we walked it through.

Two days later she was having an operation and Eileen, Mike and I were revising the plan. We didn't quite know what we should do, but agreed that some of Dorothy's planning was way out and unrealistic. We re-planned, keeping as we thought to her intentions but adapting them to our limitations. Visiting her in hospital the day after her operation, I was going to assure her, as one does hospital patients, that we'd got it all under control. However, she launched forth on some new project that she had started to discuss just before her operation with the consultant who operated on her. He had sat himself on the bottom of her bed, and they had chatted about a problem he was having with trainee Sudanese doctors and patient relationships. I never got a word in about our revised version of the 'culture' exercise.

What I didn't know was that she had already asked Eileen what our new plans were, had listened and said 'No, that won't do'. And with just two more days to go before the teaching assignment, she made up her mind to be there to do the teaching. And so she was. We were given a school hall. Raymond, armed with pillows and cushions and an armchair, helped Dorothy out of his car. We rushed to assist. She beamed at us and with measured steps between anxious guardians she walked the length of the corridor to the hall, placed herself with some difficulty onto the pillowed chair and instructed us on how she wanted the room arranged.

The class came in. The hall was already crowded with conference attenders. The students looked a little incredulous when this old invalid greeted them. She invited them to sit down on the chairs, arranged, in a semi-circle around her armchair. And she began, introducing them to Gavin, Mike and Eileen ... who were kindly going to role-play whenever they were needed. The session, during which she never left the chair, went swimmingly. We did everything as she had planned it. It all slotted into place. And some weeks later she did run a course for her consultant's trainees. She recovered well and learned a few weeks later that the cancer had been successfully removed.

The most testing part of her recovery, however, came when Joyce Simpson died soon after Dorothy's operation and she attended the funeral a day or so after her teaching engagement despite the warning by the surgeon that she should avoid being shaken in a car during a long journey, but she was determined to attend. Raymond, careful as ever, cushioned his passenger as comfortably as possible and made a slow but smooth journey to Bolton Abbey Church in Yorkshire, and Dorothy gave the celebratory address for Joyce's life as she had done, ten months earlier, for Joyce's husband, Alfred. At that time she did not know whether her cancer would spread. The whole occasion must have been distressing for her, but for Dorothy there was no choice – it just had to be done.

Raymond's death

In January 2001, Dorothy and Raymond were staying in their cottage in Steeton. Dorothy wanted to make marmalade so asked Raymond to buy a box of oranges from the village shop. While he was out she did odd jobs in the back yard, her little 'toy' garden. Her neighbour over the garden wall drew her attention to some activity at the end of the back lane. An ambulance had drawn up and a man with a bloodied head was being lifted into it. 'Poor old man', she thought, 'good job the hospital's not far away'. A little while later the neighbour went through his house and out to the road. He returned to his back yard and told Dorothy: 'D'you know ... the road's covered with oranges ... ', a scenario befitting a well-crafted film, as Dorothy herself appreciated even as she was caught up by the tragedy.

Raymond had been knocked down by an oncoming car. He was unconscious and at first the hospital suspected severe brain damage, but during some weeks of nursing and convalescence in a series of hospitals, he gradually recovered his speech and the use of his limbs. It was when Dorothy, Marianne, Kevin and Anna were with him, as he practised walking with a Zimmer frame along a hospital corridor, that he had a blood clot, collapsed and died within minutes. A post mortem revealed that at the time the car knocked him down, he had had a mild stroke, which is why this precise and careful man had stepped in front of the car. This explanation was a great relief to the the driver.

During the weeks of intensive care, slow recovery and convalescence, Dorothy had stayed at Raymond's bedside, seven to eight hours of every day. Dorothy was inundated with enquiries about Raymond to which she, as always, graciously responded. Realising that her friends at the Chester-le-Street market would be wondering what was happening, for rarely did they miss a Saturday visit, Dorothy wrote a letter addressed to: 'Marion, Saturday Market, Chester-le-Street' – which the postman delivered to the stall.

Day after day of long hospital visits relaxed Dorothy into giving what was required of her, anticipating and resigning herself to what she saw as the next phase of her life: caring for a permanent invalid. She believed that 'being there for Raymond' was to become her new life. She was accepting it and, one sensed, 'becoming' it. It would have been a full, contented life, for that is how she lives, finding wonder in whatever is demanded of her. But it wasn't to be that way. Raymond died, and her readiness to be there for him was suddenly not needed. Adjusting to this has been a long, slow hurt. Her caring has had to transfer to the disposal of his possessions, his vintage cars, cameras, tools, papers, records, maps, books, collection of journals and his orchard. 'What would Raymond want me to do with his things?'

Serendipitously, wonderful opportunities have occurred for passing these possessions on to people and places Raymond would have approved of. In turn, four youngish men have phoned and, separately, turned up at Dorothy's door in response to her enquiries. They have bought the goods themselves or arranged for their transportation to a buyer. For instance, Dorothy happened to say to the staff at the Hexham school where she was working, 'I don't suppose you know anyone that wants an orchard?' and almost in unison they replied: 'Yes, Matt's looking for one.' It turned out that apple trees were exactly what Matt wanted and he had the skill and know-how to lift them from the ground and transplant them. The sale of Old Sarah to a Lanchester owner in Germany, organised by Keith, became the subject of an article: 'Old Sarah is Emigrating' in the journal, *Driving Member*, April 2002. Paul was another who gave Dorothy support in some extra way. 'It must be Raymond', says Dorothy to me, 'he's here organising it, making sure I'm all right'. As Dorothy and I talk, we hear noises from the garage, at the back. 'I've acquired a son', says Dorothy. 'Let me introduce you to Andrew', another of the young men.

Some of Raymond's ashes were scattered by the family in the garden of High-burn House and in Nottingham. The remainder are still to be scattered at Steeton. On Saturday, 1st July, the week-end in which they would have been celebrating their 45th wedding anniversary, there was a wonderful, joyful celebration of Raymond's life. It was four months after Raymond's death, so that it was an expression of joy rather than sorrow. From all over the country people turned up for the celebration, including two past students from Denmark and California. So many of Dorothy's past students knew Raymond well. He had helped provide the sanctuary that Highburn House had been for them. Dorothy gave a witty, loving, laughing address, and we even had some Chamber Theatre!

Since Raymond's death, Dorothy has been searching for what her new life should be, testing the ground, selecting a pathway, giving herself time to choose a route. She knows there is a pathway waiting for her, and that life will be rich ... she's just looking for it. Marianne tells me that some six months after Raymond died, Dorothy became intrigued by a painting of two beached rowing boats hanging in the Shipley Art Gallery as part of the Gateshead yearly exhibition. On the spur of the moment Dorothy returned there and bought it. She explained to Marianne that she knew that Raymond would have bought it for her for Christmas: 'That painting's been haunting me ... and now I know why. The up-turned boat is the story of my life ... they're both going in the same direction, but one's upside down now ... that's me and Raymond ... and we are both going in the same direction'.

Contrasts in teaching engagements

That Dorothy accepted teaching engagements long after her retirement was not merely that she found it difficult to say no, although that was part of it. She was driven by a deep sense of 'unfinished business'. She knew that she still had not articulated a conception of education that was lying somewhere in her head. She knew that there was a new paradigm of education there, waiting delivery. Her only way of getting it out of her head was to do what she had done all her professional life – find out its meaning in a classroom.

So into classrooms she marched, always hoping that something would throw light on her new but unclear thinking. It rarely did, for the circumstances of such teaching often confined her to extending the lines she had already been following. Satisfying as that often was, she realised that her only chance of communicating her new ideas was to use selected conference platforms for voicing a new paradigm. National Drama's conference in York in 1999, at which she and I were made 'life members', presented such an opportunity, as had the Birmingham Health Networking conference organised by Lloyds Pharmacy the year before. Not until the Autumn of 2001, however, did her chance come to practice in the classroom what she was beginning to preach. But this is to anticipate the final section of this chapter.

Some of the teaching she undertook earlier in her retirement are described first, beginning with an example of 'rolling role'. Trying to explain this modified version of Mantle of the Expert requires some discussion of the feasibility of the Heathcote approach being taken up in the future. I also look briefly at the criticisms of her work that divided rather than developed drama teaching in this country, before describing two further, stylistically different examples of her teaching during retirement that give a flavour of how variously occupied she has been.

Rolling Role

Although Dorothy increasingly favoured Mantle of the Expert as a basic structure for 'true' education, she had to accept that a secondary school time-table of 35 minute or even double periods did not lend itself to the slow build-up of expertise that M of E required. Nor did it make sense for a specialist teacher working alone to try to devise an approach which aimed to meet a range of curriculum objectives belonging to a range of subject areas. In other words, M of E only seemed practical for a primary school or a special one-off programme in a secondary school. Additionally, the extensive planning for a full-blown version seemed beyond the professional capacities of a teacher working alone. Collaboration had to be the answer. Accordingly, Dorothy came up with the idea of several teachers with several classes combining on the same central concept, so that different classes operated from the same context providing work across the humanities, arts and sciences. She organised this successfully in a small number of schools, one in Jarrow during her final year of teaching, and another as part of her 'retirement' teaching in Birmingham.

I am grateful to Claire Armstrong Mills for her lively account of the Birmingham programme.

> Dorothy's work in my school has been exciting but stressful. I am aware that people who have studied with her appreciate her genius, but it can often seem very ordinary, slow and undramatic to other people, who wonder what the fuss is about. The brilliance and depth of her thinking needs a totally different mindset to the tick-box culture prevalent in much modern education, though she has shown that she can work within any prevailing orthodoxy and still develop a rich learning context for pupils.

> In 1997 Dorothy first came to work at Primrose Hill School, on a Rolling Role for several visiting primary schools. I realised that it would involve a great deal of work and that teachers of other disciplines might not understand her philosophy and resent being taken out of their usual routine. In fact, some teachers did understand and appreciate the learning: two of them, from History and Science were projected into role very successfully. Many others were simply bewildered. Teachers from UCE and drama teachers from other schools came to observe and added to the pressure in the school.

The teachers were persuaded to participate because the school numbers were declining and this was a terrific opportunity to have feeder primary pupils working in our school on something exciting with a world-famous figure.

Each of the primary schools had nominated an area of the Year 5 curriculum that they wanted Dorothy to deal with. These included: World War II, the Victorians, pulleys and levers. Each school was booked to work with her for half a day, starting Monday morning and finishing on Friday, a total of nine groups. This meant an enormous amount of preparation for Dorothy, as each group's work was different, but linked. Try as we might, the rest of us were pretty helpless, as we couldn't really keep up with her thinking.

The Rolling Role involved the replacement of a boiler in a Victorian brewery following an explosion with many fatalities; Madame Lingard's draper's and haberdasher's emporium taking orders for Queen Victoria's Jubilee celebrations; the graveyard where the children who died in the boiler explosion were buried; and a long-standing feud in the community.

The most alarming moment in the week was when one group of sixty badly-behaved pupils turned up with a supply teacher and a PE teacher who obviously wanted to hand them over and run. The work involved the sixty pupils running a rhubarb factory, not the most obviously dramatic context to work in. [The reason for the choice was that rhubarb had been used by monks in the monastery.] The level of noise was horrendous and the rest of us were terrified of the impending anarchy. Dorothy was, however, confident that all would be well. As the noise rose in a crescendo, I was instructed by Dorothy to enter in role as a Government Inspector who had come to check on the hygiene standards of the factory. I don't think I've ever been so sure that something wasn't going to work. To my amazement, as I walked the length of the room, checking the various stages of preparation, there was complete silence. They were all completely absorbed in my progress. My eyes fell on a dish of stewed rhubarb [kindly donated by the Head of Maths], and I picked up a piece to taste it. By now the sixty pupils seemed hardly to be breathing as they waited for my decision. What Dorothy had realised and the rest of us missed was the fact that the sixty pupils had all accepted the fictional context in which we were operating, and, consequently, the responsibility that went with it.

The primary school teachers and pupils were delighted with their experience, which gave them an entirely new slant on their curriculum work.

Claire's account offers us a familiar image of Dorothy's work, an image we have seen throughout this book of Dorothy working magic on seemingly uninviting undramatic material. That such an experience makes an important educational impact on her classes we accept almost as an act of faith. There is little evidence of learning, nor should we expect it, for at its most effective it opens up new capacities for understanding and for engendering new skills, a new thoughtfulness, a new sense of responsibility, a new degree of compassion, a new conception, an opening of eyes. It is an opening up of a new understanding, not a measurable quantity of newly acquired information. Any new knowledge or skills acquired by the pupils awaits further reinforcement and application in their day-to-day living. An observer cannot spot the new product like something dropped into an empty supermarket basket. I have just been to see the film, *A Beautiful Mind*. I know I have learnt something about schizophrenia that I never understood before but that new understanding remains a seed, a potential for application, waiting to be fertilized into connections with other things I understand, before I can identify what I have learnt. *A Beautiful Mind* has edged me into a new capacity for understanding. An observer listening to my comments after I saw the film might pick up clues that I have learnt something, and after drama we snatch greedily at hints of what our students are thinking and feeling. We appreciate the Maori boy in New Zealand who, after working with Dorothy in the 'Sanctuary' drama[5], commented: 'This drama is all in your mind, so it feels true', but we cannot expect anything more precise than this.

Reactions to Heathcote

Accepting therefore that the commitment and enthusiasm of her classes must mean something important is going on, what we are left with is a kind of unspecified admiration of Dorothy's work. If we press further, we might ask ourselves: when you read about Dorothy's teaching in Claire Armstrong Mills' Birmingham school, to which aspect of the account are you responding? Are you mainly identifying as a teacher with Claire's anxieties or are you enjoying a story that once more illustrates Dorothy's amazing effectiveness in the classroom? Or is your attention drawn to the methodology, because you would like to work that way? I suspect the latter wins the fewest votes. Rolling Role appears to be so far removed from an individual teacher's normal orbit of responsibility that only educationists outside the classroom are likely to consider they have the time, vision and influence to promote such a structure.

If we look at how Claire tells it, the work itself is only referred to in so far as it enables us to enjoy the drama of the occasion, with Dorothy playing the lead. Anyone really wanting to understand the nature of the work itself would learn little. Claire Armstrong Mills, more than most of us, understands Rolling Role – her M.Ed dissertation is a study of it – but she also knows that the reader of a book like this wants Dorothy, not her methodology, to be centre stage.

I have written of 'her' methodology as though the practice cannot exist apart from Heathcote. This is not so, for others will take over her practice in genera-tions to come. Nevertheless there has to be a weaning of methodology and its underlying philosophy from its inventor. John Carroll and Jerry Boland of Charles Sturt University, Australia, astutely note that when Cecily O'Neill and her Ohio students coined the phrase 'Process Drama' this 'relieved us of having to use Dorothy's name'. Since the 1950s Dorothy had developed a highly struc-tured, teacher-in-role, non-performance, living through dramatic genre. Only when its label was separated from its owner, could others begin to think 'we could do this'. 'Let's try Process Drama' replaced 'let's try the Heathcote method'.

There had always been a danger that Dorothy's work might invite a suffocating guru-worship, a gooey, gluey, unquestioning sycophancy that precludes criticism of any kind. This was immensely irritating to those who wanted to analyse the Heathcote practice critically. Some who tried to question its funda-mental principles risked being charged with heresy. One such heretic was David Hornbrook. His perception was that the only way to challenge the Heathcote orthodoxy was to declare war, and to set himself up as an alternative leader. He demanded of his followers that they should see drama education as 'black or white'. It was 'either/or'. You either followed Heathcote into what he called 'Mystifications and Dramatic Midwifery' or you followed Hornbrook into 'Dramatic Arts'. For Hornbrook, there could be no question of recognising what was worth keeping in Dorothy's work and developing from there, as other UK progressive thinkers such as Cecily O'Neill and Jonathon Neelands have done. The only hope of change, in Hornbrook's view, was to see her work as an educa-tional *cul-de-sac*, from which escape was essential. That *cul-de-sac* was ap-parently empty of artistry – as Peter Abbs, a leader in UK Arts Education chose to put it: 'devoid of art, devoid of the practices of theatre'. This is absurd to those of us who know that the fundamental basis of all Dorothy's work is dramatic art. It was certainly a costly mistake that the word 'theatre' was not retained in labels applied to her work.

It may be the very apparent cosiness of the Heathcotites' self-congratulatory armour that drives any challengers to absurd, overstated positions. At least Horn-brook's *Education and Dramatic Art*[6] is an elegantly written text, in keeping with Dorothy's own taste for metaphor and imagery. He nicely alludes to Heathcote and Bolton as starting a new breed of 'Muggletonians', those 17th century followers of the two witnesses to *The Revelation*. When reading this allusion, Dorothy wrote David Hornbrook a genuinely expressed thank-you letter, which mightily puzzled her adversary, as he had intended her to be offended. Today, Dorothy still giggles at the wit and aptness of his Muggletonian label.

Any true development from Heathcotean practice into new areas of work must be encouraged and must find its own identity. In recent years Professor Philip Taylor, formerly of Griffiths University, Brisbane and now at NYU, has experimented with a version of Heathcote's praxis under the label 'Applied Theatre'. He writes that the work has been influenced by Heathcote's praxis, especially her desire to have participants tolerate ambiguity.

> It attempts to structure work which permits multiple and diverse readings of human affairs and deliberately aims toward subtlety and incompleteness rather than descriptive didactic solutions. Heathcote's skill, one of many, was to establish moments fuelled with rich incomplete resonances. Likewise, we were keen for participants to place themselves within that incompleteness, tolerate the ambiguity of it, and work towards understanding their own and others' perspectives.

> The term 'applied theatre' has been gaining increasing currency within institutions in Australia, England and North America. It neatly characterizes that work which aims to transform human consciousness in non-theatrical settings: prisons, community centers, industry, housing estates, settings in which Heathcote would often work. When creating the applied theatre we find ways of constructing powerful and poetic scenarios, informed by detailed research.

In Philip Taylor's Applied Theatre we have an example of new thinking deriving from Dorothy's philosophy but with its own distinctive character. This does not yet seem to be the case for Mantle of the Expert and certainly not for its Rolling Role version. The main reason for this is that if it is to be seen as a viable system of teaching it cannot be left to drama teachers alone to take it on. Whereas it was appropriate that Heathcote's living through drama should be re-designated by Cecily O'Neill as Process Drama, as a new way of thinking about drama, a re-interpretation of Mantle of the Expert would require a new way of thinking about education. But if Mantle of the Expert is to become part of curriculum structure, educationists need to acquire a vested interest in fundamentally revising current conceptions of education. They must be prepared to inspire politicians, advisers, headteachers and their staff of all curriculum subjects – and introduce it into teacher-training. Left to drama teachers alone, Dorothy's M of E will die with her.

But there are positive signs. Iona Towler-Evans, now a free-lance consultant who was a curriculum adviser for Dudley, informs me that money has been allocated in Dudley for researching the effect of Mantle of the Expert on children's learning. She writes: 'I have to say it is not the *drama* teachers who are excited about the system but Primary classroom teachers who are seeking motivating approaches for learning'. Clearly, the necessary spread of interest has begun. Iona tells me also that: 'We have met up with management at Nene College with a view to accrediting a Mantle of the Expert Early Years course for their B.A. Childhood Studies'.

This discussion of how Dorothy's work will be seen in the future links with the new paradigm with which she is currently experimenting. But first, let us look at a couple of the many disparate activities she became involved in during her so-called retirement.

Dorothy Heathcote – an authoritative source for Theatre in Education teams

This is the first mention in this book of Theatre in Education. This is certainly not because Dorothy eschewed this aspect of theatre work but because it was never central to her own courses. Theatre in Education is a specifically British construct, in which a team of professional actors devises programmes for schools involving considerable audience participation. Close to Drama in Education philosophically, it is akin to teacher-in-role but with a group of actors functioning as collective teacher. At one time there were as many as thirty companies in the UK but local authorities are no longer financing such projects.

TIE teams tended to regard Dorothy as their friend, as someone they could call on for advice, and whose theory of drama education they could espouse at their own conferences. She was also willing to have a look at a design for a new programme or drop in at a rehearsal or an early performance when they could not figure what was wrong. Steve Ball of Language Arts Alive, for instance, would call on Dorothy when she was working in Birmingham. Soon after she retired she was invited by Lancaster Theatre in Education Company, then led by Warwick Dobson to have a look at their work with children on the Luddites, 19th century mill-workers who resisted the industrial revolution, wrecking machines. Dorothy combined two separate but related commitments, both taking her into 'mill' premises.

In Lancashire there is a museum, an original preserved fulling [felt] mill. Organised by Rick Lee, an ex-student of Dorothy's, it closed to the public for a week so that Dorothy could teach there. A class of children came there each day, from five different junior schools. Each day the work took an angle on an apocryphal myth about the ritual sacrifice of a straw man, ceremoniously bound to the 40 ft. diameter mill wheel. The wheel, awesomely present, was still in working order for the children to gaze at as they imagined the straw man ritual before they did their drama. The drama was about solving a mystery: one year, by mistake, a real man was sacrificed. Each evening other teachers came to plan the next day's work with Dorothy. Thus Dorothy found herself planning a different approach each day on the same topic, culminating on the last day with a wax museum presenting the tragedy.

On visiting the work at Helmshore Textile Museum in Rossendale, planned by Lancaster TIE, which was based on the early 19th century Peterloo Massacre, she criticised three aspects. While recognising the skill and background knowledge of the actors, she had to point out that they started and remained in full sail in spite of their good intentions and that however willing you are to hand over the power to the children, unless you talk at exactly the right level you will be keeping that power to yourself – the subtle talk is the hinge-pin to everything. She also suggested that the chance they gave the children to experience being at work in a mill was too quick, too shallow. Also, and this is perhaps a typical criticism of much left-wing TIE work, they tended to stereotype political sides into goodies and baddies. As someone who knew from experience how mill-owners can look after their workers, Dorothy did not respond well to an entirely one-sided presentation.

The Lancaster actors hugely respected her in spite of what amounted to fundamental criticisms, and they were pleased to do a presentation for the opening of the Lancaster Conference marking her retirement, although again it took a political slant she was not entirely comfortable with.

A day of Shakespeare

Finding a common ground for seemingly disparate groups to share is a challenge Dorothy has always welcomed. The Shakespeare project involved a company of professional actors, led by Wendy McPhee, an ex-student of Dorothy's who did her Diploma, Masters and Ph.D in Newcastle, coming up from London to perform *Anthony and Cleopatra* in the open air. The Shakespeare day was to be a kind of festival for the 84 residents of Dilston College [the MIND centre for the North-East]. There was also The Lawn Mowers, a North-east company run by and for people with learning difficulties, led by Gerry Ling, an ex-student of Dorothy's. This group spent a whole week with Dorothy at Dilston College, demonstrating to a team of architects what would be needed in the way of design should Dilston's application for a Lottery grant to build a Drama centre on the site go through. Their theme for the week was related to *Anthony and Cleopatra*. And then there was Kathy White Webster's – also an ex-student of Dorothy's – Theatre Study A-level students from Queen Elizabeth High School in Hexham, who had been studying the same play and were expected to contribute to a kind of pre-performance dramatic ritual introducing the professional performance by the Shakespeare Company.

It was all immensely complicated but its success for all the groups involved led to further annual mid-summer celebrations, using in turn *The Tempest* and *Much Ado About Nothing*.

> *This week, June 2002, Dorothy has been down in Nottingham helping Marianne, Kevin and Anna move house – and an Aga is to be installed shortly!*

A vision for education

It is now the end of June, 2002. Two weeks ago, Dorothy spent the whole week at Queen Elizabeth High School, Hexham, working with a group of 34 Year 9 pupils who have met with Dorothy and eight staff volunteers after school once or twice a month since last October. I have been careful to write 'working with' rather than 'teaching'. Next week she will be travelling to Birmingham to attend the NATD conference at which she will describe the 'Hexham Project', a commitment that has taken up more preparation time at home this last six months than anything else she has ever done. Not that she likes the word 'project' – she's seen too many projects that don't go anywhere. Her word is Commission, the Hexham Commission, implying commitment, deadlines and resolutions.

This book is Dorothy's life story – up to her 76th year. How many comparable biographies finish with an attempt to explain the subject's new paradigm in education? To understand Dorothy is to understand that she has a mission. Her story cannot be complete without it. I have tried to show through these pages that Dorothy's praxis *is* Dorothy. So there is more of Dorothy to discover. Her living through, moment of awe, a man-in-a-mess class dramas revealed Dorothy the mesmeriser, the powerful, the alluring, the tension-builder. Her person-in-role dramas showed us Dorothy the picture-making artist, the contemplator, the reader of signs, the gentle wonderer. Her Mantle of the Expert work showed us Dorothy the task deviser, the creator of signs, the colleague. But she wants to move on from there to Dorothy the ...

Aye, there's the rub. How does one explain the new conceptions in Dorothy's head that have been stirring for years but were never fully articulated and never turned into praxis until at Hexham? And even Hexham represents but a first step, the tentative journey-making into unknown territory. Getting it right hasn't been easy for Dorothy, for she doesn't know it is right until it happens. I am assured that everyone involved with the experience is thrilled with it – the pupils, the teachers, the hospital management and Dorothy herself. Conveying its essence isn't easy either.

What never changes in Dorothy's work, under whatever label, is how her major strategy is always to find a way of getting her class to take over responsibility for the work. The purpose is always to build in her pupils a desire for knowing about minute particulars – what things are, how things work, how people, institutions and societies deal with problems. She wants them to ponder on where man's responsibilities lie. She always wants her pupils to make con-nections, to see implications. And she wants to enhance their natural sense of wonder. She wants them to grasp what is universal, to have a sense of history, to be open to the mysterious, the ineffable. Whether she calls it living through drama or something else, these objectives have not changed.

In commission she appears to see a better way of achieving those same aims. Perhaps merely listing her aims and objectives does not in itself take us to where the sea-change – Dorothy's third sea-change – is going to occur. The key to com-mission as to all the other genres lies not so much in her aims as in how she per-ceives the class in front of her. She always, at least initially, regards a class as a group of interdependent, interacting individuals. And from the 1950s onwards her starting point, whatever the format, has been to *frame* them. In obvious drama sessions, they have been given a fictional role: 'Now you men in there ... throw out your guns' was the now famous beginning to *Three Looms Waiting*. In Mantle of the Expert: 'shall we design a letter-heading for our stationery?' im-plies some organisational frame in a designated locality. Is there another kind of framing altogether that she is now caught up with?

The idea for framing, originally from Goffman, conceives of a person as simultaneously following a number of social roles: for example, a father, who is also a voting citizen and has a job as a road-sweeper. And any group of people become, as it were, bracketed off into role functions – shoppers; pedestrians; citizens etc. Outside the bracket the individuals will have their own roles, but within the bracket they belong to a group of people who conform to an identifi-able code of behaviours.

In drama classes we give special meaning to roles, implying fictional ones, a bracket within a bracket. But for Dorothy's commission one dispenses with that internal fictional bracket and, by removing the stereotype school pupil bracket, one changes the expected code of learning behaviours. Take the school pupil stereotype: the difference in status between teacher and pupil as the giver and the receiver of knowledge normally defines schooling. Less obvious is the code that determines the viability of the knowledge. Imagine the difference in quality of understanding of the little English girl whose family moved to France twelve months ago, standing in front of the mirror asking her mother: '*Tu la trouve bien, ma nouvelle robe?*' and a child in England repeating the same words as an exercise in a French lesson. The former's language is contextually *derived*; the latter is contextually *contrived*. Most learning in a classroom belongs to the latter category. Whatever the subject-matter, whether Sciences or Humanities, learning rarely arises from the exigency of the moment, so can have no contingent outcome apart from a teacher's or examiner's assessment. Most learning is trapped within the teacher-pupil frame and remains stolidly contrived, with no consequences and no sense of it mattering to someone else.

Dorothy asks herself: 'Supposing the frame were to be changed ... supposing some of the classroom behaviours were to be decontextualised?' We already do this in schools when we invite children to put on a show for the public or take part in the football team that will try to defeat a rival school. Both are 'for real'; both require teachers to hand over responsibility at some point; both have outcomes that others will be interested in; both rely on group interaction and commitment. Compare these with the dead-end effect of an essay handed in for homework.

Dorothy asks: 'Supposing a team of pupils, instead of preparing to win a game, were to prepare themselves to carry out an assignment that took them along not the football pitch but several avenues of the curriculum, and that that assignment was actually *required* by someone who relied on them to complete it?' And the teacher, instead of being a coach to the team, became an agent, helping to organise the 'commissioners'. This would be the new frame: not teacher/pupils or coach/footballers, but agent/commissioners. The moment children enter school, they know who they have automatically become – pupils; the moment they enter the changing room they know they are footballers; when commissioners enter their scheduled space and/or time, they adopt the required commissioner code.

When the 34 volunteers aged 15 entered the Drama Studio at Queen Elizabeth Grammar School in Hexham after school, they knew they were framed as commissioners and adopted the code of behaviour this role seemed to require. And always waiting for them was their agent Dorothy and the eight volunteer teachers. The Drama studio was wonderfully flexible, so that each time they entered, something about the way Dorothy had prepared the space signalled the commission task – the arrangement of chairs and tables, the notices laid out, the areas labelled. As a drama studio it had associations for them of acting a role, so that taking on the mantle of commissioners seemed more appropriate as they stepped through that door. The teachers, along with Dorothy, worked hard to sustain the equal footing of the interactions, though at times it must have been tricky for teachers to obey the code – one can imagine the temptation to say: 'Marjorie Smith! Did you remember to hand in your homework?'.

But the commissioners all had a job to get on with, picking up from their last meeting. Their commission was to advise the local hospital, at the request of Northumbria Health Authority represented by Mr. Forsey, gynaecologist, on the factors that would have to be taken into account in constructing a new garden area for the hospital, one to which patients, visitors and staff would have access. The request had come to the school in September and they had to complete their recommendations by the summer.

Thus the fictional customer of Mantle of the Expert has been replaced with a real one. Instead of a series of increasingly demanding tasks invented by a teacher there is one real commission. What avenues of the curriculum they went along depended on the specialisms of the teachers involved. The eight staff, supported by Steve Sewell as video technician, were Kathy White Webster, Head of Drama; Gibby Keyes, Drama teacher; Diane Harris, Deputy Head and Physical Education; Mary Meek, Psychology; Peter Dowthwaite, Geography and Head of Year; Les Palmer, Biology and Assistant Headteacher; Mike Smith, Classics and Head of Sixth Form; and Steve Williams, English and Deputy Head of Year. From time to time, other specialist teachers were brought in as their expertise was required. The commissioners could genuinely say to such teachers: 'We need to know ... exactly what ... how ... when etc.' because they did indeed need to know.

The dimensions and levels of their enquiry emerged as they became more knowledgeable about the topic. Their first step, prompted by Dorothy, was 'who will the garden be for?' This moved to 'what varieties of gardens are there?', then to 'what does any particular kind of garden *mean*?' then 'what do people expect of a hospital garden?', to 'their garden stories, beginning, I dreamed a dream ...' and on to practical issues. The latter included designs for seating, garden levels, materials for pathways, sunlight throughout the year, the use of water as a source of harmony, peace, music, and nourishment, and the various uses of glass.

The groupings within the class, varying from session to session, were a central part of the experience. Interactions between groups, bondings within groups and the keeping of individual diaries for the archives became in themselves a cumulative learning experience.

There is not room here to describe the project in detail – that would take another book. But something of the spirit of the work is conveyed by the pupil who said: 'This is the first time something I have done in school has been important to someone'. And a member of staff remarked at the final presentation of the commissioners' findings to members of the hospital committee: 'I haven't done anything so worthwhile in the whole of my teaching career'.

'To always look for the pattern, and to find it'

This quotation given to me by Dorothy herself, is from a story[7] about an American Indian detective. However we think about the way Dorothy has lived her life or how she has sought to teach in the classroom, looking for a pattern is at the centre of what she does. The detective is speaking:

> When the dung beetle moves ... know that something has moved it. And know that its movement affects the flight of the sparrow, and that the raven deflects the eagle from the sky, and that the eagle's stiff wing bends the will of the Wind People, and know that all of this affects you and me, and the flea on the prairie dog and the leaf on the cottonwood.

> Thus one learned, gradually and methodologically, if one was lucky, to always 'go in beauty', and to always look for the pattern, and to find it.

So many people have felt it a privilege to have known Dorothy. I have been given the honour and responsibility of writing her story, or at least my version of it. From the start I knew what I wanted the last sentence of this book to be. It belongs to Bernadette Mosala, the remarkable South African who against all odds travelled to England to learn from Dorothy. At the 1993 Lancaster conference, she said: 'I wish it were possible to have pieces of Dorothy scattered all over the world ... to act as a yeast.'

Notes

1   The two publications are: *Drama for Learning: Dorothy Heathcote's Mantle of the Expert approach to Education*, by Dorothy Heathcote and Gavin Bolton, Heinemann 1995 and *So You Want to Use Roleplay?* by Gavin Bolton and Dorothy Heathcote, Trentham Books 1999

2   The International Drama and Education Association

3   National Association for the Teaching of Drama [NATD]. The other key association is National Drama [ND]

4   The last few years the NATD conference has transferred to Newman College, Birmingham

5   Referred to in Chapter 8

6   David Hornbrook *Education and Dramatic Art* Blackwell 1989

7   Tony Hillerman *Dance Hall of the Dead* Pluto Press, London and Sydney 1973

The Cast, in order of appearance in this book

Chapter One: Childhood

Mr. Andrews, Dorothy's elementary school headteacher
Margaret Freeman, Dorothy's closest childhood friend
Amy Shutt, Dorothy's mother
Aunts Ellen, Lucy and Edith
Grandad and Granny, Irving and Sarah Ann Sugden
Aunty May and Uncle Harold
Sam Clough, mill-owner
Charlie Fletcher, mill-owner
Uncles Harry and Alfred
Annie Emmet, Granny's neighbour
Mrs. Mawson, friend of Granny
Dorothy Clough, District Commisioner for the Guides, who lent Dorothy books
Miss Bray, one of Dorothy's schoolteachers
Gladys Lund, a friend
Sir Alex Keighley, Squire of Steeton Hall
Cousin Ann, Aunt Edith's daughter

Chapter Two: Three Looms Waiting

Emily, an expert weaver who taught Dorothy
Mollie Sugden, Dorothy's elocution teacher
Esmé Church, Principal of the Bradford Theatre School
J.B. Priestley, playwright, Chairman of Bradford Civic Theatre
Rudolf Laban, member of Esmé's staff of international reput
Charlie Fletcher, Dorothy's boss
Barbara Crabtree, member of staff specialising in speech
Geraldine Stephenson, member of staff and movement specialist
Lisa Ullman, member of staff and movement specialist
A.L. Stone, Physical Education organiser for West Riding of Yorkshire
Sir Bracewell Smith, Dorothy's second cousin
Annie, a neighbour of Amy and Dorothy Shutt
Margaret Robinson, artist and life-long friend
Margaret and Lola Eytel, aristocratic German sisters
Marion and Rosemary Lawrence, mother and daughter, life-long friends
Sheila Sanderson, Head of English in a Leeds comprehensive school

Chapter Three: Staff Tutor, University of Durham

Professor Brian Stanley, Director of Institute of Education at Durham/Newcastle
Mary Atkinson, Froebel expert in the Institute
Alice Hand, Dorothy's first landlady in Newcastle
Mabel Wilson, Music tutor in the Institute
Silas Harvey, Drama Organiser for Northumberland
Roger Hancock, Drama Adviser for Newcastle
Peter Slade, Drama Adviser for Birmingham
Vice-Chancellor Bosanquet, Newcastle University
Danny, owner of the stables
Flora, the Washington Grammar School teacher who introduced Dorothy to Raymond
Raymond Heathcote, Dorothy's future husband
'Old Sarah', the 1932 Lanchester, roadworthy until 1964

Chapter Four: Staff Tutor, University of Newcastle

Marianne and Richard Heathcote, Raymond's parents
Mary Earl, helped Dorothy at home, looked after Raymond's mother
Peter Slade, who played a key role in setting up the Newcastle Drama Diploma Course
Margery Peel, the first student to stay for a year in Highburn House.
Winifred Fawcus, Institute colleague of Dorothy's
Ray Verrier, student, 1965-6
Brian Way, UK pioneer of Creative Drama who moved to Canada

Chapter Five: Working mother and media star

Marianne Heathcote, daughter born June 1966
Joe Reid, BBC Education Officer for the South West
Ron Smedley, maker of school programmes for BBC, then the *Omnibus* programme
John Hodgson, Head of Drama, Bretton Hall
Tom Stabler, on staff of Hartlepool Primary School, and then a headteacher
Sister Bridget, student from 1960s course
May Spooner, the neighbour who became Dorothy's helper and friend
Gavin, Cynthia and Andrew, the 'Bolton' family
Veronica Sherbourne, movement specialist
Anna, daughter to Marianne and Kevin, born 2000
Anne Thurman, Professor of Creative Dramatics, University of Northwestern, Evanston
Joyce and Alfred Simpson, Dorothy's life-long, Yorkshire friends
The cats presiding at Highburn House: Ivan, Whisker, Jennie, Scrap, Joshua, Blaze, Emma and, now, Tabitha
Pam Bowell, member of Newham Drama Advisory team who housed Dorothy on her visits
John O'Toole, Head of English at Highfield Comprehensive School, Gateshead
A second Mrs. Dorothy Heathcote [pronounced Heethcote], headteacher, Snow Street School, Newcastle

Chapter Six: A sea-change

Jane Sallis, therapist
Iain Fraser, chief consultant at Prudhoe Hospital
Eve Carr, a student of Dorothy's, later her assistant, based at Prudhoe hospital
Wayne Balanoff from Canada who created role of 'wild man'
Chris Lawrence who created role of 'Albert'
Bill Backman, the Canadian teacher who created 'the gypsy'
Gerald Chapman, who organised Royal Court conference
John Carroll, Mitchell College, Australia
Ken Robinson, Professor of Arts Education, Warwick University

Chapter Seven: Travelling abroad

B.J.Wagner, Evanston, author of *Dorothy Heathcote: Drama as a learning medium*, 1976
Cecily O'Neill and Liz Johnson, co-editors of *Dorothy Heathcote: Collected Writings*
May Spooner, neighbour and friend
Anne Thurman, Professor Creative Dramatics, Northwestern University, Evanston, Illinois
Winifred Ward, America's renowned pioneer of Creative Dramatics
Margaret Faulkes, friend of Brian Way, University of Alberta
Bernadette Mosala, a committed follower of Dorothy from South Africa
Dorothy Loftus, a Cambridge Secondary teacher, ex-student of Dorothy's and great friend

Chapter Eight: Mantle of the Expert takes centre stage

Eileen Pennington, director, Morpeth Arts Centre
John Fines and Ray Verrier, colleagues in History education, West Sussex Institute
Roger Burgess, BBC, the man behind most of Dorothy's films
Norman Morrison, management training, Northern Gas Board and Volkswagon Audi

Chapter Nine: The authentic tutor

Roger Barnes, long-term colleague and friend
Erving Goffman, Dorothy's most influential theorist
Professor Tony Edwards, Dorothy's boss from 1979
John Fines, John West, two of her course examiners
John Crompton, lecturer in English and Drama – in the Department at Newcastle
Lesley Webb, colleague
Professor Nancy Swortzell, NYU
Mike Fleming, a Doploma student at Durham
Oliver Fiala, Australian lecturer in Drama and close friend
Derek Stevens, student of Dorothy's Advanced Diploma course and part-time M.Ed.
Brian Edmiston, a Bristol teacher, later Professor at Columbus University, Ohio
Pam Bowell, resident at Highburn House during her M.Ed year

Chapter 10: Looking forward

Marianne, Kevin, and Anna

Raymond

Pam Bowell, Head of Drama, Kingston University, London

Stig Eriksson, a leading Norwegian drama educationist, Bergen University College

David Davis, retired Professor of Drama in Education, UCE

Ken Byron, retired, lecturer Birmingham Polytechnic and Editor of *2D Journal*

Dr. Cecily O'Neill, formerly Warden of the Drama and Tape Centre, Holborn, London

Dr. Jonothan Neelands, University of Warwick

David Hornbrook, a Bristol teacher who replaced Geoffrey Hodson as Inspector for Drama, ILEA

Guy Williams, chair person of NATD

Dr. Sandra Hesten, organiser of the Lancaster conference and the initiator of the Dorothy Heathcote Archives

John Rainer, Head of Drama, Manchester Metropolitan University

Bob Hesten, computer consultant

Joyce Simpson, life-long friend of Dorothy's. Lecturer in English and Drama

Alice da Silva, ex-student of Dorothy's from Portugal

Pat Morrison, AVA Centre Newcastle University

Dorothy Croyden, AVA Centre Newcastle University

Fiona Hesten, daughter to Sandra and Bob

Dr. Mike Fleming, Senior Lecturer, University of Durham

Eileen Pennington, ex-student of Dorothy's, freelance drama teacher

Verena Balfour and Marion Proud, holders of two *bric-a-brac* stalls at Chester-le-Street Saturday market

Andrew, Keith, Matt and Paul who helped Dorothy with finding homes for Raymond's proud possessions

Philip Taylor, Professor, NYU

Claire Armstrong-Mills, Head of Drama, Kings Norton High School Birmingham

Iona Towler-Evans, consultant to Dudley Education Authority

Steve Ball, Director of 'Language Alive' Theatre in Education Company, Birmingham

Warwick Dobson, ex-director of Lancaster Theatre in Education Company

Rick Lee, ex-student of Dorothy's who organised the 'mill' experience

Wendy McPhee, ex-student of Dorothy's, director of touring Shakespeare Company: Theatre Set-up.

Gerry Ling, ex-student of Dorothy's, director of the 'Lawn-Mowers' Company of actors

Mr. Forsey, consultant Gynaecologist, Northumbria Health Authority

Kathy White Webster, Gibby Keyes, Diane Harris, Mary Meek, Peter Dowthwaite, Les Palmer, Mike Smith, Steve Williams and Steve Sewell, Queen Elizabeth High School, Hexham

Bernadette Mosala, South African teacher and ex-student of Dorothy's.

Contributors to this book

Luke Abbott, L.EA. Adviser and ex-student of Dorothy's

John Allen, Senior HMI for Drama, Principal of Central School of Speech and Drama

Verena Balfour, runs a *bric-a-brac* stall, Chester-le-Street Saturday market

Susan Battye, student of Dorothy's, 1978-9, New Zealand teacher

Roger Barnes, colleague of Dorothy's and close friend

Dr. Kathleen Berry, student of Dorothy's 1984 -5, Professor of Education in Cultural Studies, Drama and Literacy, University of New Brunswick, Canada

Cynthia Bolton, wife of the author

Pam Bowell, student of Dorothy's 1983-4, Head of Drama University of Kingston

Donna Brandes, student of Dorothy's, 1966-7, an American expert in group therapy and counselling

Margaret Burke, retired, Professor of Drama Education, Brock University, St. Catharine's, Ontario

Roger Burgess, BBC film-maker

Dr. John Carroll, Charles Sturt University, Australia

Professor David Davis, University of Central England; drama in education consultant

Helen Dunlop, retired, Ministry of Education, Ontario, Canada

Brian Edmiston, student of Dorothy's, 1983-4, Professor, University of Columbus, Ohio, USA

Doreen Feitelberg, retired Chairperson of the South African Guild of Speech and Drama Teachers

Dr. Mike Fleming, Senior Lecturer, University of Durham's School of Education

Voula Foscolo-Avis, teacher of Drama, ex student of both Durham and Newcastle Universities, now teaching the PGCE course in Newcastle School of Education

Margaret Freeman, childhood friend, now living in USA

David Griffiths, retired, LEA Inspector for South Tyneside

Dorothy Heathcote who has provided 30 hours of interview tapes

Marianne Heathcote Woodbridge, her daughter

Dr. Sandra Hesten, student of Dorothy's 1972-3, retired lecturer, Stockport and

Tameside Consortium of Higher Education and Lancaster University

Margaret Hilder, actress, a fellow student at Bradford Theatre School

Bob Hornby, ex-student of Dorothy's 1965-6, retired lecturer in Drama, Liverpool Hope University College

Kathy Joyce, retired drama lecturer, Lancaster University and trainer of business executives

Chris Lawrence, ex student of Dorothy's 1971-2, formerly Director of the Cockpit TIE company, Drama teacher in North-East and London, Editor, Drama Research

Dr. Barbara McIntyre, retired, Head of Theatre Department, University of Victoria, Canada

Libby Mitchell, fellow student of Dorothy's at Bradford Theatre School

Norman Morrison, Volkswagen Audi, personnel manager

Dr. Norah Morgan, retired from Brock University, St. Catharine's, Ontario, Canada

Dr. Cecily O'Neill, Professor of Drama and Theatre Education, Ohio State University, USA

Dr. John O'Toole, ex student of both Durham and Newcastle Universities, Professor of Applied Theatre, Griffiths University, Brisbane, Australia

Eileen Pennington, ex-student of Dorothy's 1984-86, free-lance drama teacher, formerly Director, Morpeth Arts Centre

Margaret Robinson, artist and life-long friend

Professor Juliana Saxton, University of Victoria, B.C., Canada

Peter Slade, retired Drama Adviser for Birmingham, leading figure in Child Drama

Ron Smedley, retired TV film-maker

May Spooner, Dorothy's neighbour, helper and friend

Derek Stevens, ex-student for both the Diploma course and the part-time course M.Ed, retired teacher and drama education consultant

Dr. Nancy Swortzell, retired Professor, Theatre Education, NYU, USA

Carole Tarlington, Australian teacher who set up a theatre school in Vancouver

Dr. Philip Taylor, Professor of Applied Theatre, NYU, USA

Ray Verrier, ex-student of Dorothy's 1965-6, retired lecturer in History Education, West Sussex Institute

Dr. Betty Jane Wagner, Professor, Roosevelt University, USA

Dr. Kathleen Warren, Australian lecturer in Early Childhood

Lesley Webb, member of staff, School of Education, University of Newcastle, specialising in education of young children

Calendar of principal events in Dorothy's life

1926   Dorothy is born to Amy Shutt

1931   Starts school

1940   Leaves school to start work in mill

1945   Leaves mill for Theatre School

1947   Starts to teach evening classes at Bradford Civic

1948   Completes course and takes on amateur productions in local villages

1950   Saw an Aga for the first time – and knew she wanted one

1950   Appointed to the University of Durham, based at Newcastle

1954   Met Raymond Heathcote

1954   Became Senior lecturer

1956   Married Raymond

1962   Newcastle becomes a separate University from Durham

1963/4 Dorothy's first full-time students, taking the Advanced Diploma

1964   Dorothy goes to India for six weeks on behalf of the British Council

1965   Raymond's mother dies

1966   Marianne is born

1966   First appearance before cameras: *Death of a President*

1969   Dorothy's first trip abroad to teach Drama

1972   Dorothy's mother, Amy Shutt, dies

1979   Starts full-time M.Ed course alternating with Diploma

1982   Beginning of the Dorothy Heathcote archival collection, Lancaster

1984-6 Establishes part-time M.Ed course

1985   Marianne leaves home and attends Nottingham University

1986   Retired from University of Newcastle, completing 36 years

1992   The International Centre for Studies in Drama set up in Birmingham

1993   The Lancaster Conference – to celebrate Dorothy's achievements

1996   Marianne marries Kevin

2000   Anna Heathcote Woodbridge is born

2001   Raymond dies

2001-2 The Hexham Commission

The Audio Visual Centre of the University of Newcastle-upon-Tyne is currently engaged in editing a biographical video based on interviews with Dorothy. Susan Tarlarini is the lady to contact, if you are interested in acquiring a copy. It should be out by Autumn, 2002.